READING RESEARCH

Advances in Theory and Practice

Volume 2

READING RESEARCH

Advances in Theory and Practice

Volume 2

G. E. MACKINNON
Department of Psychology
University of Waterloo
Waterloo, Ontario, Canada

T. GARY WALLER
Department of Psychology
University of Waterloo
Waterloo, Ontario, Canada

ACADEMIC PRESS 1981
A Subsidiary of Harcourt Brace Jovanovich, Publishers
New York   London   Toronto   Sydney   San Francisco

ACADEMIC PRESS, INC.
111 Fifth Avenue, New York, New York 10003

United Kingdom Edition published by
ACADEMIC PRESS, INC. (LONDON) LTD.
24/28 Oval Road, London NW1 7DX

ISSN 0191-0914

ISBN 0-12-572302-4

PRINTED IN THE UNITED STATES OF AMERICA

81 82 83 84   9 8 7 6 5 4 3 2 1

CONTENTS

WRITING SYSTEMS AND READING
Insup Taylor

READING PROBLEMS AND INSTRUCTIONAL PRACTICES
Isabel L. Beck

THE CONTENT OF SCHOOL READERS
Dale M. Willows, Diane Borwick, and Maureen Hayvren

AN EDUCATIONAL EXPERIMENT STATION FOR READING: HOW CAN LEARNING TO READ BE FACILITATED?

Edmund B. Coleman

LIST OF CONTRIBUTORS

Numbers in parentheses indicate the pages on which the authors' contributions begin.

ISABEL L. BECK (53), *Learning Research and Development Center, University of Pittsburgh, Pittsburgh, Pennsylvania 15260*

DIANE BORWICK (97), *Department of Psychology, University of Waterloo, Waterloo, Ontario, Canada N2L 3G1*

EDMUND B. COLEMAN (177), *Department of Psychology, University of Texas at El Paso, El Paso, Texas 79968*

MAUREEN HAYVREN (97), *Department of Psychology, University of Waterloo, Waterloo, Ontario, Canada N2L 3G1*

INSUP TAYLOR (1), *Division of Life Sciences, Scarborough College, University of Toronto, West Hill, Ontario, Canada M1C 1A4*

DALE M. WILLOWS (97), *Department of Psychology, University of Waterloo, Waterloo, Ontario, Canada N2L 3G1*

PREFACE

In the last decade or so the quantity of research on reading has increased rapidly. The people concerned with such research represent diverse orientations, backgrounds, and interests; i.e., psychologists, linguists, neurologists, class-room teachers, and those concerned with the assessment and remediation of reading difficulty. The extensive research which is being published on reading, and which this variety of people is trying to follow, appears in an ever-increasing and bewildering array of scholarly publications. It has become difficult for the researcher, the student, and the consumer of research on reading to keep abreast of developments in the field. In essence, both the reading community and reading research are fragmented into diverse subgroups. Communication and interaction among these subgroups are seriously lacking.

With this background in mind, this serial publication, "Reading Research: Advances in Theory and Practice," has been created. Its major purpose is to provide a publication outlet for systematic and substantive reviews and syntheses, both empirical and theoretical, and for integrative reports of programmatic research. The expectation is that such contributions will appeal to a broad, multifaceted, interdisciplinary audience, will help professionals keep abreast of growing knowledge in the various areas of reading research, will help serious students of reading come to terms with the diverse and complex field, and will help researchers by providing fresh viewpoints on areas close to their own.

The Editors have attempted to organize each volume in the publication around a particular theme or topic. The first volume was concerned with reading readiness. The chapters in this second volume, as well as those in a forthcoming third volume, focus on learning to read. The authors were asked in preparing their chapters to speak to the question, "What does a child learn when he learns to read, and how can the learning be facilitated?" Within this general framework the contributors to Volume 2 consider current educational practices and materials for the beginning reader.

The volume begins with an analysis of writing systems and their influence on learning to read by I. Taylor. By contrasting alphabetic with nonalphabetic writing systems, Taylor provides fresh insights into the question of what must be learned in learning to read and the problems children encounter in learning to read written English.

In the second chapter, I. L. Beck critically evaluates several practices and programs currently employed to instruct novice readers in learning the print-to-speech code, in developing decoding automaticity, and in comprehending what they read. Beck notes that the instructional strategies likely to be effective for word attack and word recognition skills conflict with those suitable for developing reading comprehension. To fulfill both sets of objectives, Beck suggests a two-track system of reading instruction.

D. M. Willows, D. Borwick, and M. Hayvren, in the third chapter, analyze the content of a number of widely used school readers. The text and illustrations of readers from both basal and code-emphasis programs are examined in the light of current research on factors that affect reading acquisition. These authors point out that what a child reads may play a major role in determining what he learns when he learns to read. They argue that both reading researchers and publishers of reading series must together begin to address some very important questions so that school readers may be designed that facilitate the task of learning to read.

In the final chapter, E. B. Coleman proposes a framework for designing and evaluating effective reading programs. Coleman shows how the methods of linguistics and experimental psychology can be used to provide the information required not only to design reading programs and materials but to estimate their potential effectiveness.

The Editors would like to thank Marion Tapley for her assistance in the preparation of this volume. We would also like to thank the editorial consultants of this volume, F. A. Allard, R. W. Barron, J. Rogers, and E. E. Ware, for their advice and enthusiastic support.

G. E. MacKinnon
T. Gary Waller

READING RESEARCH
Advances in Theory and Practice

Volume 2

WRITING SYSTEMS AND READING[1]

INSUP TAYLOR

Division of Life Sciences
Scarborough College
University of Toronto
West Hill, Ontario, Canada

I. DEVELOPMENT OF WRITING SYSTEMS

A. Introduction

Speech is evanescent—it must be listened to while it is happening. To overcome this ephemeral quality of speech, humans invented writing,

[1] I am grateful to M. M. Taylor for his help throughout the preparation of this article.

1

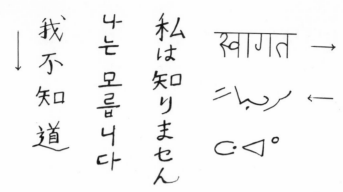

Fig. 1. A few different writing systems. From left to right: Chinese, Korean, and Japanese "I do not know" written vertically. From top to bottom: Hindi, Arabic, and Cree "Welcome" written horizontally.

which represents speech in a more or less permanent visible form. At different times, in different places, humans have developed a variety of writing systems, most of them influenced by earlier systems.

Figure 1 shows a few of the ways *I do not know* and *welcome* can be expressed in different writing systems. Some systems have a vertical arrangement of signs or letters, others a left-to-right or right-to-left horizontal arrangement. Signs or letters in some writing systems look compact and complex, while in others they appear simple and spread-out. Writing systems also differ in less obvious, more technical and fundamental ways, namely, the linguistic units they represent.

Speech can be described in terms of a hierarchy of units: They are, from lower to higher units, phonemes, syllables, morphemes, words, phrases, and sentences. The first two are basically sound-based units while the rest are meaning-based units. Different writing systems choose different basic units, some taking a phoneme, some a syllable, some a morpheme, and some a word. The smaller and lower the level of the writing unit, the greater combinatorial possibility and flexibility it possesses: a small unit can always combine with another small unit to form a large and complex unit, but not vice versa. On the other hand, the smaller the unit, the less pronounceable and meaningful it tends to become. Decomposition of speech into increasingly smaller units requires increasingly fine and abstract analysis.

Let us see the roles writing units have played in the development of writing systems. The following developmental history is based partly on Gelb (1963). A few examples of each writing system to be described are given in Table I.

TABLE I
Development of Writing Systems

Type	Unit	System	Sign	Direction	Number	Time
Logography	word (syllable)	Sumerian cuneiform	sun ⟨signs⟩	↓ →	600 (150)	3,100 B.C. −75 A.D.
		Egyptian hieroglyphic demotic	sun ⊙, man ⟨signs⟩	→ ↓ →	700? (100)	3,000 B.C. −400 A.D.
	morpheme	Chinese	sun ⊙ ⊟	↓	2,500 – 45,000	1,3000 B.C. – to date
Syllabary	syllable	Semitic Proto-Sinaitic	daleth ⟨sign⟩		31?	1,600 B.C.
		Byblos linear	daleth ⟨signs⟩		22	1,000 B.C.
		Phoenician	⟨signs⟩		22	
		Japanese	da ⟨signs⟩	↑ ↑	72	900 A.D. – to date
Alphabet	phoneme	Greek	d ⟨sign⟩	↑ ↓	23?	900 B.C.
		Arabic	ti ⟨sign⟩	↑	28	500 A.D.
		Latin	D	↑	23	700 B.C.
		English	d, D	↑	26	700 A.D.
		Cyrillic	d Д	↑	43	900 A.D.
	phoneme/ syllable	Korean	d, a 다	→	24	1,500 A.D.

B. Word Unit—Logography

A writing system in which one sign represents one word may be called a logography (e.g., Gelb, 1963) or an ideography (e.g., Diringer, 1968). Originally, a picture was drawn to represent a concrete object. Later, the same picture came to represent another less concrete word with a meaning related to the original concrete object. Eventually, the picture itself, gradually simplified and stylized over time, often lost any resemblance to the original object. Usually it is difficult to count the exact number of signs in a logography.

A limited degree of phonetization (phonetic transfer or rebus writing) arose from the need to express words and sounds which could not be adequately indicated by pictures. For example, to express 'Neil' (*kneel*), a picture of *knees* might be drawn.

According to Gelb, Sumerian, Egyptian, and Chinese are the three historically most important logographies.

1. Sumerian

The Sumerian system used cuneiform characters (wedge form). It was used in Mesopotamia (modern Iraq) between 3100 B.C. and A.D. 75, mainly to meet the need to record commercial transactions. The Sumerian system had several hundred logographs, which must have represented only some key words and not the entire vocabulary. Besides logographs, it had 100–150 syllabic signs. The syllabic system did not distinguish between voiced, voiceless, and emphatic consonants, and indicated vowels inadequately.

2. Egyptian

Egyptian writing developed from Sumerian. By around 500 B.C., there were three related forms: hieroglyphic (sacred inscription on stone) for public display, and two cursive systems, hieratic and demotic, for everyday practical purposes.

Throughout its history, between 3000 B.C. and A.D. 400, the Egyptian system was a word-syllabic writing. In its developed form, it had about 700 signs for words, and 100 signs for syllables. Each of the syllable signs indicated either one or two initial consonants, plus a vowel which was not identified.

3. Chinese

Independent of Near Eastern development of writing systems, China developed its own unique system. The first written records made their appearance in the form of inscriptions on bone, shell, and bronze, around 1300 B.C. in northern China.

Originally, the system contained at least 2500 characters, whose pictorial origins were clearly recognizable. Over centuries of continued use, the number of characters kept increasing, up to 70,000, and the pictorial origins of many became blurred.

Of the three main historical logographies, the Chinese system will be selected for further discussion in Section II for the following reasons.

1. It is the best example of logography; "the most logographic of all the writings," according to Gelb. It is a "full" logography in that it can represent any word of the Chinese language. It is a "pure" logography in that it does not have a pseudo-syllabary as an integral part.

2. It has been continuously used ever since its appearance in antiquity.

3. It is used by a huge number of people—one billion Chinese speakers, one quarter of the world population.

4. Its adoption by speakers of languages unrelated to Chinese (Japanese and Korean) poses an interesting problem.

5. It has generated a moderate amount of research into reading processes.

C. Syllable Unit—Syllabary

A writing system better suited than a logography for representing sounds is a syllabary, in which each sign represents a syllable. If a spoken word has to be phonetically analyzed, the first natural step is to divide it into its constituent syllables, as in /pə-tei-tou/. An English speaker, if asked to sound out the word *potato*, is likely to break it up in this way. Note that each of the three syllables is easy to pronounce, and can be used in other words, as the first syllable being used in *potential*. A language might have at most around a few thousand syllables, sometimes fewer than one hundred, thus reducing the required number of signs drastically from that of a logography.

Some notable syllabaries are the Semitic, two Japanese, and various syllabaries invented in modern times for some African and Amerindian languages.

1. Semitic Syllabaries

Syllabaries were used in ancient Northwest Semitic countries, stretching from Sinai to Syria. They consisted of a limited number of signs (22–30), of which 24 were identical to 24 of the 100 syllabic signs of the Egyptian system. Out of the complicated Egyptian system, the Semites evolved a simple system of their own by throwing overboard all word signs and phonetic signs with two or more consonants but retaining those with one consonant. Further, their syllable signs were restricted to a small number of open syllables.

As in the Egyptian system, each of the 22–30 signs expressed the exact consonant but not the vowel. Nonexpression of vowels did not pose a serious problem in Semitic and Hamitic (Egyptian) writings because Semitic and Hamitic languages use consonants for roots of words, and vowels for grammatical variations of these words. Ambiguities do arise sometimes. Goody and Watt (1963) point out that because Hebrew writing lacks vowels and because the consonants in question are the same, the Biblical story about Elijah leaves undecided whether the Prophet was fed by "Ravens" or by "Arabs."

The Proto-Sinaic syllabary (1600–1500 B.C.) of about 30 signs was definitely pictorial in character. Other syllabaries used nonpictorial signs: Ugaritic cuneiform (1400 B.C.) with 30 signs, and the Byblos syllabary with 22 linear (geometric) signs (1000 B.C.). When a syllabary has such a limited number of signs, it cannot have a sign for every syllable of a language.

2. Two Japanese Syllabaries

Around the ninth century A.D. Japan developed two types of syllabary. The two syllabaries will be selected for discussion in Section III for the following reasons.

1. Each of the two syllabaries is a "pure" and "full" syllabary. It does not contain any word sign, and each of its symbols represents one syllable fully, that is, its consonant and vowel. Also, it has a symbol for every syllable of the language.

2. Throughout its history, it remained as a syllabary, that is, it has not developed into an alphabet.

3. It has been continuously used by 113 million Japanese speakers, who boast one of the highest literacy rates.

4. It is used in a mixture with characters borrowed from another writing system, Chinese, thus posing an interesting problem in reading. The Japanese and Korean writing systems, though differing drastically from each other, are similar and unique in this respect.

5. The mixed use of characters and syllabaries has inspired active research into reading processes.

D. Phoneme Unit—Alphabet

In an alphabet, each symbol or letter represents a phoneme, a speech sound. The number of phonemes in any language is small, between 12

(Hawaiian) and 70 (Abkhaz), usually around 30, and hence even a "full" alphabet needs only a small number of letters. The phoneme, being the smallest and lowest common unit, has the maximum combinatorial possibility and flexibility. With only a handful signs, any sound or word of any language can be represented fully. A set of about 30 symbols can be simply shaped without limiting visual discriminability.

1. Abstracting Phonemes

When words are phonetically analyzed into syllables, the first step toward abstracting phonemes has been taken. To go the next step to an alphabet requires the decomposition of a syllable into its phonemic elements. This is relatively difficult both in historic cultures, and for modern children. The phoneme /p/ has to be mentally isolated or abstracted from the many syllables in which it occurs in various phonetic realizations. For example, the /p/ in *pit* is aspirated (a brief burst of air) whereas the /p/ in *spring* is not. Also, /p/ has to be contrasted to other similar sounding phonemes such as /b/ or /t/. Note that /p/ by itself cannot be pronounced, and a vowel has to be attached to it to form a pronounceable syllable such as /pi/. The phoneme /p/ by itself has no meaning either, although it has the potential of differentiating meanings of such "minimal pairs" as *pin* vs *tin* or *bin*.

Historically, abstraction of consonants seems to have preceded that of vowels, perhaps because the consonants are more numerous and important in most languages, especially in the Semitic and Hamitic languages which played such vital roles in the development of writing systems. Diringer (1968) considers the North Semitic writing system of the second millennium B.C. to be the first alphabet, acknowledging the fact that it abstracted and represented consonants adequately.

2. Greek Alphabet

The Greeks streamlined the cumbersome vowel representation of the Semitic system. In addition, the Greeks converted into vowels a number of Semitic signs expressing "weak consonants" which were not phonemic in Greek. Thus, Semitic *he* became Greek *e* or epsilon; Semitic *yodh* became Greek *i* or iota, and so on. In this way, consonants were truly isolated and represented separately, and vowels were differentiated adequately. The Greek system is considered to be the first genuine alphabet (Gelb, 1963). The full Greek alphabet was born around the ninth century B.C.

The Phoenician syllabary seems to have been the source of the Greek alphabet. Greek alpha, beta, gamma, delta, etc. correspond to Phoenician aleph, beth, gimmel, daleth, with the respective significance of *ox, house, camel*(?), and *door*. The Greeks eventually eliminated digamma, san, and quoppa, and added signs for phi, chi, and psi.

3. Other Alphabets

Once developed fully by the Greeks (according to Gelb), or by the Semites (according to Diringer), the idea of an alphabet has spread all over the world. Indeed, it is said that the alphabet has been invented only once in human history.

Gelb attaches great importance to the representation of vowels, and distinguishes three types of alphabets based on this feature. In type one—which includes Greek, Latin, Runic, Slavonic—vowels have their own signs on an equal footing with consonants. In type two, which includes the Semitic writings of Palestinian Hebrew and Arabic, the vowels are indicated by small strokes, dots, or circles, placed either above or below the consonant signs. These diacritic marks are written separately in Hebrew and Arabic, but in the third type, represented by Indic and Ethiopic alphabets, they are attached to consonants.

Mention should be made of the Latin alphabet, which descends from the Greek alphabet (via the Etruscan alphabet), and from which the English alphabet derives. It had 23 letters, all of which were capital letters. It did not have *J, U,* and *W.*

The Cyrillic alphabets that were developed around the ninth century A.D. have more letters, around 43, than the other alphabets. They are used by Russians and speakers of such other Slavic languages as Polish and Bulgarian.

The Korean alphabet, which is not a Roman alphabet, differs from other alphabets in design in that no sign of the alphabet can be used by itself—every sign has to be combined with other signs to form one complex or block, which then represents a syllable. The Korean alphabet will be discussed under "Alphabetic Syllabary" in Section IV.

4. English Alphabet

The English alphabet will be chosen for discussion in Section V, for the following reasons.

1. English is the most important international language, and is used either as the first or a second language by more than a half of the world's population. Further, the English alphabet is a Roman alphabet, which is today the most widely used writing system in the world. A Roman alphabet is used not only in most countries where Indo-European languages are spoken but also in such countries as Turkey where non-Indo-European languages are spoken. Even China and Japan from time to time toy with the idea of adopting a Roman alphabet.

2. The English alphabet and orthography, with their irregular and complex representation of the sound system of English, poses an interesting and unique problem of its own.

3. English orthography is associated with a host of problems in learning and usage—disordered and backward reading, and even illiteracy in spite of compulsory education. Could a comparison with other writing systems shed some light on these troubling problems?

4. Research activities into reading processes are prodigious.

5. Last but not least, the readers of this article are English speakers.

II. LOGOGRAPHY—CHINESE

A. Characteristics of Chinese Characters

1. One Character–One Morpheme–One Syllable

Chinese characters (henceforth, characters) are examples par excellence of a logography. In general, each character represents one idea, or more precisely, one morpheme, the smallest meaningful unit of a language. The overwhelming majority of Chinese morphemes are "free," i.e., each of them can be used by itself as a word. A handful of Chinese morphemes are "bound" morphemes such as suffixes and particles: a bound morpheme is not used by itself. But unlike English bound morphemes (e.g., -es, -s), Chinese bound morphemes do not inflect but remain invariant.

A word in Chinese may consist of from one to several morphemes. 火/huo/('fire') is a one-morpheme word, and so is 車/che/ ('vehicle'). When these two free morphemes are combined, a new word 火車/huoche/ ('train') is created. As a rule, each morpheme consists of one syllable, as is /huo/ or /che/ (*potato* is one morpheme but consists of three meaningless syllables). To put it in another way, each syllable in Chinese is a morpheme, is meaningful, and is represented by one character. Characters are well suited for representing the Chinese language, whose morphemes are monosyllabic and noninflecting.

2. Number and Complexity of Characters

When each character represents a morpheme, there has to be as many characters as there are morphemes in a language. The authoritative K'ang-hsi Dictionary of the eighteenth century A.D. lists around 45,000 characters. However, most of these characters are archaic, or in Wieger's (1965) words "monstrosities of no practical use." The vocabulary of daily use is only a few thousand characters.

Remember that the use of 3000 or so characters does not mean that the number of words used is restricted to 3000, because each of the 3000 characters might combine with one or two other characters to form a compound word. In Ai's (1950) count of characters and words in various readers used in primary schools in China, the number of different characters was between 2032 and 2453, while the number of different words was between 5784 and 7715. In Taiwan, the number of characters in daily use is 4532, but the number of words is 40,032 (Liu, Chuang, & Wang, 1975). Rozin and Gleitman (1977, pp. 67–68) are incorrect to suggest that "an Australian second grader [who encounters 2,747 different words in his reading series] is reasonably expected to recognize nearly as many words as a Chinese scholar acquires in a life time."

If several thousand characters are to be visually discriminable, many of them have to be complex. The complexity of a character can be measured as the number of strokes like — 亅 丿 フ 丶 . The simplest character consists of one horizontal stroke (which appropriately represents *one*), and a complex one can have as many as 50 strokes. One would think that to learn and to write complex characters with large numbers of strokes might be a strain. However, more and more complex characters may have been invented for increasingly more esoteric mean-

TABLE II

Progressively More Complex Characters with Increasingly More Specific and Infrequent Meanings[a]

Character	Meanings	Character	Meanings
虫	insects	言	words; to speak
虱	louse	訃	to announce death
螢	a glow worm	誓	to swear
蠮	a big caterpillar	讝	to speak in one's sleep
蠋	a short-legged spider	讞	to decide on judicial cases

[a] From Taylor (1976).

TABLE III
Simplification of Characters

Complex	Stroke	Simple	Stroke
燈	15	灯	6
廣	14	广	3
産	11	产	6
厰	14	厂	2
嚴	21	严	8
病	10	疒	5
Mean Stroke	**14**		**5**

ings, which are used rarely. Table II gives a few examples of characters with increasingly complex and esoteric meanings, and possibly with uncommon uses.

In modern China (mainland but not in Taiwan) and Japan, many frequently used characters have been simplified, occasionally in different ways in the two countries. Table III gives a few examples of simplified characters along with their original versions.

3. Six Categories of Characters

The American linguist Halle (1969, p.18) observed: "since strokes [in Chinese characters] are arbitrary symbols the writer's task is equivalent to that of a person trying to remember [several thousand] telephone numbers." Not exactly. The characters can be grouped into six categories based on their origins, which in turn may suggest the characters' sounds and meanings. Table IV lists the six categories.

The most important classifier of characters is the "radical," a semantic determiner or sign. In the K'ang-hsi Dictionary, characters are arranged according to their radicals, which number 214. In Table II, the radical

TABLE IV
Six Categories of Characters

Category	Example	
Pictograph	⊙ 日	sun
	☽ 月	moon
Simple Ideograph	⌐ 上	above
	⌐ 下	below
Compound Ideograph	日, 月 → 明	bright (sun, moon)
	女, 子 → 好	good (woman, child)
Analogous or Derived	网	fish net; extended to any network, cobweb
Phonetic loan	來 } /lai/	wheat ↓ come
Semantic – phonetic compound	女, 馬 → 媽	(woman) /nu/ + (horse) /ma/ = (nurse) /ma/

for *insect* and for *word* appears in a number of characters that have meanings related to *insect* or *word*. Not surprisingly, radicals are used as aids in teaching characters both in China (Ai, 1950) and in Japan (Sakamoto, 1976).

In Table IV, in the sixth category, a character contains a semantic component *woman* on the left and a phonetic component /ma/ on the right. A number of other characters containing this phonetic component would be pronounced as /ma/ or something similar to it. However, a phonetic component is not always a reliable clue to a character's sound because many other characters that do not contain this phonetic component are also pronounced as /ma/. Further, a phonetic component does not always maintain its sound element and tone as it occurs in different compound characters.

Finally, in Chinese script, no extra space is left between characters: Since each character represents a morpheme, space will be redundant.

Characters are arranged in a column, every column starting from the top of a page. Columns are arranged from right to left so that a page of a book is turned from left to right (the opposite of the Western manner). Recently, under the Western influence, horizontal writing has started to appear occasionally. Punctuation marks also have been adopted in many texts.

B. Learning Characters

1. Chinese Children Learn Characters

Characters are numerous, and have to be learned batch by batch, starting with "easy" ones and progressing to more "difficult" ones. The easy characters have the following characteristics (partly based on Ai, 1950): they occur commonly; they contain less than 10 strokes; they have "balanced" forms, i.e., when a complex character (over 13 strokes) contains two elements or subparts, each element should contain a similar number of strokes (compare the first example of complex characters to its simplified version in Table III); they are easy to discriminate from other characters containing the same element; they contain vertical and horizontal strokes rather than curvilinear and oblique strokes.

In China, about 2000 characters are learned in the first 4 years of primary school (Ai, 1950). Ai reports that the use of the six categories (see Table IV) facilitated children's learning of characters: the same children scored three times higher when the six categories were explained than when they were ignored. This was so whether the children were tested immediately or three months after learning.

Van Zian (1962) studied first graders learning characters in a Shanghai primary school. Character learning took place in three stages. In the first stage, the children related previously learned sound/meaning associations with only the global shape of written characters. In the second stage, they associated sound/meaning with parts of characters and often wrongly substituted parts from similarly shaped characters. In the third and final stage, they were able to make the correct associations between sound/meaning and the correct strokes of characters.

Character learning throughout the three stages was dominated by the visual aspects of the characters. Most of the errors (79%) made in a dictation–recall test were also visual. Confusions with semantically or phonologically similar words were few, 8 and 13% respectively. Learning the sounds of characters should be easy, because within any one dialect each character represents one syllable in a consistent manner.

2. American Children Learn Characters

Rozin, Poritsky, and Sotsky (1971) demonstrated that American children with reading problems can easily learn to read English represented in Chinese characters. Nine second-graders with reading backwardness were selected as subjects, on the basis of their inability to read a series of six simple CVC trigrams (PIP, WAT, LAG, RED, GUB) and a set of rhyming words (CAT, FAT, MAT, SAT) after being given the pronunciation for AT. Note that the children were not required to attend to the meanings of the syllables.

Thirty characters were taught to the children in six stages. In final tests, the children had to arrange the individually mounted characters to form orally presented [in English, it appears] sentences such as "A good brother does not give a man a red car." After an average of 4 hours of individual tutoring of the characters, the children were able to negotiate the final sentence and one story with relatively few errors and some comprehension.

Why did the American children succeed in learning characters after having failed to learn to read English syllables? Rozin *et al.* (1971) attribute their success partly to the novelty of characters, and partly to the intrinsic property of characters, namely, "the complete absence of sound-coding in characters," as the authors put it. The authors used the English syllables and characters in unnatural ways: They ignored the meanings of English syllables and words on the one hand, and the sounds of the chartacters, on the other. As we shall see below, characters' sounds are by no means something to be ignored. Thirty characters are only a minute fraction of the few thousand characters that a Chinese has to master to become literate. Moreover, those 30 characters were deliberately chosen for their relative simplicity or minimum confusability, and their sounds were completely ignored. Perhaps, the point of their research is not to demonstrate that the Chinese system is easier to learn than the English system but to call our attention to possible differences in processing logographs and alphabetic letters.

C. Processing Characters

Chinese characters and alphabetic letters differ in the way they appear, code sounds, map meanings, and so on. How do such differences affect the ways characters and letters are processed—perceived, remembered, read, and so on?

1. Holistic Identification of Characters

When a character represents one intact morpheme, its identification should be holistic. For one things, the necessity of sequencing a number of letters to form a morpheme or a word is eliminated. Letter/sound-sequencing is identified as one of the stumbling blocks in learning to read in English (Rozin *et al.*, 1971; Rosewell & Nachez, 1971). One of the common errors beginners make is a reversed sequencing, such as occurs when *saw* and *form* are misread as *was* or *from*.

An English word consists of a number of subunits, each of which has a semantic and/or phonetic function. Consider the word *mountain*. It is decomposable into one morpheme plus *ain*, two syllables, six phonemes, six spelling units (underscored below), and eight letters, in the following way.

$$[(\underline{mount})\underline{ain}] \text{ /maun-tən/}$$

Reading is sometimes taught by such subunits. In short, English words are potentially decomposable into a few levels of subunit; whether they are actually so decomposed in processing depends on the reader's skill with the given material.

By contrast, its Chinese equivalent 山 /shan/ is one morpheme, one syllable, and one character, which defies decomposition into subunits. A reader either identifies it as a whole or fails to identify it. One character may consist of several strokes(three in *mountain*), but they do not have individual semantic and phonetic entities as do English letters or letter groups. At most, some characters may be decomposed into a radical and a phonetic component (see Table IV).

2. Phonetic Representation of Characters

In English, visually presented letters and words seem to be phonetically represented in short-term memory (Conrad, 1964; Mark, Shankweiler, Liberman, & Fowler, 1977). Mae (1976) demonstrated that written Chinese characters too are represented phonetically in short-term memory. Mae's stimuli were 15 isolated characters, which were visually presented briefly to Chinese high school students. The characters then had to be recognized amont 90 response characters, 15 of which were "homonyms" (homophones?) (phonetic distractors), 15 synonyms (semantic distractors), 15 shapemates (visual distractors), and 45 correct items. Mae found that the largest number of errors in recognition was phonetic in nature, next visual, and then semantic.

In Tzeng, Hung, and Wang's study (1977), phonemic similarity of visually presented characters affected short-term retention of the characters. Recall was the worst for those characters that shared the initial consonant as well as the following vowel, and about the same for those that shared either only the intial consonant or only the final vowel. Further, the more phonetically similar an interference list was to a target list, the worse the recall of the target list. (An interference list is learned between the presentation and the recall of a target list.)

Taylor, Taylor, anf Coleman (submitted) discuss when and why phonetic recoding occurs. Subjects tend to resort to phonetic recoding when printed words, whether they are English or Chinese, are made phonetically similar (and hence confusable) and short-term memory requirement is explicit. In reading ordinary prose passages, confusion is sometimes based on visual aspect of characters (see Van & Zian, 1962, quoted above; also Section VI).

3. Sounds versus Meanings of Characters

Characters are devised to represent meanings primarily and sounds secondarily, while phonetic signs are devised to represent sounds primarily and meanings secondarily. Is perception of meaning direct in logographs but mediated by sounds in English words?

Wang (1973, pp. 55–56) observed: "To a Chinese [character reader,] the character for 'horse' [馬] means horse with no mediation through the sound /ma/. The image is so vivid that one can almost sense an abstract figure galloping across the page." We note that the sounds, but not the meanings, of characters change across dialects within China, and across different languages which use them, such as Japanese, Chinese, and Korean. From long disuse, I have forgotten the sounds but not the meanings of some characters.

In English orthography, letters code sounds, however erratically. English readers can sound out unfamilar, even nonsense, words. Rubenstein, Lewis, and Rubenstein (1971) and Rayner and Posnansky (1978), among others showed that visually presented English words seem to be identified via a phonetic recoding stage.

In the light of all these observations, Taylor (1980) asked: Are readers more sensitive to meanings than sounds in characters, and vice versa in English words? I prepared two lists, one consisting of character triads for Korean subjects, and another, English-word triads for English subjects. Here is an example of English-word triads.

raise

rise   rays

The subject's task was to "read" each character or English-word triad, and circle the two items "that go together." The subjects were told to do the task quickly. Would the Korean subjects circle two characters that are synonyms (or have related meanings) while the English-speaking subjects circle two words that are homophones (or rhyming words)?

Most subjects tended to connect two items on semantic rather than on phonetic grounds. Unexpectedly, this tendency was stronger for the English-speaking subjects responding to the English words than for the Korean subjects responding to the characters. It appears that meaning is more prominent than sound both in English words and in characters.

The unexpected finding that sounds are relatively more important for the characters than for the alphabetic writing means that the sounds of characters are not something to be belittled, as Wang (1973) and Rozin *et al.* (1971) seem to imply. This result is in general agreement with the implications of the studies on phonetic recoding of Chinese characters cited above.

4. Eye Movements

Emile Javal (1906) made important discoveries about visual activities in reading. The eyes of a reader do not glide along the lines of print, but perform a series of "saccadic" movements and "fixation pauses." Only during the fixation pause does visual perception of print takes place. Most of our reading time—90%—is spent in fixation pauses. In mature reading, fixation pauses move forward more or less rhythmically, but occasional "regressions" also occur for "retakes" of missed material.

Eye-movements in reading Chinese were studied by Miles and Shen (1925), Shen (1927), Wang (1935), and Gray (1956) in the United States, and by Ai (1950) in China. The results of these studies are summarized in Table V.

Before interpreting the results in Table V a confusion about what constitutes a Chinese "word" and a "character" has to be clarified. All but one of the figures given in Table V were referred to as "words" by the researchers. What is the real relation between words and characters in Chinese? Examine Chinese sentence, with an English equivalent written under each Chinese word or particle, given Fig. 2.

Two of the words, *know* and *time,* contain two characters each. As for *correct,* it contains either two or three characters, depending on whether one decides to include the accompanying suffix in the count.

TABLE V
Eye Movements in Chinese and English Readers

Author	Language	Pause duration (second)	Character/ English word per pause	Character/word per second	Regression per character/ word
Miles and Shen	Chinese	.3	2	6	
	English	—	—	5	
Wang	Chinese	.3	1.7	5.8	
Ai	Chinese			3.98	
	English			3.9	
Gray	Chinese	.37	2.5	2.8–20.7	59.8
	English	.3	1.6	—	14.5

你　　知道　　準確　　的　　時間　　嗎

you   know   correct   (suffix)   time   (particle)

Fig. 2. A Chinese sentence.

This suffix turns a preceding noun into an adjective. Finally, what do we do with the last particle? This particle transforms a declarative sentence into an interrogative sentence. The above sentence contains 5 words, 19 letters, and 5 morphemes in Chinese.

Gray's (1956) "equivalent" passages contained 146 words in English and 233 "words" in Chinese. Gray's "words" were probably characters. If so, very roughly, 1.6 characters might be counted per English word (233 divided by 146). Reinterpretation of Chinese "words" as "characters" make the results of Wang, Ai, and Gray, more comparable to those of Miles and Shen. Also, the big apparent discrepancy between Chinese and English in the number of "words" read per regression, 59.8 and 14.5, respectively, will be reduced somewhat if 59.8 is taken to refer to characters. Something like 37 words and 14.5 words were read in Chinese and English, respectively. The discrepancy between the two languages is still large.

Wang (1935) suggests a reason why eye movements tend to be more smooth in reading Chinese than English. Each character is of the same square shape and size, and occupies the same amount of space regardless of the number of strokes. This uniformity of characters causes other striking differences in the spatial distributions of fixations along a line. The square shape of the characters and their compact arrangement in a line demand smaller and more frequent eye movements than is required in the reading of English. When, however, a comparison is based on the average number of "words" [characters?] per fixation, not on the absolute spatial unit, the span of recognition is larger in Chinese than in English, while the average duration per fixation is shorter in English than in Chinese.

To attend once more to some similarities found in reading Chinese and English, Gray found that silent reading was more efficient than oral reading: more words were read per fixation, and the duration of fixation was shorter, in silent than in oral reading. Ai reports that the difference between silent and oral readings was greater in the sixth than in the third grade for both Chinese and English children. In Table V, the Chinese and English data are similar in duration of fixation, and in the numbers of words read per fixation and per second.

5. Writing Characters

Usually, those who can read can write. Slightly different processes are involved in the two skills, however: in reading, a person recognizes letters, while in writing, he recalls them. Research in human memory shows that recognition is easier. When a writing system contains many complex characters, writing is adversely affected far more than reading is.

Most characters certainly appear far more complex than most English letters. However, each character represents a morpheme, which in English requires a few letters. One way to measure the relative complexity of characters and English words is to compare the time required to write "equivalent" content in English and Chinese. Can one write 1.6 characters as fast as four or five English letters?

I chose myself as the subject for this simple test because I am a skilled writer of both characters and English. First, I randomly picked three pages of an English–Chinese conversation text (Ma, 1971), and counted the number of characters and English words in each of the three pages. In all three pages, the number of characters exceeded the number of English words. I selected the page with a median discrepancy, containing 12 sentences of the type "Have you the right time?" in English and Chinese. The 12 sentences contained 62 words (about 248 letters) in English and 98 characters. The ratio between the English words and the characters is 1:1.58, which is very close to the value of 1:1.6 calculated for Gray's (1956) longer text.

After warm-up practice with character writing, I copied the page as fast and accurately as I could. My time for English was 1.5 minutes, and for Chinese, 5 minutes. The "equivalent" content in Chinese took 3.3 times longer to write than in English.

Learning to write characters takes time and patience because of their large variety and complexity. Each character has to be written in an authorized, fixed order. However, the order of writing strokes, once learned for a handful of characters, can be applied to writing any new character.

As described earlier, many commonly used characters have been simplified to lighten the time and effort for beginning readers as well as mature writers. However, for relatively simple characters with less than, say, 14 strokes, further simplification is achieved at the risk of sacrificing discriminability (see Table III). A certain degree of simplification is desirable as long as it is done judiciously, that is, meaning-conveying radicals are retained, and visual discriminability is not sacrificed.

For typing and typesetting purposes, characters are less than ideal mainly because of their great variety. As of today, there is no typewriter for characters. Recently, two Cambridge linguists found a way to code several thousand characters into digits for computer input and output. Electronic communications using characters have been extremely cumbersome without this kind of technical breakthrough. (reported in the Globe and Mail, 1978, January 27).

III. SYLLABARY—JAPANESE

Japanese writing uses not only two types of syllabary but also Chinese characters, a Roman alphabet, and Arabic numerals.

A. Writing Systems

1. Kanji (Chinese Characters)

Japan borrowed characters from China at several times between the fifth and fourteenth centuries AD. Because of differences in the sound systems between Chinese and Japanese, the borrowed characters retain by and large their original meanings but not their pronunciations. Depending on the regions of China and the times of borrowing, Kanji take on varied pronunciations. For example, 行 can be pronounced in the following three Chinese and three Japanese ways, respectively:

Chinese	Japanese
shu*gyo*	*okona*-u
an*gya*	*yu*-ku
*ko*do	*i*-ku

Note the lack of similarity among the various pronunciations. I point out this somewhat chaotic state of Japanese pronunciation of Kanji to indicate that learning to read Japanese like a highly educated person is not as easy as one might imagine from the simplicity of its syllabaries.

In the 1950's, 1850 Kanji were designated as "official," but educated people end up learning additional 1000 "unofficial" Kanji. Kanji tend to be used for special types of word, as explained shortly.

2. Two Kana (Syllabary)

Since Japanese and Chinese are unrelated languages, Chinese characters which are suitable for the monosyllabic and isolating (noninflecting) Chinese language become at some point unsuitable for polysyllabic and inflecting Japanese. For these and other reasons, around 900 A.D. Japan developed two kinds of syllabary, Katakana and Hiragana. Each letter of Katakana is a fragment of a simple Chinese character, hence the name Kata (fragment) + Kana (borrowed name). Each letter of Hiragana (cursive or smooth borrowed name) is fashioned from a cursive form of a simple character. Table VI shows a few examples of Katakana and Hiragana.

A syllabary is well suited for the Japanese language, because Japanese has a small number of syllables all of which are simple and open: it does

TABLE VI
Katakana and Hiragana

Sound	Katakana	Kanji	Hiragana	Add (˝)	Sound: voiced	Add (°)	Semi voiced	
ha	ハ	八波	は	ば	ba	ば	pa	
hi	ヒ	比	ひ	び	bi	ぴ	pi	take both
f,hu	フ	不	ふ	ぶ	bu	ぷ	pu	(˝)& (°)
he	ヘ	⻖部	へ	べ	be	ぺ	pe	
ho	ホ	保	ほ	ぼ	bo	ぽ	po	
ka	カ	加	か	が	ga			
ki	キ	幾	き	ぎ	gi			
ku	ク	久	く	ぐ	gu		take only (˝)
ke	ケ	介計	け	げ	ge			
ko	コ	己	こ	ご	go			
na	ナ	奈	な					
ni	ニ	仁	に					
nu	ヌ	奴	ぬ		take neither (˝)nor (°)		
ne	ネ	祢	ね					
no	ノ	乃	の					

not have consonant clusters, and every syllable ends in a vowel (the only exception being /ŋ/ as a final consonant).

Katakana and Hiragana each have 46 basic letters representing 46 syllables. There are two kinds of diacritic mark that can be attached to 23 of the basic letters to create "related" or secondary letters (see Table VI). Counting both the basic and the secondary letters, 69 short syllables can be represented by 69 letters of either Katakana or Hiragana. In addition, some of the syllable signs are used in 30 or so "modified" syllable signs. Hiragana duplicates Katakana exactly in its number and the phonetic values of the letters, just as capital letters duplicated small letters in the English alphabet. The two syllabaries are put to slightly different uses, however.

In Japanese writing, space may be left between phrases, and must be left between clauses and sentences, but not necessarily between words. Recently, Japan has adopted some of the Western punctuation marks. Japanese can be written either vertically, following the Chinese tradition, or horizontally, left-to-right, following the Western tradition.

One might think that such a mixture of writing systems borrowed and developed from various sources in bits and pieces over centuries would play havoc with reading. On the contrary, the mixture turns out to be a blessing.

B. Reading Japanese

1. High Literacy and Kana

Japanese reading is interesting for two reasons: Japan enjoys one of the highest, if not the highest, literacy rates in the world, and she uses a mixture of various writing systems. Has the latter something to do with the former?

Makita (1968) reports that the literacy rate in Japan is 99%, with the illiterate 1% confined largely to the mentally retarded. He attributes the high literacy to:

1. Japanese people's respect for education
2. Compulsory education from first to ninth grade, which boasts 99.9% enrollment
3. Ready availability of good but inexpensive reading material
4. Movements to stimulate reading, such as National Reading Week
5. Initiation to reading with Kana.

Of these five reasons, I will dispose of reason (1) right away because it has little to do with writing systems. One can only speculate that

Japanese people's respect for education, coupled with their disciplined classroom behavior, may have a lot to do with their high rate of literacy. Reasons (2) and (3) apply to many advanced countries such as the United States and Canada. With respect to (3), these countries do even better than Japan in that they have many neighborhood libraries that are available to all citizens free of charge. The United States equivalent to (4) is "Right to Read," which has become a national goal for the 1970's.

Reason (5), namely, the use of Kana, seems to be unique to Japanese. Kana codes a syllable, a simply-structured one at that. As point out in Secion I, and experimentally shown by Liberman, Shankweiler, Fischer, and Carter (1974), a syllable is intrinsically easier to isolate and use than a phoneme. According to Muraishi (1976), in Japan even preschool children who could not read any letters could count syllables. By the time preschool children read 11–15 Hiragana letters, they could count syllables at 90% correct, and locate the syllable /KO/ at 65% correct.

Not only the Japanese syllables but also the Japanese syllabaries that represent them are simple. First of all, each letter represents the same syllable consistently. Second, each letter is simple in shape, containing no more than six strokes (three strokes being the most common) (Muraishi, 1976). The shape of letters is reasonably distinct between the two types of syllabary, as well as within each syllabary. For example, there are no exact mirror-image letters like the notorious b–d or q–p. Third, the number of letters in each syllabary is small, about 100 letters (46 basic, 23 secondary, and 35 modified). Thus, it is not surprising that many Japanese children learn Hiragana even before they start schooling. In Muraishi's survey, close to 90% of 5-year-olds could read 60 or more Hiragana letters. With the knowledge of these letters, preschool children can negotiate simple stories written in Hiragana only.

2. Mixture of Kanji and Kana

A Japapese cannot be considered literate unless he/she knows some Kanji, since daily newspapers, popular magazines, and street signs use them. As in China, Kanji are learned batch-by-batch: 46 in grade I: 105 in grade II: 187 in grade III, and so on, until 966 Kanji are mastered in primary school (Sakamoto & Makita, 1973). By the time children finish the compulsory 9-year education, they have mastered most of the official 1850 Kanji. As pointed out earlier, each Kanji can have several readings, and even literate Japanese people may not know uncommon pronunciations of some Kanji. In such cases, the pronunciation is often given in small Kana written along the Kanji. This method, giving pronunciation in Kana, is used in teaching the sounds of Kanji to school children. The pictographic nature of some Kanji and radicals is also a useful aid to teaching Kanji.

As for the two syllabaries, those children who have not mastered Hiragana before they start schooling will do so in short time at school. Usually Hiragana is learned before Katakana, simply because the former is far more useful, and hence is taught earlier, than the latter.

Recently, Steinberg and Oka (1978) have questioned the age-old tradition of teaching Kana before Kanji. In their experiments, preschool children in Japan learned Kanji faster than Kana. However, their Kanji stimuli were all meaningful words, whereas their Kana stimuli were all meaningless syllables. Be that as it may, the study shows that preschool children can learn a handful of common Kanji words. The best teaching method would be to teach useful words in their customary scripts, be they Kanji, Hiragana, or Katakana.

Once some Kanji, Hiragana and Katakana, Arabic numerals, and perhaps a Roman alphabet are learned, text written in a judicious mixture of the five different writing systems is easy to read, because the use of one or the other types of writing already tells the reader something about the meaning of words.

1. Words written in Kanji are roots of nouns, verbs, adjectives, and adverbs, as well as personal and geographical names. In short, they are semantically important words. Sakamoto (1976) estimates that about 25–35% of text is in Kanji.

2. Words written in Katakana are European loan words and onomatopoeic words. The proportion of words in Katakana fluctuates greatly from one type of text to another. For example, it will be relatively large in a cookbook of Western dishes which will frequently require words like "butter"and small in a cookbook of Japanese dishes. Katakana may comprise no more than 4% of ordinary text.

3. Everything else—postpositions after nouns, grammatical endings of verbs, adjectives, and adverbs, as well as some words of Japanese origin—are written in Hiragana. (Postpositions in Japanese and Korean indicate grammatical functions nouns play in sentences: for example, in Japanese, -wa or -ni after a noun indicates that the noun is a subject or an object, of a sentence.) Since these items, especially grammatical items, occur frequently in any text, Hiragana must comprise the largest proportion of text, about 65%, compared to 30% Kanji, 4% Katakana, and 1% Arabic numerals and Roman letters.

4. The use of a Roman alphabet is confined to personal names and technical terms such as cm (centimeter) of European origin.

5. The use of Arabic numerals is optional, as in other writing systems.

Figure 3 shows a Japanese sentence from a cookbook which uses all

鶏肉とベーコンは 1. 5cm の角に切る。

chicken   BACON   cube   cut

Fig. 3. A Japanese sentence.

five types of writing system, each for a special purpose. Kanji have English translations in small letters; Kana, in capital letters; 1.5 cm is obvious; the rest are Hiragana signs. ("Cut the chicken and the bacon in 1.5 centimeter cubes.")

Sakamoto (1961) photographed the eye movements of college students reading short sentences of identical meaning but written in Hiragana only or Hiragana mixed with Kanji. The all-Hiragana text required twice as much time, a shorter perception span, more frequent fixations, longer fixation pauses, and more regression. In short, the all-Hiragana text is much harder to read than text that uses both Hiragana and Kanji.

Sakamoto's results are not surprising. Texts intended for mature readers are seldom written in Hiragana only but almost always in a mixture of Kanji and Hiragana, and possibly some Katakana. Japanese readers are far more experienced in reading a mixed script than Hiragana-only text. Gray (1956), who studied a number of adults reading in 14 different writing systems, noted a large number of fixations and a slow rate of reading in his Korean subjects. The Korean readers were accustomed to reading material that included characters, but Gray's test passages did not contain them.

The question is: Why do Japanese keep Kanji when thay have two perfectly good syllabaries? There are several reasons.

1. A mixture of Kanji and Hiragana performs the function of visually separating words, since no space is left between words.

2. Kanji differentiate homophones. In general, each Kanji is associated with only one morpheme, whereas one syllable may stand for several different morphemes. For example, several morphemes such as *child, old, lone,* and *small* are all pronounced as /ko/, but each of them is represented by its own unique Kanji.

3. The roots of key words are quicker and easier to identify in a mixed script than in all-Hiragana script. Not only are they and their grammatical endings written in differently shaped signs, Kanji and Hiragana, respectively, but also Kanji with their compact and complex shapes (darker visual objects) stand out from the background of simply shaped (lighter objects) Hiragana. Kanji stand out for another reason as well—there are fewer of them than Hiragana.

4. To represent one morpheme, one needs either one Kanji or a few Hiragana letters. For example, *I* requires one character but four or three Hiragana letters /wa-ta-ku-shi/ or /wa-ta-shi/ as pronounced in a Japanese way. Physically, each Hiragana letter occupies roughly the same amount of space as each Kanji. Thus, a mixed script tends to be somewhat shorter (less to process visually) than the same contents written in Hiragana only.

5. As discussed in Section II, and below, one Kanji is more likely to be processed holistically and directly than a string of a few phonetic signs, which presents a potential for letter-by-letter processing.

6. Kanji are easy to discriminate not only from Kana in mixed text but also from other Kanji. Tanaka, Iwasaki, and Miki (1974) and Tanaka (1977) compared tasks in which subjects had to cancel one or two target Kanji or Kana among distractors of their own kind (Kanji distractors for a Kanji target.) Recognition/discrimination scores were higher for Kanji than for either Hiragana or Katakana, but only in older children. The older the children, the more experienced they are with the use of many Kanji.

In the light of the above observations which point to the semantic importance and the visual prominence of Kanji in Japanese text, what is needed is an eye-movement study that reveals that fixations in fact tend to occur more on Kanji than on Kana.

3. Selective Impairment of Kanji and Kana

When Japanese speakers suffer brain damage, do they show selective impairments in processing logographs (Kanji) and syllabaries (Kana)?

Sasanuma and Fujimura (1971) studied 32 right-handed adults who had suffered a cerebrovascular accident. In visual recognition tasks, the patients matched written words shown on a tachistoscope to line drawings of the objects which the words represented. There were three sets of words: Set I consisted of 10 words in Kanji: Set II, of 10 European loan words in Katakana: and Set III, of Hiragana versions of the Kanji words.

Group B aphasics with apraxia (who make phonological errors) made more errors than Group A (simple aphasics), who in turn made more errors than Groups C–D (hemiplegics without aphasia). The most interesting point is that Group B, but not Group A or Groups C–D, made more errors on the two kinds of Kana than on Kanji. According to the authors, a Kanji transcription can be directly identified with a word, bypassing its phonological processing, whereas a kana transcription has to be phonologically processed before the word is identified. Thus an impaired phonetic processor would affect Kana processing more than it does Kanji processing.

There seems to be another factor contributing to the differences in errors made on the three types of script. In the experiment, the words that are customarily written in Kanji were written in uncustomary Hiragana. People, especially brain-damaged patients, are more likely to make errors on words in uncustomary than in customary script. If the phonetic processing is the only factor, there should not have been differences between the two types of Kana words, but the patients made fewer errors on the Katakana words, which being European words, were in their customary script.

Later, Sasanuma (1974) made an in-depth study of one brain-damaged adult who showed serious impairment in reading but only a minor impairment in other speech functions and writing. With Kanji, the patient showed normal, instantaneous comprehension of a substantial number of words with two or more characters. With Kana, his latency in deciphering individual signs was long. Further, he had a consistent difficulty in immediately decoding a word of more than two Kana signs as an integrated visual pattern. He made a detour: he first sounded out individual Kana signs (using kinesthetic facilitation, if necessary), then combined these sounds to form an integrated sound pattern of the word, and finally arrived at the meaning. This strategy of a indirect graph-sound-meaning association was not effective for retrieving those Kanji words for which the direct graph-meaning strategy failed to work.

With "normal" adult subjects, Hatta (1978) found that single Kanji was recognized more accurately from the left visual field (right hemisphere processing). When a single Kanji was presented along with another Kanji or Hiragana as part of a word, different results were obtained: the word was recognized better from the right visual field (left hemisphere processing). Hatta hypothesizes that for a single Kanji with multiple readings, visual rather than phonetic processing is advantageous. When more than two Kanji join to form a word, usually one particular reading becomes clearer, and hence phonetic processing dominates over visual processing. (Multiple readings of a single Kanji are common only in Japan, not in China or Korea.)

4. Horizontal versus Vertical Reading

Since Japanese writers regularly use both vertical and horizontal arrangements of letters, Japanese writing is an ideal system for comparing the relative advantages of the two, with the reading habit reasonably controlled. In the study of Tanaka *et al.* (1974) on recognition/discrimination of isolated Kanji and Hiragana, a horizontal arrangement yielded a higher score than a vertical arrangement. In another study, Chan (1942) invokes the vertical–horizontal visual illusion—a vertical line appears longer than an equal length of a horizontal line; therefore reading vertically should feel more effortful. In infants, horizontal scan is more dispersed—the scan's muscles are longer and, perhaps its activities are higher—than the vertical (Salapatec, 1968).

Ultimately, one must compare the two directions of writing in real text. In Sakamoto's study (1961), eye movements for meaningless patterns were smoother for horizontal than for vertical arrangements. However, Japanese readers reading real text moved their eyes more efficiently along vertical lines of print. Shen (1927) also found that Chinese readers read comparable passages faster vertically than horizontally. In Japan, especially in China, vertical still seems to be the more prevalent direction, and reading habit is a potent influence on the relative ease of reading horizontally or vertically. Gray (1956) who compared 14 writing systems—some vertical, some horizontal, either left-to-right or right-to-left—found that the direction of writing did not make a big difference in reading.

IV. ALPHABETIC SYLLABARY—KOREAN

A. Writing System

The Korean alphabet, called Hangul (Han = Great; gul = letters), is regarded by some scholars as the most perfect phonetic system that has been called upon to stand the test of time and actual use (Diringer, 1968). Martin (1972, p.82) observes: "the Korean script is remarkable for its internal structure and for its graphic origin." It was deliberately invented in the fifteenth century A.D. by a group of scholars under their king's leadership. The scholars made a careful study of other alphabets and writing systems, and came up with an alphabet of their own after several years of deliberation.

Three uniqe and rational features of Hangul are: (1) articulatory characteristics of the sounds are reflected in the shapes that represent them; (2) Hangul starts with a few basic symbols, which are then used to create increasingly complex symbols; (3) a small number of phoneme-symbols are used as building blocks for a large number of syllable-blocks.

1. Alphabetic Symbols

To represent 19 Korean consonants (14 basic and 5 doubled), Hangul starts with five basic consonant symbols, which are shaped to depict the

ㄱ /g/ : the root of the tongue as it closes the throat passage and touches the soft palate.

ㄴ /n/ : the shape of the point of the tongue as it touches the ridge behind the teeth.

ㅅ /s/ : upper (╱) and lower (╲) tooth get together

ㅎ /h/ : unobstructed throat passage in producing /o/ is joined by two strokes.

ㅁ /m/: the shape of the closed mouth.

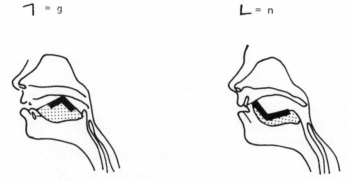

Fig. 4.   Articulation of five basic consonants.

articulators pronouncing them. For example, a small square depicts a closed mouth pronouncing /m/ (see Fig. 4 for the four other consonant symbols and their articulators).

Based on these five basic symbols, several related consonant symbols are created. For example, /d/ is articulated in the same place as /n/, and hence its symbol is created by adding a stroke to the *n*-symbol; likewise /b/ is articulated in the same place as /m/, and hence its symbol is created by adding two small strokes to the *m*-symbol.

For the articulatory feature of aspiration, a stroke is added, inside the *g*-symbol to create the *k*-symbol; over the *d*-symbol to create the *t*-symbol; and under the *b*-symbol to create the *p*-symbol (which is rotated 90 degrees in actual use). For the articulatory feature of tenseness, each of the *g*-, *d*-, *b*-, *s*-, and *ch*-symbols is doubled to make symbols for sounds that do not exist in English (see Table VII for a complete list of the resulting consonant symbols).

Vowel symbols start with a long horizontal bar, a long vertical bar, and a short bar or marker. To create a symbol for /o/, attach the marker above the horizontal bar (⊥); to create a symbol for the related /jo/, attach an additional marker (⊥⊥). To create a symbol for /a/, attach the marker to the right of a vertical bar (ㅏ); to create a symbol for the related /ja/, attach an additional marker (ㅑ). Now, if the symbols for /o/ and /a/ are combined, we have the compound symbols for /oa/ (⊥ㅏ).

2. Syllable Blocks

So far, we have talked about the phoneme-symbols for consonants and vowels. Now we talk about the "blocks" that represent syllables; these blocks are the actual reading units. A consonant symbol is never used by itself but is used always in combination with a vowel. When a vowel is used alone without a consonant, an empty circle takes the place of consonant symbol. A Hangul block then represents a syllable, which may be V, VC, CV, CVC, or CVCC. For this reason, Taylor (1980) calls Hangul an "alphabetic syllabary," i.e., a syllable is represented by a block built combining two to four alphabet symbols.

Table VIII shows how phoneme-symbols are packaged to form syllable-blocks of varying complexity. The rules for packaging are as follows. In forming a V or CV block, a horizontal vowel symbol comes under its consonant symbol, while a vertical symbol comes to the right-hand side of its consonant symbol. In a VC or CVC block, the vowel or CV part goes over the final consonant symbol; in a CVCC block, the

TABLE VII
Hangul Consonant Symbols[a]

Position	Articulation manner					Doubled
	Basic symbols					
	Continuant	(Add)	Stop (Add)	Aspirated	Lateral	Tense
Velar			ㄱ ⁻	ㅋ		ㄲ
Lingual	ㄴ	⁻	ㄷ ⁻	ㅌ	ㄹ	ㄸ
Bilabial	ㅁ	ˊˋ	ㅂ ˊˋ	ㅕ → ㅍ		ㅃ
Sibilant	ㅅ	⁻	ㅈ	ㅊ		ㅉ, ㅆ
Glottal	ㅇ		⁻	ㅎ		

[a] From Taylor (1980).

CV again goes over the final consonants (see Table VIII for examples of such syllable-blocks).

Although there is a possibility of 6400 V, CV, VC, or CVC blocks plus additional CVCCs, only around 5000 occur in practice. The beauty of Hangul is that although an experienced reader can process a syllable-block as a single unit, a beginner does not have to rote memorize all 5000 of them; he merely learns a handful of alphabet symbols and the simple rules for packaging them.

Hangul's advantage over the English system is that its reading unit is syllable rather than phoneme. When a letter codes a phoneme as in English words, a word often requires a long string of letters. For example, *entrepreneurship* requires 19 letters in English, but only 8 syllable-blocks in Hangul. A long array of letters contains not only many items to be processed visually but also it may pose a sequencing problem.

How does Hangul compare with the Japanese syllabaries? Japanese readers have to learn 100 or so syllable signs (and their duplicates) to read 100 or so CV and V syllables. Korean readers, on the other hand, learn only 35 alphabet symbols and a small number of simple rules for packaging them into syllable-blocks to read a few thousand syllables. The Korean alphabetic syllabary is eminently suited for the Korean sound system, which has a rich variety of sounds and syllables.

TABLE VIII

Hangul Syllable-Blocks in Three Complexity Levels[a,b]

Complexity level[c]	Linearly arranged				Packaged in block[d]	Syllable	Morpheme (native)
	C	V	C	C			
I		ㅏ			아	V/a/	suffix; ah
I	ㄷ	ㅏ			다	CV/da/	all
II		ㅏ	ㄹ		말	VC/al/	egg
II	ㄷ	ㅏ	ㄹ		달	CVC/dal/	moon
III	ㄷ	ㅏ	ㄹ	ㄱ	닭	CVCC/dalg/	hen

[a] From Taylor (1980).

[b] All the letters in this table, except the level III letter, could represent both native morphemes and Chinese loan morphemes; only the native ones are given here.

[c] "Complexity" is based on visual complexity, which is partly confounded with syllabic complexity.

[d] In V and VC letters, the empty circle is required to show that a vowel is alone in a syllable. The circle depicts the shape of the throat in vowel production—it is empty and wide open.

Because of its rational design, Hangul and its use in writing are easily and rapidly learned. The illiteracy rate in South Korea is 5%, which is largely confined to the mentally retarded, and to very old people who have not benefitted from compulsory education introduced in modern times. The term "developmental dyslexia" (difficulty in learning to read despite adequate intelligence) exists neither in Korea nor in Japan. According to experts on dyslexia (e.g., Boder, 1971; Vellutino, 1979), the basic difficulty of dyslexic children is word decoding in English. Note that word decoding is remarkably simple with Hangul, and also with Kana.

In Korea, knowledge of Chinese characters is useful but not vital. North Korea does not use characters, and South Korea uses only 1300 of them. Each character usually has only one reading in Korean, in contrast to its multiple readings in Japanese. As in Japanese text, so in Korean text, characters are used for key words, and phonetic signs, for grammatical endings.

Korean text can be, and often is, written completely in the Hangul alphabetic syllabary. Once practiced, all-alphabetic script in Korean is not as difficult to read as all-Hiragana text in Japanese because Korean letters come in different levels of visual complexity, and spaces are left between words.

B. Exploratory Experiments on the Korean System

Recently, I (Taylor, 1980) carried out a simple experiment to demonstrate that the three levels of visual complexity are helpful for recognizing and discriminating syllable-blocks. Korean readers' task was to spot and cancel one target block among other blocks. There were two experimental conditions: (1) a block was recognized/discriminated among other blocks of one complexity level, its own; and (2) a block was recognized/discriminated among other blocks of all three complexity levels. The target blocks could come from any of the three complexity levels. The subjects indeed recognized/discriminated a target block better in condition (2).

In another experiment, I (Taylor, 1980) compared linear arrangement to packaged arrangement of Hangul symbols. Test words were eight CVCV words and eight CVCCVC words. In the linear arrangement, the two types of word require four and six alphabet symbols, respectively; in the packaged arrangement, both types require two blocks. With only 5 minutes of explanation on the principle of block formation and pronunciation, English-speaking subjects could pronounce the words reasonably fluently. The CVCV words had shorter pronunciation times than the CVCCVC words, but the differences narrowed over 18 trials. The linear arrangements resulted in shorter pronunciation time than the packaged one throughout the trials, but again, the differences almost disappeared on the final eighteenth trial.

The experiment needs to be carried out over many more trials, and with Korean children who do not have a long-established habit of linear reading.

Park and Arbuckle (1977) found that the Korean words presented in Kanji were recognized and recalled better than the words presented in Hangul. Why? The authors themselves invoke Craik and Tulving's (1975) "depth of processing hypothesis": "a more informative stimulus [Kanji] elicits more elaborate encoding operations, yielding a more elaborate memory trace, than does a less informative stimulus [Hangul]."

I would scrutinize the test material of Park and Arbuckle before endorsing such an interpretation. In Korean, some native words can be written only in Hangul, and some Chinese loan words are written customarily in Kanji. The Hangul test words of Park and Arbuckle appear to be transcriptions of Kanji words. In that case, their words may have been Chinese loan words written in uncustomary Hangul. Their results remain equivocal: If a Hangul word is less well remembered than its Kanji version, is it because the Hangul word is in an uncustomary script or because it is intrinsically less memorable than the Kanji version?

They overlooked another point: Some Hangul syllable-blocks (level III in Table VIII) are almost logographs in that each of them represents a unique morpheme. How do such blocks compare with level I blocks which are not logographic?

Only a modest beginning has been made in research on the Korean writing system, both in Korea and in North America.

V. ALPHABET—ENGLISH

The principle of an alphabet is to represent each phoneme with one grapheme.

A. English Orthography

1. Grapheme–Phoneme Noncorrespondence

The English alphabet and orthography fall far short of being ideal. To begin with, only 26 letters are available to represent 40 or so phonemes. Second, one letter can represent a few sounds, and different letters can represent the same sound. According to Dewey's (1971) count based on 100,000 running words, English orthography has 219 spellings for 24 consonants, or 9.1 spellings per consonant, and 342 spellings for 17 vowels, or 20.7 spellings per vowel. For pronunciation, count 2.4 sounds per consonant letter, and 8.2 per vowel letter. Such vagaries in the orthography have arisen partly because of a faster change in speech than in spelling since the fifteenth century. Another cause is a profuse infusion of loan words, whose original spellings are sometimes retained, and sometimes not.

Who can blame Lawrence of Arabia, who, when asked by his perplexed publisher to try to spell his foreign words and names more uniformly, answered: "I spell my names anyhow, to show what rot the systems are" (1935, p. 25). Or, listen to a hapless reader: "How on earth do you spell pearl?—and don't ask me to look up in the dictionary because I've already looked under 'pir,' 'pur,' and 'per' without finding it" (Rosewell and Natchez, 1971, p. 103).

Here is a short catalogue of the vagaries of English orthography.

1. One letter for several different sounds: as *a* in *fall, far, fat, fame, about, hurrah*; *t* in *native, nation, nature, listen*;
2. Double letters for one sound: *sh, th, mm*;
3. Redundant letters: *x, q, c* for /k/;
4. Letters or letter clusters for no sound: *Psalm*, dra*ch*m;
5. Nonexpression of a sound: *lieutenant* /leftenənt/ (in Canada and Britain);
6. Representation of another sound than its own: *comptroller* /controlə/.

The relation between graphemes and phonemes is not as anarchic as it appears. An English speaker will have no trouble sounding out such a pseudoword as *phlought* using an analogy from *phrase* and *brought*. (But he might say *fluffed,* as easily as *flaut*.) On the other hand, he may or may not pronounce such real words as *indict* and *Pontefract* correctly. An analogy from *predict* will mislead him to mispronounce the former, and no analogy will help him to pronounce the latter (the correct pronunciations are: /indait/ and /pʌmfri/.

2. Functional Spelling Unit

Venezky (1967) derived spelling-to-sound correspondences, or 65 functional spelling units, for 20,000 most common English words. To relate graphemic patterns to sound patterns in a regular fashion, he maps via an intermediate unit between phoneme and morpheme, i.e., morphophonemic level. (In determining sounds of a word, consider the word's morphemes.) For example, the sound of *ph* in *sapphire* and *shepherd* differs: in the former, it occurs within one morpheme and is pronounced as /f/, and in the latter, at a morpheme boundary and is pronounced as /p/. The functional units do not transcend such morpheme boundaries.

Prediction of sounds from spellings may be more regular with Venezky's functional units than with grapheme–phoneme units, but prediction still is not fully regular. Venezky's book contains over 70 pages of rules, plus many exceptions to the rules.

Even when we take a word's morphemes into consideration, recovering sounds from spellings does not seem always straightforward. Take *phase, haphazard, shepherd,* and *goatherd.* A reader must learn:

(1) *f* is pronounced as /f/.

(2) *ph* too is pronounced as /f/.

(3) But wait—there can be exceptions to (2) in the following cases.

(3a) *ph* = /p + h/ in *haphazard,* which consists of *hap* and *hazard.*

(3b) Drop /h/ of /p + h/ in *-herd* of *shepherd,* which too consists of two morphemes *shep* and *herd.*

(4) Wait again—there can be exceptions to (3b) too. In *goatherd,* /h/ in *-herd* is retained.

3. Underlying Phonetic Representation and Vowel Shift Rule

Chomsky and Halle (1968) contend that English orthography is a "near optimal" system for the lexical representation of English words. It ignores surface phonetic variations, such as vowel or consonant alternations (which can be predicted from general phonological rules), and maintains a close correspondence between semantic units and orthographic representations in abstract, underlying phonetic representations. In word derivation, a vowel sound but not its letter may change, as in:

Underlying vowel /li:n/

Diphthongization [lain]

Vowel shift rule and laxing rule *linear* /liniə/

An example of a consonant shift is: *anxious–anxiety* /ks/–/gz/.

Even if it does represent underlying lexical units rather than surface phonetic units, there is no reason why English orthography should hold on to its many vagaries. All words using the letter *c* could have either *k* or *s* substituted without causing any additional difficulty. For example, *compose/composite* could be spelled *kompose/komposite* without losing their lexical relations (the second *o* is retained despite its differing pronunciations), but using one consistent letter *k* instead of allowing two letters, *c* or *k,* for one sound.

There are also groups of words that show different spelling patterns despite their same lexical and phonological relations.

candy–candies
play–plays

On the other side of the coin, *night* and *knight* share the irregular spelling pattern of *night* without sharing any obvious relation. Both come from earlier forms in which the *gh* was pronounced, as in the modern German *Nacht* and *Knecht*.

Moskowitz (1973) points out that those word pairs which show vowel shifts constitute a small percentage of the total vocabulary. They are also among the most literary and abstract types of word, and occur very infrequently in speech.

Taylor, Coleman, and Taylor (in preparation) looked for words that undergo a vowel shift among 1000 frequently occurring words in Grade I children's speech. We found none. In adults' speech sample, we found several words. But we wish to emphasize the fact that, in word derivation, there are far more words that undergo sound **and** spelling changes (e.g., *sing–sang–sung*) than those that undergo only sound but not spelling changes (*anxious–anxiety*).

According to Moskowitz, other factors that complicate the vowel-shift rule are: some related word pairs do not show vowel shifts (*stupid–stupidity*); some word pairs that show vowel shifts are not related (*rape–rapture*); some word pairs that do not have semantic and historical relations follow the same phonological pattern (*dime–dimity*).

Moskowitz points out that children come to use the vowel shift rule from learning to read and spell. Simons (1975) conducted a limited test of children's use of the vowel shift rule. Second and third graders were given paired-association learning on two types of material: (1) morphologically related word pairs (*hide–hid*) with the same vowel spellings; (2) morphologically unrelated word pairs (*pine–pin*) with the same vowel spellings; and (3) filler pairs. The related word pairs were not learned better than the unrelated word pairs, and the grade levels did not make any difference.

Steinberg (1973) tested adults' use of the vowel-shift rule in word derivation. For example, given the base *trout* in a meaningful context, which suffix, *-cal* or *-ify*, would people choose, and how would they pronounce the suffix chosen? For *troutical,* no subject said [trʌtikəl], which is what Chomsky and Halle predicted; the subjects all said [traᵂtikəl].

Another phonetic information that is not explicitly indicated in orthography is stress. Chomsky and Halle proposed a set of complex rules for assigning stress in words. Some of the factors that influence stress assignment are:

1. Vowel quality—in two-syllable words, a tense (long) final vowel attracts stress: *témpest* vs *domáin*.
2. Number of consonants—two-syllable words ending in two consonants have stress on the second syllable: *édit* vs *eléct*.
3. Affix—the prefix *com-* causes stress to move to the second syllable: *cáncel* vs *compél*.
4. Silent *e*—the final silent *e* attracts stress on the penultimate vowel in three-syllable words: *dámask* vs *arabésque*.
5. Noun vs verb—extra rules operate on nouns derived from verbs: *súrvey* (noun) vs *survéy* (verb).

Smith and Baker (1976) tested adults and Groat (1979) tested 7-year-old children for their abilities to use these rules. All of the above factors had large and significant effects on the assignment of primary stress in the word. Roughly the same results were obtained for the adults and the children, except on the silent *e,* to which the adults were far more sensitive than were the children. In both studies, Chomsky–Halle's phonology accounted for some but not all the effects. In particular, there was no strong evidence for the underlying phonology.

All considered, Trammel's (1978, p. 93) conclusion seems reasonable: "While the orthography may be 'near optimal' for a formal system of rules, the speaker's internalized rules are not nearly so well defined or consistently applied as those of SPE [Chomsky and Halle's book]."

As Rogers (1979, personal communication) points out, Chomsky and Halle's complex phonological rules may be largely irrelevant for nonlinguists, but preserving the same spelling *-s* for plural morpheme in spite of its changing sounds is convenient.

cats	/s/
dogs	/z/
bases	/iz/

The same observation can be made of the past-tense morpheme *-ed*.

walked	/t/
moved	/d/
mended	/id/

It might be instructive to ponder how the other phonetic writing systems considered in this article solve the problem of sound changes.

Japanese and Korean systems solve it by simply representing sounds as they sound. In the two languages, there is little sound change within the roots of words across different dialects and morphological forms. All kinds of sound change— grammatical, dialectic, honorific, historic—seem to occur more in grammatical endings than in roots of words.

4. Concluding Remarks

English orthography represents the English language in several levels— phonemic, morphophonemic, morphemic, and lexical. This fact itself is not unique to English orthography. What is unique about it is that it does so in a highly irregular, complex, and even abstract, way. To grasp fully the relations between graphemes and phonemes, a reader must consider stress patterns, the number of syllables and morphemes, form class, etymology, underlying phonetic and lexical representation, morphological and phonological derivations, and the interrelations among all of these. Usually, it takes a lot of exposure to English orthography before the reader grasps some of the more obvious relations. As for the abstract ones, only trained linguists seem to be aware of them. All the same, English orthography is the key to the vast treasures of printed material in English. Obviously, it is not something to be tinkered with, but neither is it something to be exalted; it is simply something to live with.

B. Learning to Read English

The amount of research into reading in English is prodigious: indeed, it is overwhelming. My coverage is more concerned with beginning than with skilled reading. The influence of writing systems on reading seems to be strongest at the initial stage of learning to read. Bewilderingly numerous systems for teaching English reading have been proposed, only because English orthography is complex and difficult.

1. Short Perceptual Span

The span of visual perception is smaller in children than in adults. During a fixation pause a child can perceive two to three letters, usually not enough to form a morpheme or a word. First-grade children make two fixations per word, as compared to skilled readers who make one fixation per two words. A child also makes frequent regressions—once for every two words, as compared to a skilled reader who makes one for every two lines of print. Around the tenth or twelfth grade, children's eye movements in reading approximate those of adults (Taylor, Frackenpohl, & Pattee, 1965; Rayner & McConkie, 1977).

The short span of perception does not seem to pose a problem in the three other writing systems already discussed in this article. In the Japanese syllabaries and the Korean alphabetic syllabary, two to three letters perceived during one fixation may very well form a morpheme or a word. In these two languages as well as in Chinese, recall that one Chinese character represents one morpheme-syllable.

In English reading, a child's short span of visual perception necessitates decoding graphemic strings into auditory percepts, for which he has a larger span, according to Gasper and Brown (1973). In any case, a child has normally already learned his mother tongue by listening and talking, and the first stages of his learning to read will tend to be based on his oral repertory.

2. Phonics versus Look–Say

Four difficulties a beginning reader of English faces are:

1. A letter or a grapheme represents a phonetic unit rather than a meaning unit.
2. The phonetic unit represented is a small and abstract unit, phoneme, rather than a more accessible and concrete unit, syllable.
3. The grapheme–phoneme relation is irregular and complex.
4. Some letters—b/d and q/p—are mirror-images.

The phonics method of teaching grapples with all these difficulties while the look–say method avoids them altogether. By the phonic method, a child learns to pair letters and letter-clusters with spoken phonemes and syllables, and by the look–say method, he learns to read each word at sight, as a whole. The two methods have been compared in numerous experiments in the past few decades.

To cite one typical experiment, Jeffrey and Samuels (1967) compared phonics and look–say training on transfer to reading new words. Kindergarten children were given phoneme blending training and then assigned to phonics, look–say, and control (irrelevant task). All three groups were then given the same list of transfer words, whose constituent letters had occurred in the original training. The phonic group was significantly better than the other two groups in the number of words read without any help, and in the speed of learning the entire list. No significant difference was found between the look–say and control groups on either of these measures.

Most laboratory experiments comparing the two teaching methods use an extremely limited number of sounds and words, whose sound–letter correspondence is perfect. Such stimuli do not reflect the English orthography. Nevertheless, one may conclude that phonics is better than the look–say method in teaching children to read new words.

In classrooms, teachers have noted that, at first, learning is rapid with look–say, but this does not last for too long. Presumably only so many words can be recognized by such visual cues as length, initial and final letters, possibly shape, before the whole-word strategies prove ineffective. A small number of very common but irregularly spelled words like *come, walk, laugh, the* might be suitable candidates for look–say method. The current practice in English-speaking countries seems to be eclectic, with a somewhat heavier emphasis on phonics than on look–say method.

A few thousand Chinese characters by necessity have to be taught by look–say. But characters are suited for look–say teaching because each of them is visually and semantically more integrated and distinct than a word consisting of a few phonetic signs, as discussed in Sections II and III. To recapitulate, since any of individual strokes of a character does not code a phoneme (or any other information), it is futile to process a character stroke-by-stroke.

3. i.t.a. and T.O.

The initial teaching alphabet (i.t.a.) was developed by Sir James Pitman in Britain beginning about 1960. Now its use has spread to the English-speaking countries such as the United States, Canada, New Zealand, and Australia. Aukerman (1971, p. 342), after comparing a variety of teaching and (English) writing systems, declares: "i.t.a. . . . has created an impact upon education and upon reading in particular that far surpasses anything that has happened since the introduction of the first basal reader series."

The system consists of 44 graphemes, 24 of which are identical to those in the Roman alphabet (minus *q* and *x*), and 20 additional graphemes, 14 of which are ligatured ones. It has two separate symbols for the two different sounds of *th.* It has no upper case letters, and sentences begin with a larger version of the lower case. The sounds are based on a "standard" dialect. The principle of i.t.a. is to have one consistent grapheme for one sound. Occasionally, this principle is violated so as not to deviate too drastically from traditional orthography (T.O.).

According to Gasper and Brown (1973) who compared i.t.a. and T.O. in Britain, a child taught to read by means of i.t.a. learns not only to translate the individual graphemes into corresponding phonemes but also to blend these into spoken words relatively quickly and with little need for oral drill. The authors consider that the mere possibility of attributing meaning to printed signs by means of a phonemic notation is beneficial to a child in two related ways: in the formation of a positive attitude toward the activity of reading, and in the development of his vocabulary.

In the United States, i.t.a groups are found to be superior to T.O. groups only in the initial stage of learning, and only in specific word-decoding skills (e.g., Gillooly, 1976). Perhaps teaching material, methods, and the time and method of transfer to T.O. may have differed in the two countries. The i.t.a. system is a writing system, and can be taught by either phonics or look–say, just as T.O. can be. However, i.t.a. does not require excessive oral drill because of its relatively regular correspondence between grapheme and sound, while T.O. does. After the first year, a child begins to work toward a transition to T.O. starting with familiar words now expressed in T.O. Advocates of i.t.a. claim that by the end of 1 year, the great majority of children can and do easily transfer to T.O. at a level of reading comprehension far beyond that possible with traditional basal series. Further, there are only half as many very poor readers in the i.t.a. group as there are in the T.O. group (Downing, 1965, 1973).

The i.t.a. system promotes word decoding, and it does so without excessive oral drill, which might later get in the way of developing comprehension in silent reading. Although a child does not automatically become a Reader by learning merely to "bark at print," grapheme-to-sound decoding is an important basic skill of reading. Calfee, Lindamood, and Lindamood (1973) found that the ability to perform word-segmentation and construction continues to distinguish successful from unsuccessful readers all the way through twelfth grade.

Word-decoding should be easy with alphabets that have regular phoneme–grapheme correspondence. Among Roman alphabets, Finnish orthography is noted for this feature. Accordingly, Finnish children, at the end of Grade I, can read nearly all words in the language. In test with pronounceable nonwords, they showed a high level of word-decoding ability, although decoding ability was correlated with reading only moderately in Grades II and III (Venezky, 1973).

4. Reading Disorders

A number of factors singly or jointly may cause developmental dyslexia. Genetic and constitutional factors (family history, brain-damage, abnormal laterality, being male); social factors (disadvantaged home); psychological factors (low motivation, hyperactivity); cognitive factors (perceptual and/or memory deficits); linguistic factors (limited vocabulary and syntax) have been suggested by various authors as possible causes (e.g., Boder, 1971; Bryden, 1970; Witelson, 1977; Morrison, Giordani, & Nagi, 1977; Benton & Pearl, 1978; Vellutino, 1979).

Here we are concerned about a writing system being a contributing factor. The observations that, while learning the same system, many more boys than girls, and many more children from disadvantaged than advantaged homes have reading problems, rule out the possibility of the writing system being the sole important contributing factor. On the other hand, there is almost no illiteracy and reading disability among "normal" Japanese-speaking people, while the English system in the United States produces 10–20% functional illiterates and disabled readers. One suspects that already unfavorable learning conditions are aggravated by a complex orthography. Thus, a dyslexic child may read such an irregular word as *laugh* as *log* or *loge,* and spell it as *laf* (Boder, 1971).

Guthrie (1973) showed that normal readers in the third grade had mastered all of the subskills measured in the Kennedy Institute Phonics Test. For these readers, the eight subskills such as Nonsense-word production, Short or Long vowel production, and Initial letter recognition were highly correlated. Disabled readers at age 9 manifested a group profile that was virtually indistinguishable from that of young normal readers. However, the interrelation among the subskills was low for the disabled group, suggesting that a lack of interfacilitation among skills is debilitating for them. A disabled reader is likely to have a profile in which one or two of the simple skills are likely to have a high level of strength (80% or more) whereas all of the more complex skills in the hierarchy will have a low level of development (40% or less).

All the subskills Guthrie examined seem to be concerned with word-decoding. Such word-decoding problems are peculiar to English orthography.

VI. MATURE READER

A mature reader reads silently 300–400 words a minute with good comprehension. How does he perform such a feat? Since other contributors to this volume will be discussing this topic, I will present a mere sketch of a mature reader of English text, and presumably of text written in any other systems.

A. Perceptual Span

A mature reader spends on average .25 seconds in a fixation pause, during which he can perceive 4 letter positions to the left of the center of vision and no more than 12 letter positions to the right. He also makes an efficient use of peripheral vision, with which he can obtain some gross visual characteristics of words (shape, space, initial and final letters). Word-length patterns are noticed somewhat further to the right of fixation (Rayner & McConkie, 1977).

Peripheral vision apparently plays an important role in reading, as it does in visual perception in general. According to Hochberg (1970), fast readers ordinarily pick up an interword space in peripheral vision and use it to program the next fixation to center on, or near, the initial letters of words, which usually convey maximum information. A second possible cue—word length—might serve to distinguish short function words from longer content words. The reader is more likely to look at the latter since they are high information words (Rayner, 1977).

Readers of different writing systems may pick up different kinds of gross visual features from their peripheral vision. For example, what a Japanese or a Korean reader picks up in reading mixed scripts might be distinction between Kanji and Kana or Hangul. Most of the gross visual features of English text, such as word length and initial letter, are lacking in Chinese text.

B. Processing Unit

Potentially, letter, spelling patterns, syllable, morpheme, word, phrase, clause, or sentence can be used as processing units in reading. As Huey in 1908 observed: "we read by phrases, words, or letters as may serve our purpose best. But . . . the reader's acquirement of ease and power of reading comes through increasing ability to read in large units" (p. 116).

The kind of text and task is also a factor in the choice of unit in reading. Terry (1976) found holistic, parallel processing of familiar words with up to three to six letters. The same readers reverted to serial letter-by-letter processing, however, when the words were presented in unfamiliar mirror-image orthography. Average response latency increased from three to six letters for the transformed but not for the regular orthography. Proof readers often resort to letter-by-letter processing.

A cluster of graphemes which has an invariant pronunciation might be a useful unit too. Gibson, Pick, Osser, and Hammond (1962) showed that accuracy of report from tachistoscopic exposures was higher when six-letter arrays contained only regular spelling patterns at customary positions (e.g., *GLURCK*) than for letters randomly arrayed (*CKURGL*). In another kind of task, Santa and Santa's (1977) subjects judged whether a word (*BLAST*) and a probe (e.g., *BL, L, BC*) were the same or different. Initial consonant clusters were processed as quickly as single letters, and only slightly faster than whole words.

Let us consider a larger unit, a phrase. In reading aloud, the eye is usually ahead of the voice, because visual and cognitive processing is faster than the motor process of reading aloud. The span between the eye and voice, usually measured in words, is eye–voice span (EVS).

Levin and Kaplan (1970) showed that EVS extended to a phrase boundary regardless of the age of the reader and the size of the phrase. The ages of their subjects ranged from about 7 to adult, and the phrase sizes from two to four words. When readers inserted words that were not really in the text, their insertions usually completed phrases.

Processing by phrase means that individual words within a phrase are held in short-term working memory, with varying degrees of partial processing, until the entire phrase is completed. This is an efficient method of processing because the meaning, sound, and syntactic function of an individual word are sometimes ambiguous until other words in a phrase provide a context. It also may mean that some low-information function words such as *the* and *to* that are regular parts of phrases are processed scantily or not at all (Schindler, 1978). This kind of procedure can be repeated for a unit still higher than a phrase, such as a clause, as long as it does not tax the working memory.

C. Phonetic Recoding and Subvocalization

In their extensive review of the literature on phonetic recoding and subvocalization, Taylor, Taylor, and Coleman (submitted) gave the following summary.

There are several routes for extracting meaning from words on a page, and they may derive from a common developmental sequence. The foundation for the sequence is laid in the first auditory images the child uses to recognize spoken words. For example, a young child has the auditory image of *fish* though he can pronounce it only as *fis* (Brown & Berko, 1960). Later, the sequence proceeds from learning to read aloud, to subvocalization, to phonetic recoding, to direct semantic coding of the visual input. One learns to read by reading aloud, gathering meaning through the well-practiced auditory channel. Later, the overt vocalization may be omitted, although covert control of the vocal musculature still occurs in the form of subvocalization. Subvocalization seems to provide a redundant channel for perceiving printed words, and it is associated with poor readers, difficult material, or early stags of learning to read (e.g., Edfeldt, 1959; McGuigan, 1970). At the subvocalization stage, the child's articulatory control patterns may complement the auditory images and the two may gradually replace the heard vocalization of the reading-aloud stage.

Next is the development of phonetic recoding—the formation of auditory images with little or no subvocalization. People who read faster than 300–400 words per minute simply have not enough time to articulate all they read, because a reader can pronounce only 150 words a minute.

A decisive piece of evidence that reading can go on without articulation is provided by Pintner (1913). He required subjects to read while repeating aloud numbers 13, 14, 15, 16 indefinitely. Counting hampered the reading at first but with practice the subjects read more efficiently with the counting than they had read under normal conditions.

Internal auditory representation can move more quickly than the muscles and bones of articulation. Further, not every letter or word has to be auditorily represented, any more than it has to be visually perceived.

For example, in my silent reading, I must have formed and stored an auditory image of *Zangwill* as /Zangvil/ considering it to be a German name. When it was mentioned by other people as /zængwil/ in an American pronunciation, I failed to recognize it immediately, presumably because it deviated from my stored auditory image.

In its turn phonetic recoding may be superseded during easy reading by direct semantic coding of the printed words. Even at this stage, phonetic recoding will still be used to suspend the words in short-term memory (Huey, 1908; Kleiman, 1975). Good readers resort to phonetic recoding more than do poor readers (Liberman, Shankweiler, Fowler, & Fischer, 1977; see also Section VI,B).

D. Use of Context

A mature reader makes use of semantic, syntactic, orthographic, and phonological context. An ordinary text is full of such contextual information. Readers' sensitivity to semantic and syntactic context has been shown by Kolers (1970). College students reading aloud pages of transformed text (inversion, mirror-reflection, and rotation in the plane of page) made many errors, which were not random. In general, when one word was mistaken for another, the incorrect reading was consistent both semantically and syntactically with the antecedent text in about 90–100% of cases. Here is a good example. "Emerson once said that every man" might be misread as *suggested*, which has little visual similarity to *said* but is semantically and syntactically compatible with the antecedent context. In fact, incompatibility with context alerts a reader to his misreadings.

A word provides a context for identification of its contituent letters. A letter such a *C* or *J* is perceived more accurately in a tachistoscope when subjects attend to the whole word (*COIN* or *JOIN*) in which either of the two letters occurs than when the subjects focus their attention on just the letter they want to see, or see each of the two letters by itself. This "word-superiority" effect obtains best with real words, next with pseudowords (*PIDE, NART*), and not at all with unrelated letters (*CPRD,*

JPRD) (Barron & Thurston, 1973; Johnston & McClelland, 1974; McClelland, 1976). If deaf subjects also show the same effect for real words and pseudowords (Gibson *et al.*, 1970). the phonetic constraint is not always crucial. On the other hand, letter sequences which are unrelated to English phonology or orthography in total, but which contain high-frequency bigrams or even trigrams (*KTER*), yield no clear word-superiority effect (McClelland & Johnston, 1976).

Context facilitates the perception of any item by reducing the number of alternatives and providing a sequential constraint to the item to be perceived. It enables a reader to expect a certain type of (not necessarily a specific) item, and what he expects, he perceives with low threshold, with a minimum visual cue. At least half of the visual cues, if not more, seem to be redundant in English text. For example, text in which every other letter is deleted can be read with fair comprehension (Shannon, 1951). Text with only the upper or left half of words is also reasonably intelligible (Huey, 1908).

Readers of any writing system have probably developed semantic, syntactic, orthographic, and phonological structures of their own writing systems and languages, as well as general knowledge about many things, making them experts in the use of context. The more a reader makes use of context, the less he relies on visual cues; and the less he relies on visual cues, the less it matters in which writing system he is reading. Multilinguals read silently in different writing systems without having to make any major readjustment. What differ in various writing systems are the kinds and loci of visual cue contained in graphemes and their arrangements.

VII. SUMMARY AND CONCLUSIONS

Writing systems emerged only about 5000 years ago. First, pictures represented objects and events. Rudimentary phonetic signs were available from the early stage. These eventually developed into full-fledged syllabaries. Finally, an alphabet developed out of a syllabary; it then spread all over the world. The linguistic unit adopted in writing systems was first a word/morpheme, then a syllable, and finally a phoneme.

Chinese characters were originally pictures of objects, but are now stylized symbols representing morphemes. Each character is visually and semantically an integrated and distinct entity. Characters represent meanings primarily and sounds secondarily, and hence, they are relatively immune to sound changes across different dialects and languages. But their sound coding within each dialect or language is not something to be ignored.

Characters are necessarily complex and numerous. Learning a handful of them is not difficult, but learning the entire system takes time. They are inconvenient for type-setting and electronic communications, but perhaps this technological constraint will be overcome before long.

By using a limited number of characters for the roots of key words, Japanese and Koreans take advantage of the virtues of characters without inheriting all of their difficulties. The two languages had to devise phonetic systems because their words require grammatical endings. Japan developed two simple syllabaries, and Korea, a rational alphabetic syllabary. By using two kinds of writing systems, but each for its particular function, Japan and Korea have the best of both worlds.

The English alphabet itself is simple, but its orthography is not. English orthography represents the English language at several levels, from phonemic to lexical, in a complex way. The skill to decode grapheme-to-sound and to sequence graphemes and/or sounds into words has to be specifically learned. Deficiency in this skill is often associated with reading disabilities. Much research is being done on ways of teaching English orthography to normal as well as to disabled readers. On the other hand, the simplicity of the alphabet makes typewriters possible.

A mature reader reads rapidly and silently with good comprehension, using any writing system. He does so by making expert use of contextual and visual information.

What features must a writing system possess to be described as "optimal"? A system must:

1. Represent its particular language adequately.
2. Be easily and rapidly learned.
3. Not produce a high proportion of reading casualties.
4. Be processed efficiently by mature readers.
5. Be attuned to technological conveniences (typewriters, electronic communications).

Which writing system discussed in this article is "optimal"?

REFERENCES

Ai, J-W. A report on psychological studies of the Chinese language in the past three decades. *Journal of Genetic Psychology,* 1950, **76,** 207–220.

Aukerman, R. *Approaches to beginning reading.* New York: Wiley, 1971.

Barron, R.W., & Thurston, I. An analysis of the word-superiority effect. *Cognitive Psychology,* 1973, **4,** 207–228.

Benton, A.L., & Pearl, D.(Eds.) *Dyslexia: An appraisal of current knowledge.* New York: Oxford Univ. Press, 1978.

Boder, E. Developmental dyslexia: Prevailing diagnostic concepts and a new diagnostic approach. In H.R. Myklebust (Ed.), *Progress in learning disabilities* (Vol. II). New York: Grune & Stratton, 1971.

Brown, R, & Berko, J. Psycholinguistic research methods. In P.H. Musson (Ed.), *Handbook of research methods in child development.* New York: Wiley, 1960.

Bryden, M.P. Laterality effects in dichotic listening: Relations with handedness and reading ability in children. *Neuropsychologia,* 1970, **8,** 443–450.

Calfee, R.C., Lindamood, P., & Lindamood, C. Acoustic-phonetic skills and reading— kindergarten through twelfth grade. *Journal of Educational Psychology,* 1973, **64,** 293–298.

Chan, C-Y. A study of the relative merits of the vertical and horizontal lines in reading Chinese print. *Archives of Psychology,* 1942, 276.

Chomsky, N, & Halle, M. *The sound pattern of English.* New York: Harper, 1968.

Conrad, R. Acoustic confusions in immediate memory. *British Journal of Psychology,* 1964, **55,** 75–84.

Conrad, R. Speech and reading. In J.K. Kavanagh and I.G. Mattingly (Eds.) *Language by ear and eye: The relationships between speech and reading.* Cambridge, Mass.: MIT Press, 1972.

Craik, F.I.M., & Tulving, E. Depth of processing and the retention of words in episodic memory. *Journal of Experimental Psychology: General,* 1975, **104,** 268–294.

Dewey, G. *English spelling: Roadblock to reading.* New York: Teachers College, Columbia University, 1971.

Diringer, D. *The alphabet* (2 volumes). New York: Funk and Wagnalls, 1968.

Downing, J. The i.t.a. reading experiment. *Reading Teacher,* 1965, **18,** 105–110.

Downing, J. Linguistic environments, II. In J. Downing (Ed.), *Comparative reading.* New York: Macmillan, 1973.

Edfeldt, A.W. *Silent speech and silent reading.* Chicago: Univ. of Chicago Press, 1960.

Gasper, R., & Brown, D. *Perceptual processes in reading.* London: Hutchinson Education, 1973.

Gelb, I.J. *A study of writing* (2nd ed.). Chicago: Univ. of Chicago Press, 1963.

Gibson, E.J., Pick, A., Osser, H., & Hammond, M. The role of grapheme–phoneme correspondence in the perception of words. *American Journal of Psychology,* 1962, **75,** 554–570.

Gillooly, W.B. The influence of writing system characteristics on learning to read. *Reading Research Quarterly,* 1973, **8,** 167–199.

Goody, J., & Watt, I. The consequences of literacy. *Comparative Studies in Society and History,* 1963, **5,** 304–345.

Gray, W.S. *The teaching of reading and writing.* Paris: UNESCO, 1956.

Groat, A. The use of English stress assignment rules by children taught either traditional orthography or with the initial teaching alphabet. *Journal of Experimental Child Psychology,* 1979, **27,** 395–409.

Guthrie, J.T. Models of reading and reading disability. *The Journal of Educational Psychology,* 1973, **65,** 9–18.

Halle, M. Some thoughts on spelling. In K.S. Goodman & J.T. Fleming (Eds.), *Psycholinguistics and the teaching of reading.* Newark, Delaware: International Reading Association, 1969.

Hatta, T. Recognition of Japanese Kanji and Haragana in the left and right visual fields. *Japanese Psychological Research,* 1978, **20,** 51–59.

Hochberg, J. Components of literacy: Speculations and exploratory research. In H.Levin & J.P. Williams (Eds.), *Basic studies on reading.* New York: Basic Books, 1970.

Huey, E.B. *The psychology and pedagogy of reading*. Cambridge, Mass.: MIT Press, 1968 (original print, 1908).

Javal, E. *Physiologie de la lecture et de l'ecriture*. Paris: Felix Alcan, 1906.

Jeffrey, W.E., & Samuels, S.J. The effect of method of reading training on initial reading and transfer. *Journal of Verbal Learning and Verbal Behavior*, 1967, **6**, 354–358.

Johnston, J.C., & McClelland, J.L. Perception of letters in words: Seek not and ye shall find. *Science*, 1974, **184**, 1192–1193.

Kleiman, G.M. Speech recoding in reading. *Journal of Verbal Learning and Verbal Behavior*, 1975, **14**, 323–339.

Kolers, P. Three stages of reading. In H.Levin & J.P. Williams (Eds.), *Basic studies in reading*. New York: Basic Books, 1970.

LaBerge, D. Beyond auditory coding. A discussion of Conrad's paper. In J.K. Kavanagh & I.G. Mattingly (Eds.), *Language by ear and by eye: The relationships between speech and reading*. Cambridge, Mass.: MIT Press, 1972.

Lawrence, T.E. *The seven pillars of wisdom: A triumph*. London: World Books, 1935.

Lee, J-H. *Hun-min Jeoung Eum (correct pronunciation of letters for teaching people): An explanation and translation*. Seoul, Korea, 1972 (in Korean and English).

Levin, H., & Kaplan, E.L. Grammatical structure and reading. In H. Levin & J.P. Williams (Eds.), *Basic studies in reading*. New York: Basic Books, 1970.

Liberman, I.Y., Shankweiler, D., Fischer, F.W., & Carter, B. Explicit syllable and phoneme segmentation in the young child. *Journal of Experimental Child Psychology*, 1974, **18**, 201–212.

Liberman, I.Y., Shankweiler, D., Liberman, A.M., Fowler, C., & Fischer, F.W. Phonetic segmentation and recoding in the beginning reader. In A.S. Reber & D.L. Scarborough (Eds.), *Toward a psychology of reading*. Hillsdale, N.J.: Erlbaum, 1977.

Liu, I-M, Chuang, C-J, & Wang, S-C. *Frequency count of 40,000 Chinese words*. Taiwan: Lucky Books, 1975 (in Chinese).

Ma, D. *A talking book of elementary conversation* (in Chinese and English). Hong Kong: Wan Li Book Co., 1971.

Mae, C-C. *Even Chinese ideograms are phonologically encoded in STM!* Paper given at First Annual Boston University Conference on Language Development, Boston, October 1976.

Makita, K. The rarity of reading disability in Japanese children. *American Journal of Orthopsychiatry*, 1968, **38**, 599–614.

Marks, L.S., Shankweiler, D., Liberman, I.Y., & Fowler, C.A. Phonetic recoding and reading difficulty in beginning readers. *Memory & Cognition*, 1977, **5**, 623–629.

Martin, S.E. Nonalphabetic writing systems: Some observations. In J.F.Kavanagh & I.G. Mattingly (Eds.), *Language by ear and by eye*. Mass.: The MIT Press, 1972.

McClelland, J.L. Preliminary letter identification in the perception of words and nonwords. *Journal of Experimental Psychology: Human Perception and Performances*, 1976, **2**, 80–91.

McClelland, J.L., & Johnston, J.C. *The role of familiar units in the perception of words and nonwords*. Unpublished manuscript, University of Pennsylvania, 1976.

McGuigan, F.J. Covert oral behavior during the silent performance of language tasks. *Psychological Bulletin*, 1970, **74**, 309–326.

Miles, W.R., & Shen, E. Photographic recording of eye movements in the reading of Chinese in vertical and horizontal axes: Method and preliminary results. *Journal of Experimental Psychology*, 1925, **8**, 344–362.

Morrison, F.J., & Giordani, B., Nagy, J. Reading disability: An information-processing analysis. *Science*, 1977, **196**, 77–79.

Moskowitz, A.I. On the vowel shift in English. In T.E. Moore (Ed.), *Cognitive development and the acquisition of language*. New York: Academic Press, 1973.

Muraishi, S. The reading ability of preschool children in Japan. In J.E. Merritt (Ed.), *New horizons in reading*. Newark, Delaware: International Reading Association, 1976.

Park, S., & Arbuckle, T.Y. Ideograms versus alphabets: Effects of script on memory in "bis‌criptual" Korean subjects. *Journal of Experimental Psychology: Human Learning and Memory*, 1977, **3**, 631–642.

Pintner, R. Inner speech during silent reading. *Psychological Review*, 1913, **20**, 129–153.

Rayner, K. Visual attention in reading: Eye movement reflect cognitive processes. *Memory and Cognition*, 1977, **5**, 443–448.

Rayner, K., & McConkie, G.W. Perceptual processes in reading. In A.S. Reber & D.L. Scarborough (Eds.), *Toward a psychology of reading*. Hillsdale, N.J.:Erlbaum, 1977.

Rayner, K., & Posnansky, C. Stages of processing in word identification. *Journal of Experimental Psychology: General*, 1978, **107**, 64–80.

Rogers, J. Comments on I.Taylor's working paper on "Writing systems and reading," 1979 (personal communication).

Rosewell, F., & Natchez, G. *Reading disability* (2nd ed.). New York: Basic Books, 1971.

Rozin, P. & Gleitman, L. The structure and acquisition of reading II: The reading process and the acquisition of the alphabetic principle. In A.S. Reber & D.L. Scarborough (Eds.), *Toward a psychology of reading*. Hillsdale, N.J.: Erlbaum, 1977.

Rozin P., Poritsky, S., & Sotsky, R. American children with reading problems can easily learn to read English represented by Chinese characters. *Science*, 1971, **171**, 1264–1267.

Rubenstein, H., Lewis, S.S., & Rubenstein, M.A. Evidence for phonemic recoding in visual word recognition. *Journal of Verbal Learning and Verbal Behavior*, 1971, **10**, 645–647.

Sakamoto, T. *On reading skills of vertical versus horizontal sentences*. Paper read at the 3rd Annual Congress of the Japanese Association of Educational Psychology, Nagoya 1961. (Mentioned in Sakamoto & Makita, 1973.)

Sakamoto, T. Writing systems in Japan. In J.E. Merrit (Ed.), *New horizons in reading*. Newark, Delaware: International Reading Association, 1976.

Sakamoto, T., & Makita, K. Japan. In J. Downing (Ed.), *Comparative reading*. New York: Macmillan, 1973.

Salapatec, P. Visual scanning of geometric figures by the human newborn. *Journal of Comparative Physiological Psychology*. 1968, **66**, 247–258.

Santa, J.L., & Santa, C. Units of word recognition: Evidence for the use of multiple units. *Perception and Psychophysics*, 1977, **22**, 585–591.

Sasanuma, S. Kanji versus Kana processing in alexia with transient agraphia: A case report. *Cortex*, 1974, **10**, 89–97.

Sasanuma, S., & Fujimura, O. Selective impairment of phonetic and non-phonetic transcription of words in Japanese aphasic patients: Kana vs. Kanji in visual recognition and writing. *Cortex*, 1971, **7**, 1–18.

Schindler, R.M. The effect of prose context on visual search of letters. *Memory & Cognition*, 1978, **6**, 124–130.

Shannon, C.E. Prediction and entropy of printed English. *Bell System Technical Journal*, 1951, **30**, 50–64.

Shen, E. An analysis of eye movements in the reading of Chinese. *Journal of Experimental Psychology*, 1927, **10**, 158–183.

Simons, H.D. Transformational phonology and reading acquisition. *Journal of Reading Behavior*, 1975, **7**, 49–59.

READING PROBLEMS AND INSTRUCTIONAL PRACTICES

ISABEL L. BECK

Learning Research and Development Center
University of Pittsburgh
Pittsburgh, Pennsylvania

Over the years, it has been my experience that teacher's descriptions of students' reading problems come in three packages. Package one contains descriptions of student behaviors such as "guesses at the pronunciation of words," "can't remember his sight words," "doesn't know her vowel sounds," and numerous other behavior descriptions symptomatic of children who are having difficulties with the print-to-speech code. In instructional terms, children exhibiting the kinds of behaviors just noted are described as not having learned their "decoding skills" or as having "word attack" problems.

Package two contains descriptions of children's behaviors such as "reads word by word," "often pauses before pronouncing words," "isn't able to finish a reading assignment," and other indicators of slow word processing. I have heard practitioners describe children who manifest accurate but slow decoding as "hesitant readers," "nonconfident readers," "children lacking a positive reading self concept."

Package three contains assertions that a given child cannot comprehend what he or she reads. Since a child's comprehension cannot be directly observed as can behaviors associated with inaccurate decoding or slow word processing, a teacher infers that comprehension has been poor when a student is unable to perform a variety of traditional postreading activities, such as recapitulating or answering questions about what has been read. Along with other researchers and practitioners, I believe that inaccurate decoding and slow word processing are often implicated in comprehension difficulties. However, it is not uncommon to hear about children who exhibit both decoding accuracy and word recognition fluency, but who still encounter problems in comprehending. When this is the case, and if lack of motivation can be ruled out as a contributor, then my first candidate as the source of the comprehension problem is the child's lack of important prior knowledge about the content of the material that is not being understood.

In this article, the three general areas just described will be addressed in turn, with varying levels of analysis. The differing levels of discussion reflect differences in the state of affairs of instructional practice and scientific investigation in each area. First, a number of traditional practices associated with breaking the print-to-speech code will be described and assessed. This part of the article can be viewed as one more attempt to clarify some of the continuing controversy concerning appropriate strategies to use during the early stages of the learning-to-read process. This is the area that has been most frequently addressed in instructional, experimental, and evaluative literature, yet skirmishes continue. It is hoped that the level of analysis that will be used here to describe certain practices will serve to better discriminate the practices that may be most facilitative in beginning reading instruction.

Next, I will consider the problem of accurate but slow decoding. The area of word processing fluency or decoding automaticity is a relatively new area of investigation. Although the need for such a capability has been suggested theoretically and implied empirically, work has just begun to investigate how this capability develops and whether direct intervention can facilitate its development. In this section, then, I will present hints that can be gleaned from the literature in terms of practices that might promote word processing fluency.

In the last section, I will look at knowledge. Of course, the role of prior knowledge in comprehension is not a new discovery, but recently it has been in the forefront as one of the components of comprehension being actively studied. Although the relationship between knowledge and comprehension is under active investigation, there is currently no empirical work that links lack of prior knowledge to problems in reading instructional practice. Therefore, in this section, I will tentatively thread my way through some instructional notions for considering prior knowledge requirements in relationship to specific texts.

I. DECODING INSTRUCTION IN BEGINNING READING

That beginning reading has received the lion's share of attention is reflected in the fact that for well over a century, there has been discussion concerning appropriate strategies for initial reading instruction. One can find references to a variety of instructional approaches in the historical literature, virtually all of which have modern counterparts. In 1967, Chall proposed two general families of instructional approaches, meaning–emphasis methods and code–emphasis methods. As a starting point, the two general categories are quite useful, as they allow discussion of distinctions among strategies in principle as well as distinctions in practice.

A. Distinctions in Principle

Proponents of various meaning–emphasis approaches stress the communication aspects of reading from the beginning of instruction. To a large extent they believe that initial reading instruction should be arranged to put the learner into a position where she/he emulates skilled reading performance as closely as possible. It follows, then, in the meaning–emphasis approaches that, since skilled readers process units such as words and sentences, so should beginning readers, even if they can manage only a few words and sentences. Since skilled readers interpret and evaluate what they read, so too should beginning readers. By contrast, a code emphasis in early reading assumes that the fundamental task of initial reading is to learn the structural relationships between written and spoken language. Proponents of various code–emphasis approaches do not see initial instruction as concerned primarily with arranging conditions for the beginning reader to behave as a "miniature skilled reader." They find it reasonable to engage a beginning reader in behaviors that are not totally comparable to the skilled performance, such as, overt analysis of the structural relationships between written and spoken language.

B. Distinctions in Practice

In practice, the whole word and language experience approaches fall under the label of meaning emphasis; the phonic and linguistic approaches fall under code emphasis. While there are many internal variations among current programs that fall under the same general label (and this point will be important to the later discussion), there are sufficient similarities to allow them to be grouped together.

All beginning reading instruction is concerned with the teaching of decoding. There is consensus among professionals associated with reading that many factors come into play in the translation of print to speech. Predominant among these factors are two types of clues that can help unlock the print-to-speech code: (a) clues that come from outside the particular word that is being decoded at the moment, such as the syntactic and semantic clues that surround the word, picture clues, etc.; and (b) phonological clues within the word that come from knowing expressly that letter–sound relationships do exist and can be employed specifically to unlock the code. Once again, no professional associated with reading would argue that decoding is not facilitated by using both sets of clues and relationships. An important difference between the two general approaches has been the type of clue each stresses more emphatically. Indeed, this was one of the dimensions along which Chall (1967) drew her meaning–emphasis and code–emphasis distinction. She pointed out that the more meaning–emphasis programs stressed the use of the surrounding context and picture clues. While these programs did eventually teach phonological clues to words, they did so late in their instructional sequences and they were of less importance than syntactical, semantic, and picture clues. On the other hand, the more code–emphasis programs stressed the derivation of major decoding clues from the phonological features of the words, with less emphasis placed on clues that surrounded the words.

C. Methods in the First Half of the Twentieth Century

As noted earlier, for virtually every modern method seen and discussed, one can find in the literature over the past century an "old" method that bears a striking resemblance to the modern one. However, despite the variety of word methods, experience methods, sentence methods, and phonics methods that surfaced in the literature from time to time, phonics was the prevailing method of beginning reading instruction through the early decades of this century. The major objective of reading instruction during this period seems to have been mastery of word pronunciation and fluency of oral reading.

It appears that the kind of phonics practiced in the early part of this century was of an elaborated and elongated "drill and practice" nature. Diederich (1973) describes the scene as follows:

> Initial instruction in letter-sound relationships and pronunciation rules was done to death . . . children had to learn so much abstract material by rote before doing any significant amount of reading. (p. 7)

The whole-word approach came into being in the 1920s. Compared to the extended drill on letter–sounds, their synthesis into often meaningless syllables, and the recitation of rules of pronunciation, the whole-word method must indeed have been a relief. Diederich describes his own response to the whole-word method when he first saw it as a graduate student in education at the University of Chicago. Diederich reports:

> When [this] writer began his graduate study of education in 1928, he was told by no less an authority than Walter Dearborn that it was quite possible to learn to read without first learning the alphabet. This seemed preposterous, and Dearborn had to send his students to observe several classes that were learning to read by the new "look-say" method before they would believe that it was possible. When prospective teachers like the students of Walter Dearborn discovered what a relatively painless process the teaching of reading could be, using the . . . whole word approach, they were not disposed to demand evidence of superior results. It was enough to show that the new method worked about as well as the old and with far less agony. (p. 7)

By the 1930s, the whole-word method prevailed and continued virtually unchallenged until the 1950s. In this decade, the whole-word method received challenges from two quarters—the academic world and the public sector. The academic challenge was launched by linguists who revived the notions Bloomfield (1942) had discussed several decades earlier. The linguists argued that the whole-word approach as exemplified in the basal readers of the period made it difficult for the child to discover the structural relationship between written and spoken language. That is, since the words for the basals were chosen for their frequency in the language and their meaningfulness to the young child, they were not of the sort that displayed the regularity of the written code. Hence, the task of learning to read was made unnecessarily difficult. The challengers urged that instructional materials be arranged to expose beginning readers to words that maximize the regularities of print-to-sound mapping (e.g., *man, pan; men, pen*) rather than to those that exacerbate the irregularities (e.g., *come, hot, stove, coat*).

In the public sector, Rudolph Flesch's best-selling book, *Why Johnny Can't Read* (1955), sparked a challenge to the whole-word method. Flesch vehemently attacked the prevailing method of reading instruction and demanded a return to phonics. Although the general public and press reacted favorably to Flesch's book, it was rejected by reviewers of educational journals—chiefly because it took the form of a propagandistic argument rather than a carefully reasoned presentation of evidence.

D. Chall's Conclusions

Amid this atmosphere of controversy over approaches to beginning reading instruction, Jeanne Chall in 1962 undertook a landmark study of reading methods. Her work, published in 1967, included an exhaustive examination of existing research and an investigation of various practices. She analyzed comparative studies of beginning reading methods and synthesized correlational studies of early reading achievement. She explored the relationship between children's reading failures and the methods of instruction used. She conducted field work consisting of interviews of leading proponents of reading programs and observations of the practices in use.

On the basis of her review of the research and literature over a 50-year period, Chall concluded that the evidence indicated that a code-emphasis approach to reading produced better results. As Chall (1967) stated:

> My review of the research from the laboratory, the classroom, and the clinic points to the need for a correction in beginning reading instructional methods. . . . the research from 1912 to 1965 indicates that a code-emphasis method—i.e., one that views beginning reading as essentially different from mature reading and emphasizes learning of the printed code for the spoken language—produces better results, at least up to the point where sufficient evidence seems to be available, the end of the third grade. (p. 307)

By the late 1960s, Chall's conclusions had made an impact, an impact which did not pass unheeded by the publishers of reading programs. Two trends began to appear in the commercial reading programs of the day. First, houses that had previously published what Chall would term meaning–emphasis programs (i.e., extended whole-word instruction before phonics instruction) began to incorporate substantial phonics instruction very early in the instructional sequences of their newer editions (Popp,

1975). Second, reading programs were developed and marketed that adhered to code-first principles from their inception.

Presently, it has become quite fashionable to describe current approaches as "eclectic" and to suggest that the differences described by Chall between meaning–emphasis approaches and code–emphasis approaches have become blurred in contemporary programs. For instance, Pikulski (1978) contends that "no widely accepted current approach to teaching reading advocates using either a whole word *or* phonics approach; rather, popular approaches to teaching reading differ on the relative emphasis placed on each" (pp. 128–129). On this same issue, Venezky (1978) suggests that the distinction between the two types of approach is in the timing of letter–sound instruction.

E. Important Distinctions between Approaches Remain

Some work recently completed (Beck & Block, 1979; Beck & McCaslin, 1978) points to differences among current reading programs well beyond those in "emphasis" and "timing of instruction"[1] (see also Beck, 1979). Beck and McCaslin analyzed selected dimensions of eight widely used commercial reading programs to study how instruction is arranged in the first two grades of elementary school for teaching beginning readers to break the code; i.e., to understand that printed letters represent particular sounds and words in oral language.

The eight programs analyzed were: (1) *Distar Reading I* and *Distar Reading II*, SRA (1974); (2) *Programmed Reading*, Sullivan Associates, McGraw-Hill (1973); (3) *The Palo Alto Reading Program*, Harcourt Brace Jovanovich (1973); (4) *The Merrill Linguistic Reading Program*, Charles E. Merrill (1975); (5) *Reading 720*, Ginn (1976); (6) *The Houghton Mifflin Reading Series*, Houghton Mifflin (1976); (7) *The Bank Street Readers*, Macmillan (1973); and (8) *The New Open Highways*, Scott Foresman (1974).

The first four programs were initially developed in the 1960s and followed one of the earlier-mentioned trends by adhering to code–emphasis principles from their inception; these four programs will here be labeled code programs. Three of the remaining four (excepting Bank Street) were developed by publishing companies with long histories of producing whole-word programs. Indeed, Chall (1967) used the 1961 Ginn and 1956 Scott Foresman programs as exemplars of meaning–emphasis ap-

---

[1] Beck and Block (1979), which preceded Beck and McCaslin (1978), analyzed the Ginn and Palo Alto programs along a number of dimensions: decoding, sight word instruction, and aspects of comprehension. Beck and McCaslin extended the analysis to include the study of six additional reading programs along a reduced set of dimensions.

proaches. Had she included the 1960s edition of Houghton Mifflin, it would unquestionably also have been classified as meaning emphasis. The first Bank Street Readers did not enter the market until the mid-1960s, but they clearly constituted a whole-word program. However, the latest editions of all four of these programs followed the other trend mentioned earlier by including substantial phonics instruction from the very beginning of their instructional sequences. Thus, the last four programs in the listing above are exemplars of basal programs with phonic components; to distinguish them from the code programs, they will here be labeled basal programs. Some results of comparisons between the two sets of programs and comparisons among programs will be summarized in the following sections.

F. Flow of Instruction and Initial Content in the Lessons of the Programs

Within the books or levels or storybooks of the eight programs is the more basic unit of content, the lesson. One of the obvious differences between the code programs and the basal programs concerns the initial content of a lesson and the temporal order of the elements within a lesson. In the basal programs, the initial content of a lesson is a set of high-frequency words; in the code programs, the initial content centers around letter–sound relationships and/or a set of words that exemplifies particular letter–sound relationships. The flow of instruction within the lessons of the programs determines the instructional relationship and temporal order of story reading and phonics instruction.

In the four code programs, the bulk of phonics instruction takes place prior to story reading. In these programs, the exercises that precede story reading most often introduce a new letter–sound correspondence and the subsequent story uses words that contain that correspondence. This kind of sequencing suggests that, for code programs, the story is viewed primarily as an occasion for the child to apply learned correspondences to words in connected text. Through repeated exposure, words that start out being decoded through word attack are supposed to become familiar enough to begin to be recognized as wholes. This notion of proceeding from word attack to word recognition is central to the code programs.

In contrast, for three of the four basal programs, story reading precedes phonics instruction. The new words to be encountered in the upcoming story are identified by word recognition techniques (sights word teaching as whole word units). Very often, the new words are placed in sentences and the children are encouraged to use the surrounding context as decoding clues. Story-reading first seems a logical sequence, therefore, since stories are the optimal place to find contextual clues. The conceptualization of story reading in basals seems to be that stories are the best place to present the earlier encounters with new words. It is not until after story reading that phonics instruction occurs.

Bank Street is alone among the basals studied in that it seems to "hedge its bets." Bank Street presents some phonics instruction prior to story reading, the story is then read, and after that, another set of word-attack activities is presented.

Thus, in the temporal ordering of a lesson, the basal programs (with the exception of Bank Street as just noted) go from story reading to the teaching of word-attack skills. The code programs move from activities that promote word attack to story reading.

G. Decodability of the Texts on the Basis of Knowledge of the Sound Elements within Words

The previous discussion implied one of the major differences between code and basal programs; that is, the basis for selecting words that children encounter in their readers. The current basals continue to select their words from high-frequency words and words that are likely to be in the young child's experiential store. The order of the introduction of words is not constrained by the letter–sound correspondences or letter–patterns that are introduced in the basals' phonics components. On the other hand, the words introduced in the code programs are to a large extent constrained by the correspondences or letter–patterns introduced.

To compare and contrast the eight programs along this dimension, the letter–sound sequences of the eight programs were extracted and comparisons were made between the letter–sounds introduced and the words children encounter in their readers. In this manner, percentages of words that are decodable solely on the basis of knowledge of the sound elements within the words were determined for two time segments during the first grade.

In the analyses presented below, a word was considered decodable if any kind of explicit attention had been given to all its constituent letter–sound correspondences, spelling patterns, or syllables. Explicit attention was interpreted very broadly here to include not only direct letter–sound instruction (such as when the teacher points to a letter in isolation or in a word and tells the children its sound) but also more indirect procedures (such as those related to inductive and discovery learning). For instance, the word *man* would be considered decodable in these analyses if the children had encountered other words beginning

TABLE I

Percentage of Decodable Words in the First Third of First Grade in Four Code and Four Basal Reading Programs[a]

Program	Percentage decodable words
Code programs	
Distar	100
Sullivan	93
Merrill	79
Palo Alto	69
Basal programs	
Houghton Mifflin	13
Ginn	3
Bank Street	0
Open Highways	0

[a] Finding the percentage of decodable words in Distar, Sullivan, and Gin was not difficult as these programs provide the necessary information in the teacher's manuals or in listings in the children's readers either in direct form or in easily extractable form. For the other five programs, the correspondences taught through the first third of first grade were charted and related to each unique word in that time period. Because of special characteristics in several programs, the decision rules developed resulted in somewhat of an underestimate of the phonologically decodable words for Palo Alto.

with *m* and other words ending with *an* and they had discussed the fact that the *m* words began the same way and that the *an* words all ended alike.

Table I shows the percentage of decodable words for each of the eight programs through the first third of first grade. The difference between the first four programs on the table, the code programs, and the last four, the basal programs, is immense in terms of the degree of relationship between the letter–sound generalizations taught and the words used in the readers at corresponding times. In the code programs, there is a high percentage of decodable words found in early first-grade texts; in the basal programs, the percentage is extremely low or nonexistent. The major factor affecting the difference between the two sets of programs in this time period is that the code programs include several vowels along with the introduction of consonants in their instructional sequences, thus enabling the generation of decodable words. The basal programs, however, mostly conform to the traditional pattern of introducing many consonants before any vowels are introduced. Strictly speaking, then, during this time period, the words children encounter in the basals are not decodable on the basis of knowledge of all the sound elements in their constituent

TABLE II

Percentage of Decodable Words in the Last Full Book or Level of First Grade in Four Code and Four Basal Reading Programs

Program and unit designation	Percengage of first-grade material included in the unit	Percentage decodable
Code programs		
Distar, Book 3	17	89
Sullivan, Book 7	14	97
Merrill, Book C	35	85
Palo Alto, Book 6	17	78
Basal programs		
Houghton Mifflin, Level F		
Ginn, Level 5	30	59
Bank Street, Level 4	45	43
Open Highways, Book 1,	39	38
Part 2	38	53

parts. Of course, the first third of the first year of instruction is a very restricted time period, so another analysis was performed to see how the programs fared on this dimension toward the end of first grade.

Table II shows the percentage of decodable words for the last full first-grade unit of each of the eight programs. Several qualifiers need to be noted concerning the data for this table. First, since the division of material into units differs from program to program, the amount of instructional material included in this analysis is different from program to program. The second column in Table II indicates the percentage of the total first-grade material for each program that is included in this analysis. For example, Palo Alto's first-grade material is divided into six units of equal length. Therefore, the last Palo Alto unit constitutes approximately 17% of the total first-grade material. Ginn, on the other hand, has unequal amounts of material in its four first-grade units, with the last first-grade unit constituting approximately 45% of the total first-grade material. As a second qualifier, the percentages of decodable words reflected in Column 3 of Table II were derived solely from those words introduced in the last unit of first grade. In the case of Sullivan, for example, only new words in Book 7, not the cumulative vocabulary of Books 1–7, were used. Third, because of the decision rules adopted, the percentages of decodable words in Houghton Mifflin, Bank Street, and Open Highways are somewhat overestimated, while the percentage for Palo Alto is underestimated. The last qualifier only makes the distinction between the code programs and the basal programs somewhat greater than the percentages that Column 3 of Table II report. While the difference between the two sets of programs is not as stark toward the end of first grade as it was in the first third of first grade, the difference is still large. The basal programs continue to employ greater percentages of nondecodable words in their readers. This, however, is perfectly consistent with their notion that other clues (syntactic and semantic) are more important or at least equally important for decoding as phonological clues.

The point of the above analyses has been to note that there is a difference in the kind of words encountered between code and basal programs. That is, the code programs relate their phonics content to their textual selections, whereas the basals do not. The code programs show letter–sound or letter–pattern control of their vocabulary; the basals do not. In the basal programs, the letter–sound sequence appears to have been designed independently of the word sequence. In the code programs, the letter–sound or letter–pattern sequences determine the words that will be used. To the extent just noted, then, the four current basal programs are quite similar to their older counterparts in that their words are not chosen to maximize the regularities of print to sound mapping. The lack of letter–sound control in the basal vocabulary makes it more difficult for beginning readers to recognize that certain letters have certain sounds, and that words encountered in reading can be decoded on this basis.

H. The Pedagogy for Teaching Letter–Sound Correspondences

Unlocking the pronunciation of an unfamiliar word solely by phonological clues requires knowing the letter–sound correspondences in that word. The importance of such knowledge has been noted by many. For instance, Carroll (1964) suggests that "when the learner has mastered the important grapheme/phoneme correspondences . . . the learner may be said to have 'broken the code' of English orthography" (p. 340). It needs to be pointed out, however, that it is possible to master the letter–sound correspondences without their having been directly taught. Indeed, tens of millions of children who learned to read successfully through the older whole-word programs described by Chall (1967) did sooner or later acquire the letter–sound knowledge needed for independent reading. Those programs assuredly did not make the induction of letter–sound knowledge easy since words were not selected to maximize the regularities of the coding system and phonics instruction was postponed until quite late in the instructional process.

Although it was noted that current basals resemble their forebears by not selecting words that maximize the regularities of the coding system, in contrast to their forebears, the four current basals do initiate phonics instruction from the very beginning of their instructional sequences. They all thereby give immediate attention to letter–sound learning. Indeed, each of the eight programs, the four basals and the four code programs, spends a substantial amount of time attempting to teach the major letter–sound correspondences in the language. However, analyses of the pedagogy used to teach letter–sound correspondences point to some major differences between the two sets of programs in **how** the correspondences are taught.

The teacher's manuals of each of the eight programs studied contain very definite suggestions to the teacher regarding strategies for presenting the letter–sound correspondences. To compare the instructional strategy suggestions, Beck and McCaslin (1978) analyzed the teaching directions for either short *i* or *e* lessons in each of the eight programs.

1. Differences in Labels and Phoneme Availability

One of the major differences among the programs is the way that the target phoneme is labeled and referred to by the teacher. In three of the basal programs (the exception is Houghton Mifflin), the target phoneme is always referred to as a member of a class of sounds. In three of the code programs (the exception is Merrill), the phoneme is explicitly produced.

To be more specific about the code programs, at various places in a given Distar, Sullivan, or Palo Alto lesson, the teacher directly tells the children the sound of the target grapheme. Using the short *e* as an example, the teacher brings attention to a printed *e* (e.g., she/he underlines or points to the *e* in a word or presents the *e* in isolation) and produces the phoneme. That is, the teacher models the exact association to be learned: *e* to /e/.

In Merrill, the other code program, the phoneme for the target letter is never produced in isolation, but is referred to by letter name as a word containing the target grapheme is compared and contrasted with a known word. Merrill's instructional strategies adhere strictly to the linguistic approach proposed by Bloomfield and Barnhart (1961), which attempts to have children induce letter–sound correspondences by consistently sequencing and displaying words that maximize similar and contrasting features of major spelling patterns.

By contrast, the major way of referring to a target phoneme in the four basal programs is to say that it is a member of a class of sounds.[2] In these programs, the phoneme is not isolated. Although there is variation within basal programs, in general, a grapheme–phoneme correspondence is taught as follows: First, a word (e.g., *get*) or a set of pattern words (e.g., *met, wet, let*) or a set of nonpattern words (e.g., *sled, wet, egg*) is read. Then, depending upon the program, the target phoneme is variously referred to as "the vowel sound you hear in *get*" and/or "the short sound of *e*" and/or "the same vowel sound that's found in all those words" and/or "the unglided vowel sound heard in *get*."

The differences between the two sets of programs in how the target phoneme is labeled make important differences in the chances that the correspondence will be acquired. What needs to be learned is that, in certain words, when one sees an *e*, one will overtly or covertly produce an /e/. In at least three of the code programs, since the grapheme–phoneme correspondence is made explicit, precisely what needs to be learned is quite clear. In the basal programs learning the *e* to /e/ association has, depending on the program, difficult to enormously difficult task requirements. Think of what is involved in learning *e* to /e/ under the following stereotypic but representative circumstances: The teacher writes *get* on the board, reads the word, points to the *e* and tells the children that the sound produced by the *e* in *get* is the "short vowel sound of *e*." First, the child has to relate the label "vowel sound" to one of the sounds in the auditory stream; second, she/he must extract from the auditory stream the /e/; third, she/he must hold /e/ in memory; fourth, the child has to link /e/ to the letter *e* in the printed *get*; and fifth, she/he has to translate the label "short vowel sound of *e*" into /e/. While all five of these steps are not always required in each of the four programs at one time, there is one task that is virtually always required. This task is the extraction of a phoneme from a word. This may well be one of the most problematic aspects of the basals' phonics instruction, as there is much evidence that many 5- and 6-year-old children have difficulty analyzing spoken words for phonemes and other speech segments (e.g., Bruce, 1964; Calfee, Chapman, & Venezky, 1972; Liberman, 1973; Rosner, 1973).

Liberman, Cooper, Shankweiler, and Studdert-Kennedy (1967) have noted that phoneme segmentation is difficult since a spoken word rarely

---

[2] Houghton Mifflin is the one basal program that does allow the teacher to produce an isolated phoneme. However, calling an *e* an /e/ is not the major way that a target letter is referred to in Houghton Mifflin. This occurs only for vowel correspondences and is only done once or twice per lesson. For the most part, the grapheme is labeled as a member of a class of sounds as in the other basal programs.

has an acoustic marker for determining where a particular phoneme ends and another starts. Therefore when the teacher points to the *e* in *get* and tells the children that it is the "short *e* sound heard in *get*," we have no assurance that the children have focused on the /e/ in the auditory *get*. Some children may focus on the /g/ or /ge/ or /et/ or /t/ rather than the true target. If the correct target phoneme is not extracted the whole point of the lesson is lost.

The letter–sound correspondence instruction found in programs that do not make the phoneme directly available requires sophisticated phonemic analysis skills. One has to question seriously whether children are likely to acquire the correspondence from such instruction. Indeed, those children most in need of explicit instruction in letter–sound correspondences are precisely the children who are likely to get little or nothing from these kinds of instructional procedures since they are least likely to possess the prerequisite phonemic analysis skills. If this is true, then, these children are left to induce the letter–sound correspondences from their sight word repertoires, a far from easy task since the basals do not select and sequence their sight words in such a way as to make induction easy.

There is a better chance that children lacking sophisticated auditory analysis skills will learn letter–sound correspondences when they are made explicitly available. Programs that make the phoneme directly available do not presuppose well-developed auditory analysis skills since they do not require the child to extract phonemes independently. Rather, direct help is provided in the programs by indicating the units upon which the child should focus. The child's attention is directed to the grapheme and the phoneme is sounded; she/he need not discover the relationship independently.

There is evidence from laboratory studies that there is greater positive transfer (i.e., ability to read new words) from isolated letter–sound training as compared with whole-word training (Bishop, 1964; Jeffrey & Samuels, 1967). It would seem that isolated letter–sound training is preferred not only for increased transfer but also for ease of initial acquisition. Telling a child that an *e* makes the sound /e/ is far closer to the point than telling him or her that the *e* in *get* is the short *e* vowel sound.

The programs that restrict the production of phonemes in isolation reflect the admonitions of Bloomfield (1942), Fries (1963), and more recently Gibson and Levin (1975), all of whom point out that most English phonemes, particularly the noncontinuant consonants, cannot be produced in isolation without the addition of a *schwa*. Therefore, they would maintain that if the child learned the letter–sound associations for *c* and *a* and *t,* she/he would really have learned /kuh-a-tuh/. If the child then came across *cat* for the first time and attempted to apply his or her letter–sound knowledge, the result would not be *cat*, but *kuhatuh*. In this regard, two points need to be made. First, it is indeed true that synthesizing phonemes into a word is a difficult task for some children. Therefore, the discussion will shortly turn toward determining the kind of attention that is given in the eight programs toward the development of synthesizing ability. The point that needs to be made for now is that the production of the phonemes in a word does not guarantee a perfect pronunciation. Resnick and Beck (1976) have noted that phoneme production provides only a candidate pronunciation, a pronunciation that must be tested in order to determine whether a recognizable word has been generated. Even if the word *cat* were read in isolation, a child who had any knowledge of what reading is about would not be satisfied with /kuhatuh/ as a pronunciation. With any kind of context, it would indeed be a rare child who read "dogs and kuhatuhs" or "Puff is a kuhatuh."

2. Blending

In addition to the acquisition of correspondence knowledge, there is a second element that is also needed for producing the pronunciation of an unfamiliar word. This element has variously been termed blending, sounding out, and sequential decoding; it appears time and again in task analyses for reading a new word (e.g., Bateman, 1979; Golinkoff, 1978; Resnick & Beck, 1976; Venezky, 1975). Clearly, many children develop this capability spontaneously. But several studies have indicated that some beginning readers need to be taught explicitly how to blend (Haddock, 1976; Marsh & Sherman, 1970; Muller, 1973; Silberman, 1964).

Based upon the method of presentation of the short *e* or short *i* correspondences in the eight programs studied, Beck and McCaslin (1978) also looked to determine whether attention was given to teaching this necessary synthesizing ability. It was found that only two of the programs, Distar and Palo Alto, attended to the development of synthesizing ability in any consistent and systematic fashion.[3]

Distar has a definite instructional strategy for teaching blending. It consists of having children frequently perform the following procedures: Upon seeing a word such as *if*, they are directed to say the sounds in an extended manner /iiifff/ and then synthesize those extended phonemes

---

[3] The Sullivan Program does indeed want children to synthesize phonemes into words, but it does not have a strategy for teaching them to do so. Rather, Sullivan directs the teacher to help students sound out words. This is not adequate since one does not know how teachers will operationalize this advice. The teacher needs a strategy, not merely advice.

into the word. This is a simple strategy, but it occurs consistently several times within a lesson over 45 lessons. With such extended practice, children are likely to develop synthesizing ability. On the negative side, one needs to question whether this extent of overlearning is necessary even for poor prognosis children.

Palo Alto may get at aspects of synthesizing ability through numerous word-building exercises. The program materials included a device called a Spelling Pocket, which is a cardboard card-holder that each child receives. In addition, each child also receives his or her own letter card for every correspondence introduced. At any place in the program, then, each child has a collection of all the letters introduced to that point. Words are built at various times within a lesson by inserting letter cards into the Spelling Pocket. For example, as directed by the teacher, the children place *h* and *m* in their Spelling Pockets; the teacher says *him* and each child is then responsible for inserting the correct letter card between the *h* and *m*; the teacher says *ham* and the children replace the *i* with an *a*; the teacher says *Sam* and the children replace the *h* with an *S*. There are many variations in Palo Alto on the general theme of placing letters in various orders and of exchanging letter positions within words followed by reading the resultant word.

Letter substitution is a traditional activity and also occurs in several of the other programs studied. There are, however, two differences between Palo Alto's use of this activity and its use in other programs. In the other programs, letter substitution is a whole-group activity. That is, for the most part, the teacher substitutes one letter for another and the children read the resultant word. As noted, in Palo Alto, however, each child manipulates her/his own letter cards for each word that is built. When it is the child who exchanges letters and places them in various positions, the chances are better that attention is focused where is belongs. The second, and perhaps even more important difference between Palo Alto's use of this traditional letter substitution activity and the other programs' use, is that in Palo Alto word building is frequently and consistently employed. Indeed, word building consumes a large portion of every correspondence lesson. In the other programs, word building appears a little here or a little there, but not consistently and not very often.

In summary concerning the kinds of attention that the various programs devote toward the development of synthesizing ability, Distar has an overt instructional strategy for teaching children to blend sounds into words. Palo Alto may get at the process by providing each child with many opportunities to manipulate letters and to read the result of each manipulation. This kind of manual manipulation may be a useful prompt for externalizing the sequential ordering of phonemes, a subskill that is important in blending. The other six programs neither include instructional strategies that overtly teach blending nor consistently provide instructional activities that can be interpreted as getting at aspects of synthesizing capability.

Before leaving blending, it is important to point out that just as letter–sound correspondences can be induced, so too can blending. But just as some children need to be taught letter–sounds directly, so too do some children need to be explicitly taught to blend.

I. Several Other Strategies Used in Phonics Instruction

The previous discussion has been concerned with how beginning reading programs label the target correspondences and whether they address the need to develop synthesizing abilities in beginning readers. There are numerous other strategies used in the phonics instruction of the eight programs. In this section, several of these will be discussed.

1. Letter-Naming

A number of studies have found high correlations between letter–name knowledge and success in first-grade reading (Bond & Dykstra, 1967; DeHirsch, Jansky, & Langford, 1966; Durrell, 1958). However, the results of several training experiments (Jenkins, Bausell, & Jenkins, 1972; Samuels, 1972; Ohnmacht, 1969) have indicated that letter–name training does not transfer to decoding. From these training studies, one can infer that the high correlations between letter–name knowledge and reading success are a correlational artifact rather than a causal relationship.

There is, however, absolutely no evidence that letter–name instruction is harmful. What needs to be specified in terms of determining whether letter–name instruction should be included is the functional use of letter–name knowledge. It would seem that there are two obvious reasons for children to know letter names: First, it is part of being literate; parents expect that their first-graders will indeed learn their ABCs when they go to school. Second, the letter name is a useful label for certain instructional purposes, such as writing and spelling. What needs to be made clear is that instruction in letter-naming does not facilitate the acquisition of initial reading. Venezky (1975) suggests that if there is a danger in letter–name instruction, it is that it is overemphasized "at the expense of other essential learning experiences" (p.20).

Among the eight programs analyzed, letter–name instruction occurs in first grade in seven of the programs; it is not included in Distar until second grade. While letter–name instruction is present in all the programs, some teach letter names to a greater extent than do others. Beck and McCaslin (1978) did not detect any program that seemed to go overboard in letter–name instruction.

There was, however, one problematic aspect detected. In one of the code programs, children are required to say a phoneme in the absence of the printed stimulus, after its letter name is presented orally. That is, the teacher says *e* and the children are required to say /e/. Since this is not a reading requirement (in reading the printed *e* would be the stimulus), one must wonder why instructional time is spent on this task. Such a task could be considered harmless, but it is a difficult task in that developing the desired response probably requires a lot of instructional time. One should consider the functional use of an instructional task along with the time required to perform the task. Knowledge of letter names does not facilitate decoding, but as has been indicated, it does not facilitate decoding, but as has been indicated, it does have a function in areas such as writing and spelling.

2. Writing

In all of the code programs and in several of the basal programs, students are required to write the target letter and/or words containing the new letter.

Several investigators have suggested that a sensory-motor task such as writing may serve to focus attention on the shape of the letter being taught (Fernald, 1943; Gillingham & Stillman, 1966; Ross, 1976). Tasks that help a child to focus attention selectively on relevant stimuli are positive, and the writing of the letter may indeed help to focus such attention. In general, more time is spent writing in the code programs than in the basal programs.

3. Rules, Pictures, and Objects

Scattered throughout the programs are some practices that seem worthless in that they are not related to reading behavior and also seem to have no other useful functions. First, consider the teaching of rules of pronunciation. For example, children may be instructed that when they see the letter *e* followed by one or more consonant letters, they should respond with the short sound of *e*. In the course of a lesson, when the child encounters a word such as *bed*, the teacher elicits the pronunciation rule from the child. There is no evidence that stating a pronunciation rule facilitates the ability to apply that rule. In fact, Venezky (1975) negated the hypothesis that children apply such rules. He said, "The . . . hypothesis that the child generalizes from a verbalization of a rule is inconsistent with experimental data reported by Venezky and Johnson (1973) for English letter-sound patterns" (pp. 7–8). This author has witnessed many children who enter remedial reading clinics with the ability to recite such rules, but who are unable to apply them to unlock the pronunciation of a new word.

Next consider the questionable strategy of providing practice on a phoneme by having children identify pictures whose names contain the target phoneme of the lesson. The value of this kind of task has been well described by Bateman (1979) who states that "circling a thousand worksheet pictures of things that start with [/i/] provides exactly zero practice in looking at [i] and responding with [/i/]" (p.39). The ability to focus on the grapheme and produce the phoneme should be the objective of the phonics lesson, not extended practice in this type of auditory analysis task.

A third highly questionable practice is related to the just-mentioned auditory analysis task of providing practice in phonemes by having children respond to pictures. In this extended case, however, some programs suggest using actual objects whose names contain the target phoneme as instructional devices. Children respond to the objects by naming them. Once again, the criticism is that this type of auditory analysis has no relationship to reading a word containing the target phoneme. Production of a word containing a target phoneme in response to the object carrying that label does not facilitate reading, which requires that phonemes be produced in response to their graphemic representations.

To this point, the discussion has drawn on some rational analyses of certain instructional procedures and has introduced in support of those rational analyses evidence from some small scale basic studies that touched on a particular element under discussion. We turn now to a summary of the evidence that exists from post-Chall, large-scale evaluative studies.

J. Research on Instructional Emphasis in Beginning Reading

The National Institute of Education recently sponsored a project to investigate the locus and nature of reading problems in elementary schools. The final report included three studies (Guthrie, Samuels, Martuza, Seifert, Tyler, & Edwall, 1976). In one study, Samuels and Edwall surveyed the data from reports of successful programs for the purpose of identifying the characteristics of successful programs. Data for the survey were drawn from the following reports: American Institute for Research (Bowers, Campeau, Roberts, & Oscar, 1974), Weber (1971), New York State Office of Education (1974), the CRAFT Project (Harris & Serwer, 1966), and the RMS Research Corporation (Tallmadge, 1974).

Samuels and Edwall found that the inclusion of a "phonics" component frequently characterized successful programs.

Another section of the NIE document contained a reanalysis of the first-grade studies sponsored by the U.S. Office of Education (Bond & Dykstra, 1967). Here Guthrie and Tyler reported that code-oriented approaches were shown to be more efficient for teaching decoding and word recognition. In the third study, Guthrie, Martuza, and Seifert reanalyzed data collected by the Educational Testing Service for a study of compensatory reading programs (Rubin, Trismen, Wilder, & Yates, 1973). One of their findings was that, for lower SES children, programs with high skill-emphasis were superior to programs with low skill-emphasis for producing gains in comprehension as measured by the Reading Subtest of the Metropolitan Achievement Test.

A major problem with the findings from the studies just noted is that the instructional procedures discussed are identified in a totally global way, such as "a phonics components" or "a skill-emphasis." Indeed, a major point in this present article is that a variety of procedures, some of which may be inappropriate, go on under the same label. Further, Guthrie *et al.* (1976) clearly noted that they were unable to get appropriate specifications for discussing instructional approaches.

From the Follow Through evaluations (Stebbins, St. Pierre, Proper, Anderson, & Cerva, 1977) comes support for a code program whose procedures are quite well specified. A number of instructional models used in classrooms of disadvantaged children were evaluated. The one model that has more regularly shown advantage over its control group is the University of Oregon's Distar program, a program that stresses a code-emphasis. While the instructional procedures are quite clear in the Distar program, a number of other instructional conditions that can affect outcomes, such as time devoted to reading, are not specified.

The large-scale evaluation studies of instructional programs in natural settings such as those just noted are beset with pragmatic problems. Because of the problems inherent in such research, the studies have been faulted on a variety of methodological points, thus allowing their conclusions to be questioned. (See for instance House, Glass, McLean, & Walker, 1978 for a critique of the Follow Through evaluation studies.) However, other researchers, along with the present author, find enough evidence in these studies to believe that they are one other source of converging evidence that recommends a code-emphasis approach to beginning reading instruction.

Quite recently, Resnick (1978) and Williams (1978) independently reached similar conclusions about the relationship between theory and research, and instructional practices. Partly from their reviews of the studies previously discussed, they made recommendations favoring a code-emphasis approach to beginning reading. Williams concluded:

> It seems to me that the evidence suggests that you might as well provide the child with a good decoding program. Clearly, such instruction teaches basic skills more effectively. As far as the ultimate goal of comprehension is concerned, it hasn't been demonstrated that decoding instruction helps; but it certainly doesn't seem to hurt. (p.9)

Resnick concluded in a similar fashion:

> First, as a matter of routine practice, we need to include systematic, code-oriented instruction in the primary grades, no matter what else in also done. This is the only place in which we have any clear evidence for any particular practice. We cannot afford to ignore that evidence or the several instructional programs already in existence that do a good job of teaching the code. The charge . . . that too early or too much emphasis on the code depresses comprehension, finds no support in the empirical data. On the other hand . . . there is no evidence that code-emphasis programs alone will ''solve'' the reading problem. (p.13)

The independent conclusions of these prominent researchers are remarkably similar, as they both point out that: (1) there is evidence that a code-emphasis approach teaches the word recognition aspect of reading more effectively and (2) while there is no evidence that code-emphasis facilitates comprehension, there is no evidence either that it inhibits comprehension. Thus, the more meaning-emphasis approaches have not succeeded in teaching comprehension any better than the code-emphasis approaches in that meaning-emphasis approaches do not result in higher test scores.

It is appropriate to conclude this section by noting that I am in complete agreement with Mathews (1966) who, in an excellent historical account of reading instruction, noted:

> No matter how a child is taught to read, he comes sooner or later to the strait gate and the narrow way: he has to learn letters and the sounds for which they stand. There is no evidence whatever that he will ultimately do this better from at first not doing it at all. (p.208)

It is my conclusion that children will learn letter–sound relationships more easily if they are taught some of the letter–sound correspondences in an explicit and direct way and if they encounter decodable words in their beginning reading materials.

II. AUTOMATICITY

The previous discussion has been concerned with instructional dimensions that may affect independent and accurate decoding. The point to be made in this section is that whether initial decoding is taught through whole words or through direct letter–sound knowledge, it must be developed to the point that it is **automatic**. The word *automatic* is used to describe a skill that can be carried out without receiving overt attention. The recognition of a need for automaticity is based on the theoretical position that a limited capacity processor cannot attend to many things at once without hindering at least some of its processing activity (Kiss & Savage, 1977). Therefore, if attention is more than occasionally focused on getting through the words during reading, too much processing capacity will be taken up with decoding and that will interfere with the higher level components of the reading process (i.e., constructing meaning).

There are few researchers or practitioners who would not agree that the reader who literally stops and attacks the pronunciation of too many words (e.g., sounding out, /ch/ /chick/ /en/ /chicken/) in a text will have difficulty with the meaning of the material. A more subtle problem is the reader who does not appear to be initiating word attack procedures, but who is simply slow at reading. Teachers worry about such children because they do not finish a silent reading assignment; they tend not to be concerned about the material that was read, however slowly, only about the material that was not read. Yet, there is evidence that comprehension of texts that are read too slowly will be weak. Work by LaBerge and Samuels (1974) and Perfetti (1976) indicated that slow word recognition is related to poor sentence processing. Perfetti and Hogaboam (1975) have demonstrated that fast word recognition is correlated with better reading comprehension.

With theory and some data pointing to the importance of automated word processing, we turn to a discussion of how this ability develops. The answer of course is obvious—through practice. Clearly, many children develop automatic decoding ability as they proceed through formal reading instruction with no special attention given to its development. Other children going through the same formal reading instruction come away lacking automatic decoding ability. Of course, a vicious cycle is probably at work here. Those children who develop effective word processing skills early in the learning to read process are the ones likely to read more both in and out of school. This extra practice in reading may exacerbate the skill differences between the more fluent readers and those who are less efficient at word processing. It would seem then that early instructional intervention aimed directly at building word processing fluency might be important to those students who do not develop the ability independently.

Beyond a global directive to read more, is there any kind of direct intervention that contributes to the development of word processing fluency? Unfortunately, a specific instructional prescription is not readily available. However, some general suggestions can be gleaned from the literature. The first hint concerns the positive effects of repeated encounters with the same words in varying contexts; the second is closely related but concerns repeated encounters with the same passages.

Data supporting the first general suggestion concerning repeated encounters with the same words in varying contexts appear in a longitudinal study now in progress at the Learning Research and Development Center. Several cohorts of children are being followed as they learn to read.[4] At certain achievement-related curriculum intervals, each child receives a battery of tests, including tests of reading and tests of speed of word processing and recognition. (See Lesgold, 1978 and Lesgold, Resnick, & Beck, 1978 for a description of the longitudinal study and a summary of the first year's results.)

In a word processing task known as Category Matching, the child is told the name of a category (e.g., *animals*) and decides if a word that is flashed on a screen is an instance of that category (e.g., *rabbit*). The child's speed in making a "yes" or "no" response is measured. All the words that the child sees are drawn from words used in the instructional materials completed by the point of testing. The first year's results for the initial cohort of first-grade children show that mean response time was much lower for words frequently encountered in the reading materials (Beck, 1979). Correlations between frequency of occurrence of words in the child's reading program and speed of recognition for each word in the experimental task, controlling for the number of letters in the words, show $r(11) = -.65$, $p<.01$ at the first testing point and $r(11) = -.62$, $p<.05$ at the second testing point. These are healthy correlations which hint at the usefulness of frequent encounters with the same words toward the development of rapid word processing in beginning readers. These data only suggest that a lot of previous encounters with a word increase the young reader's speed of processing that word. However, the important question remains: whether a first-grader's faster word processing speed leads to general reading facility, or whether general reading facility increases word processing speed.

This chicken or egg dilemma has been discussed by Lesgold (1978):

> We have not completely solved the problems of which comes first, word processing speed or reading facility. We have, however, shown even in this preliminary set of data that the two are closely tied together and are not, for example, jointly the

---

[4] Three cohorts of children are receiving instruction through the New Primary Grades Reading System, developed at LRDC. (For a description of NRS, see Beck and Mitroff, 1972 and Beck, 1977.) The study was extended in 1978 to include cohorts of children who are learning to read through a commercially available basal program.

result of some general intelligence or other entering characteristic of the children. Further, the lack of any delay between changes in word-processing RT and improvements in reading efficiency is consistent with the notion that adequate processing speed means a decrease in the cognitive load on a limited capacity system, allowing the appearance of performance levels of higher-level processing for which competence may have existed all along. (p.11)

The second general suggestion for contributing to word processing fluency mentioned earlier was demonstrated by Samuels (1979). In a method of repeated readings, children read outloud a short, meaningful passage to an adult several times until a satisfactory level of fluency had been reached. In between reading the passage to the adult, the children practiced reading the passage on their own. When a satisfactory level of fluency was reached, the procedure was repeated on a new passage. In Samuels' study, students not only improved in fluency on each passage, but they also showed a transfer of training effect in that the first reading of each new passage was faster than the previous initial reading had been, and also the number of readings to reach criterion decreased. Samuels points out that this procedure may be particularly useful with poor prognosis readers; it should not supplant the traditional methods of teaching beginning reading, but rather should be employed as a supplement to the reading program in use.

The successful use of repeated encounters with the same words or passages suggests that practice on a limited set of words may be an effective path to decoding automaticity. Unfortunately, the current trend in reading programs seems to be directed toward presenting a much more diverse set of words than had been done in earlier editions. Rodenborn and Washburn (1974) reported that in the older basals "a word was repeated from 6 to 10 times on the pages immediately following introduction" (p. 886). Those authors then found the following rates of repetition for 240 words used in the first book of a 1970 basal: 37 words occurred more than 11 times; 29 occurred between 6 and 10 times; 174 occurred fewer than 6 times; and 85 occurred only once in the entire book. Clearly the majority of words sampled in the 1970 basal program occurred fewer times than the 6 to 10 word repetition noted in the earlier basals.

Beck and McCaslin (1978) did not specifically count word repetitions in the eight programs they analyzed, although they certainly concur from general impressions of current programs that more diverse sets of words are being presented, rather than repeated practice on a more limited set. Yet solely to call for program developers to provide more encounters with their words toward facilitating automatic decoding is not the appropriate remedy. The issue needs attention from several quarters. More research is required that draws attention to automatic, as opposed to accurate, word recognition as an essential part of a reader's repertoire. Hard evidence is also needed to show that direct intervention is helpful, and in some cases required, if automaticity is to develop. Notions on the specific type of practice that will contribute most effectively to the development of automaticity need to be clarified.

There are two sides to the idea of refining instructional practice. One is that practices that seem nonhelpful for automaticity should be closely examined or eliminated. Such a candidate seems to be the practice of moving children through their reading materials at a constant pace, proceeding on to harder and harder selections, regardless of a child's ease and fluency in reading. A word pool that is constantly increasing in size and difficulty may allow little opportunity for rapid word recognition to develop.

The other side of the practice coin is to investigate the practices that seem promising. Promising practices share the characteristic of presenting repeated encounters on a set of words. Further research could show whether repeated encounters are best accomplished with frequent repetitions of a subset of words occurring in instructional materials, with materials written entirely around a limited corpus of words, or with supplemental techniques such as repeated readings or game-like activities under speeded conditions.

Up to this point, the discussion in this article has been concerned with instructional practices that may affect the development of word attack skills and rapid word recognition. The focus then has been on the development of skills that are unique to reading rather than a part of all language comprehension. These skills provide prerequisites for the comprehension of printed materials.

III. THE ROLE OF KNOWLEDGE IN COMPREHENSION

Now we move to comprehension, which is, of course, the *sine qua non* of reading. The view of reading comprehension that will be espoused here and that will govern the discussion in this section is drawn from the theories of Fries (1963), Sticht, Beck, Hauke, Kleiman, and James (1974), and Carroll (1977) and is also related to the ideas of Mattingly (1972) and Liberman and Shankweiler (1979) who share the assumption that reading comprehension is a specific case of language comprehension.[5] This position holds that, apart from decoding skill, reading

[5] The following discussion of the role of knowledge in comprehension draws upon my recent work at LRDC (Beck, McKeown, McCaslin, & Burkes, 1979).

comprehension is dependent upon linguistic, conceptual, cognitive, and general knowledge abilities that are similar to those required for aural language comprehension.

In virtually all reading programs, be they code or basal, children are required to interact independently with connected textual materials early in the process of learning to read. That is, they are assigned to read silently connected discourse.[6] To be sure, at the very beginning, the texts read are just a sentence or two, but within a short time period, the assigned silent reading gets longer. It is during the time that each child interacts with the text by him/herself that comprehension is constructed and the meaning of the text gets represented in memory. The notion that the meaning of a text is constructed as opposed to being extracted from the textual materials serves to point out that comprehension is an interactive process between previously acquired knowledge and the content of what is read. Prior knowledge is seen as providing the framework that helps the reader to assimilate new information. For example, it provides guidelines for recognizing what is important about a given topic and it allows appropriate inferential elaboration to be made about that text. (See Anderson, 1977, Brown, Smiley, Day, Townsend, & Lawton, 1977, Carroll, 1977, and Spilich, Vesonder, Chiesi, & Voss, 1979, for further discussion of the relationship between prior knowledge and comprehension.) Anderson, Reynolds, Schallert, and Goetz (1976) point out that a lack of knowledge about specific content can be a source of problems in comprehension; specifically, "it may turn out that many problems in reading comprehension are traceable to deficits in knowledge rather than deficits in linguistic skill narrowly conceived." (p.19).

Since children have a more limited knowledge base than do adults, such a limitation should be considered in the preparation of their reading materials. Yet some of the basals in their more recent editions have been including texts that require specialized or sophisticated previous knowledge in order to be understood. As early as the second grade, and certainly by the third grade, one begins to find stories in children's texts in which knowledge beyond everyday experiences is required for comprehension. As the materials begin to progress into unfamiliar territory by including concepts that the children have not even vicariously encountered, there is both positive and negative potential. The materials provide increased opportunities for elaborating upon the child's knowledge structures, but they also provide increased opportunities for com-

---

[6] To the best of my knowledge, Distar is the only program that has all textual materials read orally, before they are read silently.

prehension to go awry if unfamiliar concepts are not clarified during the reading lesson.[7]

By including conceptually more difficult material, the reading programs have acted with good intentions. In an attempt to allay criticism directed at earlier editions for being too stilted, the basals have included literature in grades three through six that has been drawn from recognized published children's works. In order to provide materials encompassing the diverse interests of a pluralistic society, the programs have included selections focusing on a range of special interests. In this sense, the basal programs are trying to be everything to everybody. The use of a broader base of general knowledge meets one aim of reading instruction, i.e., that such instruction should build knowledge. Yet the sophistication of the selections in the newer basals exacerbates the problem that some prior knowledge of a domain is prerequistite to understanding a reading selection about that domain.

Reading programs could reduce this problem inherent in some of their selections by better utilizing the structure of the directed reading lesson, the traditional format for reading instruction in the elementary schools, to supply the information needed for understanding specific selections. The directed reading lesson typically involves preparing children for an upcoming selection, reading the selection, and then questioning and discussing the selection. The prereading preparation is an appropriate place to begin to build in the students the knowledge structures required for comprehending the upcoming text. In the newer basals, precisely where the preparation component of the directed reading lesson should be expanded to build knowledge required for understanding the texts, what seems to have occurred instead is a reduction of prereading activities. Yet there is strong evidence (Sticht *et al.*, 1974) that new concepts are better acquired through oral/aural presentation than through printed presentation, until children are able to comprehend as efficiently by reading as they are by listening, which Sticht *et al.* suggest occurs around the seventh or eighth grade.

A. Building Knowledge through Prereading Discussion

There are several levels of knowledge problems. Small knowledge gaps might effectively be filled by the teacher during prereading discussion. From examination of several programs along this dimension, it was found

---

[7] It is important to note that the concern here is stories, not other discourse types. While recent work has shown that children do understand narratives in terms of their structure, it should not be construed that children therefore can always comprehend the content of narratives.

that programs sometimes provide information to fill small knowledge gaps and sometimes they do not. Knowledge structures to fill larger knowledge gaps cannot effectively be developed in 10 or 20 minutes. In these cases, either the story should be excluded from the reading program or the necessary knowledge structures built up over at least several days time. I will elaborate by presenting some examples.

An example that effectively provides information for a small knowledge problem was found in a third-grade Houghton Mifflin story; it shows the kind of care that can be taken to try to build the knowledge required for children to comprehend stories incorporating unfamiliar material. The story under consideration is set in China in 1913 and concerns a maker of rat-traps who becomes the official kite-maker for the Mandarin ("The Wooden Cat Man," Level J). In the selection, the Mandarin and his subjects live in a remote village and have never seen an airplane. When a Western pilot lands his plane near the village, the Mandarin and his people are astounded. Inspired by the unprecedented event, the Mandarin declares a contest in which kites resembling the airplane are to be made. The winner will become his official kite-maker.

The story opens, "In the Year of the Water Ox, a long time ago" (p. 271, Teacher's Guide). Such an introductory line is unusual and perhaps needed to clue children that they are entering a different world from the one they know. Importantly, however, the children are prepared to encounter this atypical story opening. In the prereading discussion, the teacher has explained:

> In the old Chinese calendar, each year is named for an animal. . . . The story you are going to begin reading today . . . took place in the Chinese Year of the Water Ox. The Year of the Water Ox was the same as the year 1913 on our calendar. (p.270, Teacher's Guide)

Later in the story, the idea that the characters are so astounded by the sight of an airplane might be puzzling for some children since airplanes are so ubiquitous today. The teacher tries to preclude possible confusion by explaining prior to reading:

> There are many things we are accustomed to seeing today that were unusual sights in the year 1913. Automobiles and airplanes had been invented—but many people had never seen or even heard of them. (p. 270, Teacher's Guide)

In this example, therefore, through pertinent prereading discussion, several potentially unfamiliar concepts are introduced, thereby providing information that would contribute to the knowledge needed for comprehension. In addition to most likely facilitating comprehension of this particular story, this kind of information is generative, as it adds to the store of knowledge about an unfamiliar cultural milieu.

In contrast, consider a third-grade story from another program in which no attempt was made to fill a small knowledge gap. In this tall tale selection, one of the characters ends a drought by tipping the Little Dipper over, thus releasing the water inside of it. Background information should have been presented about dippers, both about the function of dippers in general and also about how that particular constellation of stars likely came to be termed the "Little Dipper." Since dippers are all but anachronistic in today's world, it may be assumed that not all children will be aware of the use of the dippers in ladling water. It also may be assumed that not all third-graders who read this story will already know that constellations are named after objects or people that they seem to resemble. In order for children to understand the clever trick that solves the problem of this story, they must be able to follow the logic that since the dippers hold water, a "dipper" spanning the sky must hold a lot of water. Thus, the initial premise that dippers hold water and the connection between dippers in general and the Little Dipper in particular are important ingredients for a complete understanding of the story. The teacher should be alerted by the program to make certain that the children have this information in prereading discussion. Unfortunately, discussion around this concept is not specified by the program as a prereading activity.

As was pointed out earlier, the reason that the prior knowledge gaps in the first story about China could likely be successfully addressed was that the gaps themselves were not enormous. Of much greater concern are stories that require an array of working knowledge that many target-age children are unlikely to possess.

Without elaborating, consider a fifth-grade story that assumes a working knowledge of the lifestyle of the antebellum South and an understanding of various facets of a slave's life. Without an appropriate background in which to fit such concepts as: Quaker, Underground Railroad, free states, overseer, trader, bloodhounds, runaway, patrol, and hummocks, comprehension of the story seems likely to suffer. Or consider a sixth-grade story that is heavily dependent upon nautical and sea-related knowledge. Or, think for a moment about a fourth-grade story that relies upon knowledge of the interdependence of animals in nature. The knowledge structures that are needed to comprehend this kind of sophisticated content are not developed in a 10-minute prereading discussion. Yet the crucial point here is that the programs under consideration do not appear to provide any systematic differential preparation for those texts that are obviously more difficult than others in terms of the prerequisite knowledge they require for understanding. In general, setting the stage for comprehension through the prereading discussion appears rather perfunctory in some recent programs. For texts that require considerable prior knowledge, the prereading discussion should certainly be given more serious consideration.

A prevalent notion purports that reading can be taught through the content subjects. Relatedly, an examination of background knowledge serves to suggest that reading instruction should deal with more than just reading, i.e., that attention should be given to teaching about the content that is being presented in the reading selections. Acknowledging the oracy-to-literacy sequence of language development, prereading time should involve oral experiences aimed at developing new knowledge frameworks pertinent to the upcoming reading selection.

Before developing prereading activities, programs should carefully monitor the knowledge requirements for the texts,[8] and they should provide specifications for helping the teacher to develop background knowledge for at least those texts where it is obviously necessary. Careful editing should alter the stories to delete extraneous terminology. If some stories cannot be adapted to fit the knowledge levels of the students, those particular selections should be omitted from the programs.

Of course, wide individual differences make it impossible for programs to accommodate to the multitude of variations in backgrounds of the students who use the programs. But it would appear that designing more suitable prereading activities, editing out unncecessary terminology, or discarding certain selections would make the selections more appropriate for general use. Then, the programs also have the duty of alerting teachers that children come to texts with varying degrees of relevant previous knowledge, and that their own teaching must be adjusted accordingly. Teachers need to evaluate their students and attempt to determine what they know, and then attempt to teach whatever they need to know for a particular story, providing the information through oral/aural experiences.

Reading programs can preclude some comprehension problems by helping children to acquire knowledge appropriate to a specific reading selection. However, Anderson and his colleagues (1976) have also cited other ways that the relationship between a reader's knowledge base and textual content may lead to comprehension problems. For example, a reader may possess pertinent knowledge but may not have enough facility to bring it to bear in comprehending what is read. A traditional element in the preparation component of the directed reading lesson, termed "purpose" for reading, provides an opportunity for activating children's existing knowledge so that it can be applied to constructing meaning.

[8] I must admit that I know of no way of establishing appropriate matches between the previous knowledge needed for a given text and the knowledge possessed by target-aged children other than the use of "informed judgment." Better of course would be actual tryouts of the materials.

B. Activating Knowledge through Purpose–Direction Setting

In most reading programs, the "purpose" for reading is established by the teacher who follows the program's specifications; it comprises a few introductory remarks to the students about the content of the story lesson to be read that day and then a guiding statement such as "read to find out . . ." or "you will find out . . ." that suggests some particular information for the student to look for during reading. The term "purpose" is somewhat of a misnomer for this activity since the whole directed reading lesson is intended to establish and probe the purpose of reading the selection, not just the brief introductory remarks and guiding statement made by the teacher. Therefore, for this discussion "purpose" has been renamed "setting the direction for story lesson reading" or in shortened from "direction setting."

To illustrate more concretely the form of the direction setting activity, let us examine one example from the Ginn program. In a late first-grade story in which a farmer goes to the city to sleep in order to escape the constant noise made by his farm animals, the Ginn manual directs the teacher to:

> Tell the children that Mr. Big has a problem. Let them try to guess what the problem may be . . . Suggest that they read the story with the purpose of finding out what Mr. Big's problem is and what he does to solve it. ("Mr. Big," Level 5, p. 102, Teacher's Guide)

Note the presence of the introductory remarks (concerning Mr. Big's problem) and the guiding statement (to read to find out specifically about the problem and its solution).

In closely examining the direction setting activity through the intermediate grades in several programs, many examples of what appear to be two grades of quality of the activity were found: examples that might have a positive effect on the reader's comprehension of the text, and examples that might have a generally negative effect on reading behavior and, in turn, on comprehension. By identifying interfering direction-setting activities, there is concurrence with a statement made by Frase (1977) that "purpose in reading may lead a reader to stray from, as well as move toward, desirable learning outcomes" (p.43). In the present discussion, the "desirable learning outcome" is, of course, good comprehension of the text.

Let us first consider some examples of interfering direction-setting activities and the reasons they have been judged as likely to affect comprehension negatively. Interfering direction setting activities seem to err in establishing the appropriate framework for the reader in three different ways. In the first case, instances were found where the direction-setting activities could set the reader off in what can be considered the wrong direction; these misdirective activities seem likely to evoke inappropriate expectations in terms of what will be discovered later by reading the story. For example, in preparation for a third-grade story, children are told by the teacher that a particular king is always firing his chefs. After beginnig to read the story, however, it becomes clear that the king never did actually fire a chef. He would provide them with suggestions for improving their cooking, and because of their pride, they would resign in a huff. Direction-setting activities that provided conflicting information of this sort were found in several lessons within several programs.

Second, activities were identified in which the direction may be right but the scope is too narrow considering the passage to be read. That is, the focus of the direction-setting activity is on only a small portion of text found at either the beginning or ending of the selection. The activity therefore excludes most of the story's content from its focus. Guiding statements that focus on the beginning of a story and may be fulfilled by reading the title alone or just the first few lines of text, seem insufficient both as motivational and direction-setting devices. For those guiding statements that focus on the end of the story, too many pages of text intervene between the posing of the guiding statement and the textual location of the information it requested.

One example, selected from the many available, of a direction-setting activity geared toward information contained at the end of a story comes from a selection about an old African woman who is driven from village to village because she is believed to be a witch responsible for widespread floods. Near the conclusion of the story, the woman teaches the art of rainmaking to a villager, who treats her with courtesy in contrast to the treatment to which she is accustomed. The guiding statement for this story was to find out how the villager learned the art of rainmaking. The villager, however, does not even enter the story until the ninth page of the 12-page selection, let alone learn how to make rain. Frase (1977) has noted that "the effects of questions are diminished when they are placed some distance from the relevant text content" (p.48).

Third, there are instances of direction-setting activities that in themselves give away pertinent information in the selection, information that should be determined by **reading**. While giveaway activities do indeed set the reader off in the right direction concerning the story situation, they often take him or her through the whole journey.

As an example, a direction-setting activity that gives away a major part of the textual content occurs in a second-grade story about two children who decide to trade names and lives. The introductory statement gives away a major and highly interesting element of the story: the identity switch. By giving away key concepts about a selection or a major portion of the story content, it appears that the direction-setting activity supplants the reading role.

Thus far in this section, direction-setting activities that may inhibit comprehension for varying reasons have been discussed. It will be helpful here to break the activity into its two component parts, the introductory remarks and the guiding statement, and to attribute to each part its major weakness.

In general, the activities seem to go astray for one of two reasons. First, they rely too heavily on information-gathering specifications that may focus the reader's attention on severely limited and possibly non-critical story elements. The guiding statement is the more vulnerable of the two component parts in this respect. The very format of specifying a piece of particular information to be acquired through reading is delimiting since children can be told to "read to find out . . ." only a small amount of information at one time. Second, they set the reader off along the wrong path of reasoning or they set him/her off along the right track but then go on to provide excessive information and give away the story. In this respect, the introductory statement seems the more guilty, but examples have been found in which the guiding statement also is culpable.

If the arguments presented above are accepted, then it follows that a good direction-setting activity would activate the correct context in which to view the story. It also follows that the guiding statements should be watched carefullly; they should either be formulated in more general terms or possibly be omitted entirely. Let us move now to examine good direction-setting activities.

In the view of Frase, "purpose in reading gives rise to unique per-ceptions, memories, and understandings . . . . [which can] influence learning" (1977, p. 42). This line of reasoning, then, suggests that di-rection-setting activities should prepare children to construct the meaning of a text by evoking a network of relevant associations. Instead of being designed to elicit one or two bits of information, the direction-setting activities should provide a framework for the organization of events and concepts in the text so that many aspects of the text become interrelated, and thus, more memorable. In attempting to identify the key ingredient of the direction-setting activity that would further these objectives, the notions of Anderson (1977) and others about schemata are very helpful.

Schemata, which have variously been called *scripts, frames*, or *plans*, are ideational superstructures into which concepts can be incorporated to delineate their interrelationships. Anderson specifically indicates that a schema is a framework for ideas that can be thought of as containing "slots" to be filled.

In an experiment by Anderson and Pichert (1977), subjects were given one of two perspectives prior to reading the same textual passage. One group was alerted to read the passage from the perspective of a potential house buyer; the other group was told to read the passage from the view of a potential burglar. On an immediate recall test, subjects with the house-buying perspective remembered such details as the condition of the roof and basement. Subjects with the burgling schema remembered details such as unlocked doors and the location of valuable items. Thus, certain elements of the text assumed importance because of the predesignated schemata which provided an organizational frame for the subjects' recall. In Anderson's words, schemata are useful for "directing attention to text elements that are significant in light of the schema" (1977, p. 22).

Accordingly, then, the recommendation is that direction-setting activities be formulated in terms of schematic design. A schema promoting a network of ideas relevant to the content of a text might transform a direction-setting activity from an information-gathering directive eliciting one or a few details into a plan for attention in reading that would help children to identify, interrelate, and remember important story elements. However, it must be noted that the schema to be activated for a particular story may not always be clear cut. The selection of the schema should be determined by what the instructional designer believes to be the most meaningful associations to activate. Implicit in the recommendation that direction-setting activities employ schematic design is the assumption that the schema that is evoked will be appropriate and, indeed, central, to the story at hand. The adoption of just any schematic format will not necessarily circumvent all the potential problems of direction-setting activities as they have been outlined in preceding protions of this section; the appropriateness of a schema is highly dependent upon story content. The notions just discussed may be clarified by an example.

This example illustrates a direction-setting activity that attempts to activate what appears to be the single most important schema in light of the story to follow. The story conerns a schoolgirl who successively convinces a male companion that she **can** be a doctor, a pilot, or a president, and that her job possibilities are not determined by her sex (Houghton Mifflin, "Girls Can Be Anything," Level G). To introduce the story, the teacher says:

> How many of you think that you know just what jobs you want to have someday? . . . Let's hear about some of these jobs . . . Following these responses, go around the group asking pupils the questions, "How would you like to be a _____? Why or why not?" Ask the girls about occupations that have often been associated with boys—pilot, firefighter, police officer, football coach, engineer, dentist, farmer, etc. Ask the boys about occupations that have often been associated with girls—

nurse, kindergarten teacher, nursery school teacher, baby sitter, secretary, dietitian, etc. Through questioning and discussion, guide them to arrive at the conclusion— or to begin thinking in the direction—that there are really no valid reasons why a boy can't be a nurse or a girl can't be a pilot, provided that each is trained or prepared or educated for the job.

In today's story, you're going to read about a boy and a girl who have some disagreements. You'll find out what those disagreements are and how they are settled. (p.127, Teacher's Guide)

The discussion of jobs and of the possibility of not falling into de facto sexually determined job roles may indeed provide the children with an orientation that will help them to read the story with understanding.

The schematically oriented direction-setting activity for reading differs from the earlier-cited information-gathering types in that it is more concerned *with setting children thinking in ways that will help them to understand the story* than in specifying a particular story element to be located and remembered. In the example, an idea central to the story content is discussed prior to reading so that children might have an appropriate and specific frame of reference for reading and understanding the selection. It would appear that the crucial element of a direction-setting activity is an orientation or ideational framework that prepares a child to recognize important story elements as they are encountered and to relate them to each other under some larger design.

This discussion has focused on two aspects of the relationship between prior knowledge and reading comprehension, that is, the prerequisite knowledge needed for understanding specific content, and the activation of appropriate knowledge already possessed to facilitate an understanding of what is read. To be sure, other factors such as linguistic and conceptual abilities, are clearly involved in comprehension. Yet my experience with young readers and reading materials, in concurrence with recent work on knowledge cited in this article, has emphasized the importance of prior knowledge as a contributor to comprehension. Instructionally, the area of knowledge is a most useful place in which to begin to examine practices because the prereading preparation that can build knowledge and set a direction for reading occurs before the child is left on his/her own to construct meaning, and thereby may affect the constructive processes of comprehension.

IV. A RESOLUTION OF CONFLICTING RECOMMENDATIONS

This article has addressed two factors that are seen to underlie comprehension of a text, that is, lower level processing (word attack and automaticity of word recognition) and prior knowledge. It must be noted that there is a major conflict for instructional practice between polishing lower level skills and adding to the knowledge store through reading. Instruction aimed at polishing lower level skills must be kept conceptually easy, while instruction focused upon adding to a student's knowledge store must carry a greater conceptual load. Perhaps what is needed is a two track system of reading instruction: a daily reading assignment of an interesting but conceptually easy selection and also a regular presentation of conceptually more difficult selections grouped around the same knowledge domain. The easier selections would allow children to build reading fluency since the conceptual load would not require a great deal of processing. The stories with a greater conceptual load would help to build students' knowledge structures. Grouping stories along the same knowledge domain, e.g., nautical stories, would efficiently use the time spent preparing children to read about specific content. Each successive story in the strand could serve to reinforce the children's previous knowledge of the topic and then proceed to build on that knowledge base.

V. IN SUMMARY

At the beginning of this article, three areas of reading problems frequently noted by practitioners were set forth. Some instructional practices associated with each area were then described and assessed.

The problem area characteristic of the earliest stages of reading involves learning the print-to-speech code. This area has virtually dominated research and curriculum development for the past half century. The key issue here is whether initial reading should emphasize more heavily the structural relationship between oral and printed language or the meaning of the printed message. An uneasy consensus favoring phonics instruction has arisen over the last decade. Many program developers have added earlier and more substantial phonics components to their meaning-oriented programs. Analyses presented here of several such programs have shown that conditions have not been arranged for the most efficient learning of letter–sound correspondences. To be most effective, phonics instruction should make the grapheme–phoneme correspondence explicitly available, provide an instructional strategy for blending sounds into words, and sequence instruction so that the reading selections provide practice with words containing the newly acquired letter–sound correspondences. In addition, the reading selections should include a vocabulary chosen to maximize the regularities of the coding system.

The second area of reading problems examined was characterized by hesitant oral reading or slow silent reading. A probable cause for these behaviors is a lack of word-processing fluency or decoding automaticity. Recent theoretical and experimental work was cited suggesting that decoding automaticity is a necessary part of a reader's repertoire. Instructional practices centering on repeated encounters with the same words appear to be helpful in the development of automaticity. The recognition of automatic word-processing skills is a relatively new research topic, and as such, requires more investigation, both to draw attention to its importance and to refine the notions of how instructional practice can promote its development.

The third area of reading problems identified in this article was characterized by poor comprehension of what has been read. Though problems in the first two areas are also often implicated in poor comprehension, a frequently occurring problem of the intermediate grades is a lack of comprehension manifested apart from difficulties in word processing. Deficits in prior knowledge about the content of the reading material may be an important contributor to poor comprehension. While current research has emphasized the crucial role of a reader's prior knowledge in comprehension, recent editions of reading programs have increased the conceptual load of their selections. Of course, one goal of reading is to increase knowledge, yet this goal can hardly be accomplished if readers do not have the knowledge framework to allow comprehension of the new material. It was suggested that reading instruction include, through a teacher's oral presentation, content information necessary to build such knowledge frameworks.

In assessing current instructional practices associated with each problem area, recommendations were made concerning practices viewed as likely to be effective. It was noted, however, that the instructional prescriptions for the lower level processing involved in word attack and word recognition conflict with those for adding to the knowledge store through reading. Facility with lower level processing can best be gained through the use of conceptually easy reading material while an increase in knowledge is best achieved through a heavier conceptual load in the reading material. To fulfill both sets of objectives, a two track system of reading instruction was suggested which would combine daily reading selections of conceptually easy material with the regular presentation of more difficult selections organized around a single knowledge domain.

While certain instructional practices have been negatively assessed in this article, it must be noted that many children do learn to read under those very conditions. It must be recognized equally, however, that there are also children who have difficulty learning to read. For those children, reading instruction should be carried out in the most effective way possible. This does not mean the application of some instant instructional panacea, for none exists. Fluent reading ability develops slowly, over time. Improvements in instructional practice must be matched to this gradual evolution. A refinement of strategies, aimed at more careful development of each daily lesson, seems an appropriate course to follow.

REFERENCES

Anderson, R. C. *Schema-directed processes in language comprehension* (Tech. Rep. No. 50). Urbana, Illinois: University of Illinois at Urbana-Champaign, Center for the Study of Reading, July 1977.

Anderson, R. C., & Pichert, J. W. *Recall of previously unrecallable information following a shift in perspective* (Tech. Rep. No. 41). Urbana, Illinois: University of Illinois at Urbana-Champaign, Center for the Study of Reading, April 1977.

Anderson, R. C., Reynolds, R. E., Schallert, D. L., & Goetz, E. T. *Frameworks for comprehending discourse* (Tech. Rep. No. 12). Urbana, Illinois: University of Illinois at Urbana-Champaign, Center for the Study of Reading, July 1976.

Bank Street College of Education. *The Bank Street Readers.* New York: Macmillan, 1973.

Bateman, B. Teaching reading to learning disabled children. In L. B. Resnick & P. Weaver (Eds.), *Theory and practice of early reading* (Vol. 1). Hillsdale, New Jersey: Erlbaum, 1979.

Beck, I. L. Comprehension during the acquisition of decoding skills. In J. T. Guthrie (Ed.), *Cognition, curriculum, and comprehension.* Newark, Delaware: International Reading Association, 1977.

Beck, I. L. *Instructional ingredients for the development of beginning reading competence.* St. Louis: CEMREL, 1979.

Beck, I. L., & Block, K. K. An analysis of two beginning reading programs: Some facts and some opinions. In L. B. Resnick & P. Weaver (Eds.), *Theory and practice of early reading* (Vol. 1). Hillsdale, New Jersey: Erlbaum, 1979.

Beck, I. L., & McCaslin, E. S. *An analysis of dimensions that affect the development of code-breaking ability in eight beginning reading programs.* Pittsburgh: University of Pittsburgh, Learning Research and Development Center, 1978 (LRDC Publication 1978/6).

Beck, I. L., McKeown, M. G., McCaslin, E. S., & Burkes, A. M. *Instructional dimensions that may affect reading comprehension: Examples from two commercial reading programs.* Pittsburgh: University of Pittsburgh, Learning Research and Development Center, 1979. (LRDC Publication 1979/20).

Beck, I. L., & Mitroff, D. D. *The rationale and design of a primary grades reading system for an individualized classroom* (LRDC Publication 1972/4). Pittsburgh: University of Pittsburgh, Learning Research and Development Center, 1972 (ERIC Document Reproduction Service No. ED 163 100).

Bishop, C. H. Transfer effects of word and letter training in reading. *Journal of Verbal Learning and Verbal Behavior,* 1964, **3**, 215–221.

Bloomfield, L. Linguistics and reading. *Elementary English Review,* 1942, **19**, 125–130.

Bloomfield, L., & Barnhart, C. L. *Let's read, a linguistic approach.* Detroit: Wayne State Univ. Press, 1961.

Bond, G. L., & Dykstra, R. The cooperative research program in first-grade reading instruction. *Reading Research Quarterly,* 1967, **2**, 5–142.

Bowers, J. E., Campeau, P. L., Robert, A., & Oscar, H. *Final report: Identifying, validating, and multi-media packaging of effective reading programs.* Palo Alto, California: American Institutes for Research, 1974.

Brown, A. L., Smiley, S. S., Day, J. D., Townsend, M. A. R., & Lawton S. C. *Intrusion of a thematic idea in children's comprehension and retention of stories* (Tech. Rep. No. 18). Urbana, Illinois: University of Illinois at Urbana-Champaign, Center for the Study of Reading, February 1977.

Bruce, D. J. Analysis of word sounds by young children. *British Journal of Educational Psychology*, 1964, **34**, 158–169.

Buchanan, C. D. *Programmed reading (3rd ed.): A Sullivan Associates program.* New York: McGraw-Hill, 1973.

Calfee, R. C., Chapman, R. S., & Venezky, R. L. How a child needs to think to learn to read. In L. W. Gregg (Ed.), *Cognition in learning and memory.* New York: Wiley, 1972.

Carroll, J. B. The analysis of reading instruction: Perspectives from psychology and linguistics. In E. R. Hilgard (Ed.), Theories of learning and instruction. *The Sixty-third Yearbook of the National Society for the Study of Education* (Pt. 1), 1964, **63**, 336–353.

Carroll, J. B. Developmental parameters of reading comprehension. In J. T. Guthrie (Ed.), *Cognition, curriculum, and comprehension.* Newark, Delaware: International Reading Association, 1977.

Chall, J. *Learning to read: The great debate.* New York: McGraw-Hill, 1967.

Clymer, T., Christenson, B., & Brown, V. *Reading 720.* Lexington, Massachusetts: Ginn, 1976.

DeHirsch, K., Janksy, J. J., & Langford, W. D. *Predicting reading failure: A preliminary study.* New York: Harper, 1966.

Diederich, P. B. *Research 1960–1970 on methods and materials in reading* (TM Report 22). Princeton, New Jersey: Educational Testing Service, 1973.

Durr, W. K., LePere, J. M., & Alsin, M. L. *The Houghton Mifflin Reading Series.* Boston: Houghton, 1976.

Durrell, D. Success in first grade reading. *Boston University Journal of Education,* 1958, **3**, 2–47.

Engelmann, S., & Bruner, E. C. *Distar Reading I (2nd ed.): An instructional system.* Chicago: Science Research Associates, 1974. (a)

Engelmann, S., & Bruner, E. C. *Distar Reading II (2nd ed.): An instructional system.* Chicago: Science Research Associates, 1974. (b)

Fernald, G. *Remedial techniques in basic school subjects.* New York: McGraw-Hill, 1943.

Flesch, R. *Why Johnny can't read and what you can do about it.* New York: Harper, 1955.

Frase, L. T. Purpose in reading. In J. T. Guthrie (Ed.), *Cognition, curriculum, and comprehension.* Newark, Delaware: International Reading Association, 1977.

Fries, C. C. *Linguistics and reading.* New York: Holt, 1963.

Gibson, E. J., & Levin, H. *The psychology of reading.* Cambridge, Massachusetts: MIT Press, 1975.

Gillingham, A., & Stillman, B. *Remedial training for children with specific disability in reading, spelling, and penmanship.* Cambridge, Massachusetts: Educators Publishing Service, 1966.

Glim, T. E. *The Palo Alto Reading Program (2nd ed.): Sequential steps in reading.* New York: Harcourt, 1973.

Golinkoff, R. M. Critique: Phonemic awareness skills and reading achievement. In F. B. Murray & J. J. Pikulski (Eds.), *The acquisition of reading.* Baltimore: University Park Press, 1978.

Guthrie, J. T., Samuels, S. J., Martuza, V., Seifert, M., Tyler, S. J., & Edwall, G. *A study of the locus and nature of reading problems in the elementary school.* Washington, D.C.: The National Institute of Education, 1976.

Haddock, M. Effects of an auditory and an auditory-visual method of blending instruction on the ability of prereaders to decode synthetic words. *Journal of Educational Psychology,* 1976, **68**(6), 825–831.

Harris, A., & Serwer, B. The CRAFT Project: Instructional time in reading research. *Reading Research Quarterly,* 1966, **2**, 27–57.

House, E. R., Glass, G. V., McLean, L. D., & Walker, D. F. No simple answer: Critique of the Follow Through evaluation. *Harvard Educational Review,* 1978, **48**, 128–160.

Jeffrey, W. E., & Samuels, S. J. Effect of method of reading training on initial learning and transfer. *Journal of Verbal Learning and Verbal Behavior,* 1967, **6**, 354–358.

Jenkins, J. R., Bausell, R. B., & Jenkins, L. M. Comparisons of letter name and letter sound training as transfer variables. *American Educational Research Journal,* 1972, **9**, 75–86.

Kiss, G. R., & Savage, J. E. Processing power and delay—limits on human performance. *Journal of Mathematical Psychology,* 1977, **16**, 68–90.

LaBerge, D., & Samuels, S. J. Toward a theory of automatic information processing in reading. *Cognitive Psychology,* 1974, **6**, 293–323.

Lesgold, A. *Word-memory access and reading: Toward more explanatory evidence.* Paper presented at the annual meeting of the American Educational Research Association, Toronto, March 1978.

Lesgold, A. M., Resnick, L. B., & Beck, I. L. *Preliminary results of a longitudinal study of reading acquisition.* Paper presented at Psychonomic Society Meeting, San Antonio, November 1978.

Liberman, A. M., Cooper, F. S., Shankweiler, D., & Studdert-Kennedy, M. Perception of the speech code. *Psychological Review,* 1967, **74**, 431–461.

Liberman, I. Y. Segmentation of the spoken word and reading acquisition. *Bulletin of the Orton Society,* 1973, **23**, 65–77.

Liberman, I. Y., & Shankweiler, D. Speech, the alphabet, and teaching to read. In L. B. Resnick & P. Weaver (Eds.), *Theory and practice of early reading* (Vol. 1). Hillsdale, New Jersey: Erlbaum, 1979.

Marsh, G., & Sherman, M. *Transfer from word components to words and vice versa in beginning reading* (Tech. Rep. No. 23). Los Alamitos, Cal.: Southwest Regional Laboratory, 1970 (ERIC Document Reproduction Service No. ED 042 587).

Mathews, M. *Teaching to read historically considered.* Chicago: Univ. of Chicago Press, 1966.

Mattingly, I. G. Reading, the linguistic process, and linguistic awareness. In J. F. Kavanagh & I. C. Mattingly (Eds.), *Language by ear and by eye: The relationship between speech and reading.* Cambridge, Massachusetts: MIT Press, 1972.

Muller, D. Phonic blending and transfer of letter training to word reading in children. *Journal of Reading Behavior,* 1973, **5**(3), 13–15.

New York State Office of Education. *School factors influencing reading achievement: A performance review.* Albany, New York: Author, March 1974.

Ohnmacht, D. D. *The effects of letter-knowledge on achievement in reading in the first grade.* Paper presented at the American Educational Research Association, Los Angeles, 1969.

Otto, W., Rudolph, M., Smith, R., & Wilson, R. *The Merrill Linguistic Reading Program (2nd ed.).* Columbus, Ohio: Merrill, 1975.

Perfetti, C. A. Language comprehension and fast decoding: Some psycholinguistic prerequisites for skilled reading comprehension. In J. T. Guthrie (Ed.), *Cognition, cur-*

riculum, and comprehension. Newark, Delaware: International Reading Association, 1976.

Perfetti, C. A., & Hogaboam, T. The relationship between single word decoding and reading comprehension skill. *Journal of Educational Psychology,* 1975, **67,** 461–469.

Pikulski, J. J. Critique: Translating research in perception and reading into practice. In F. B. Murray & J. J. Pikulski (Eds.), *The acquisition of reading.* Baltimore: University Park Press, 1978.

Popp, H. M. Current practices in the teaching of beginning reading. In J. B. Carroll & J. S. Chall (Eds.), *Toward a literate society* (The report of the committee on reading on the National Academy of Education). New York: McGraw-Hill, 1975.

Resnick. L. B. *Theory and practice in beginning reading instruction.* Pittsburgh: University of Pittsburgh, Learning Research and Development Center, 1978 (LRDC Publication 1978/15).

Resnick, L. B., & Beck, I. L. Designing instruction in reading: Interaction of theory and practice. In J. T. Guthrie (Ed.), *Aspects of reading acquisition.* Baltimore: Johns Hopkins Univ. Press, 1976.

Rodenborn, L. V., & Washburn, E. Some implications of new basal readers. *Elementary English,* 1974, **51**(6), 885–888.

Rosner, J. Language arts and arithmetic achievement and specifically related perceptual skills. *American Educational Research Journal,* 1973, **10,** 59–68.

Ross, A. O. *Psychological aspects of learning disabilities and reading disorders.* New York: McGraw-Hill, 1976.

Rubin, D., Trismen, D. A., Wilder, G., & Yates, A. *A descriptive and analytic study of compensatory reading programs* (Phase I Report—PR–73–28). Princeton, New Jersey: Educational Testing Service, August 1973.

Samuels, S. J. The effect of letter-name knowledge on learning to read. *American Educational Research Journal,* 1972, **9,** 65–74.

Samuels, S. J. The method of repeated readings. *The Reading Teacher,* 1979, **32,** 403–408.

Scott, Foresman, & Company. *The New Open Highways (2nd ed.).* Glenview, Illinois: Author, 1974.

Silberman, H. *The use of exploratory research and individual tutoring techniques for the development of programming methods and theory.* (Tech. Memorandum No. 895/200/00). Santa Monica, California: Systems Development Corporation, 1964.

Spilich, G. J., Vesonder, G. T., Chiesi, H. L., & Voss, J. F. Text processing of domain-related information for individuals with high and low domain knowledge. *Journal of Verbal Learning and Verbal Behavior,* 1979, **18,** 275–290.

Stebbins, L. B., St. Pierre, R. G., Proper, E. C., Anderson, R. B., & Cerva, T. R. *Education as experimentation: A planned variation model* (Volume IV-A: An evaluation of Follow Through). Cambridge, Massachusetts: Abt, 1977.

Sticht, T., Beck, L., Hauke, R., Kleiman, G., & James, J. *Auding and reading: A developmental model.* Alexandria, Virginia: Human Resources Research Organization, 1974.

Tallmadge, G. K. *The development of project information packages for effective approaches in compensatory education.* Los Altos, California: RMC Research Corporation, 1974.

Venezky, R. L. *Prereading skills: Theoretical foundations and practical applications* (Theoretical Paper No. 54). Madison: Wisconsin Research and Development Center for Cognitive Learning, May 1975.

Venezky, R. L. Reading Acquisition: The occult and the obscure. In F. B. Murray & J. J. Pikulski (Eds.), *The acquisition of reading.* Baltimore: University Park Press, 1978.

Venezky, R. L., & Johnson, D. Development of two letter-sound patterns in grades one through three. *Journal of Educational Psychology,* 1973, **64,** 109–115.

Weber, G. *Inner-city children can be taught to read: Four successful schools.* Washington, D.C.: Council for Basic Education, 1971.

Williams, J. *Has the psychology of reading helped the teaching of reading?* Paper presented at the meetings of the American Psychological Association, Toronto, August 1978.

THE CONTENT OF SCHOOL READERS[1]

DALE M. WILLOWS, DIANE BORWICK,
AND MAUREEN HAYVREN

Department of Psychology
University of Waterloo
Waterloo, Ontario, Canada

When a child fails to learn to read well, it has been common to attribute that failure to a lack of ability or effort on the part of the child, to incompetency or insensitivity on the part of the teacher, or to the "method" of reading instruction—be it a meaning- or code-emphasis approach. Rarely have educators or researchers looked to the content of school readers as a source of potential causes of reading failure.

Trends over a period of 40 years suggest that publishers of reading series have been progressively reducing the textual load in first-grade

[1] We would like to express our sincere appreciation to all of those who contributed to the preparation of this article. Very special thanks are extended to Nancy Gorewich, Peter Boos, Rosita Lam, and Karen Leitner for their assistance with the content analysis, and to Bonnie Lee Bender for typing the manuscript.

books while simultaneously increasing the amount of text in the teachers' manuals. In comparing various characteristics of five editions of Scott Foresman first-grade readers and the associated guidebooks (the editions published in 1920, 1930, 1940, 1956 and 1962), Chall (1967) found that the number of new words per average story in the highest level first-grade readers had come down from 8.0 in 1920 to 4.2 in 1962 and that the number of new words in the entire book had diminished from 425 in 1920 to 153 in 1962. At the same time the teachers' manuals had increased in length from 157 pages in 1920 to 256 pages in 1962, and the number of words of instruction to the teacher per average lesson had mushroomed from 561 in 1920 to 2000 in 1962. These two concurrent trends appear to reflect an emerging attitude among the publishers of reading series (and, by inference, among educators) that what the teacher says and does in a beginning reading program is more important than what the child reads. In other words, the method of reading instruction seems to be considered by publishers and educators to be a much more significant factor in children's learning to read than the amount and type of textual content in the readers.

A similar point of view seems to be held by reading researchers. Although the literature of research on reading is voluminous, only a very small proportion of the studies have any relevance to the content of school readers. From the early 1920s when behaviorism first had its impact on experimental psychology until the 1960s when it began to lose favor, basic research on reading was almost nonexistent in the literature (Venezky, 1977). During that period, however, innumerable applied studies of reading were conducted. By far the majority of these addressed the question "What is the best method of teaching reading?" Educational researchers conducting these studies apparently hoped that by pitting the various approaches to reading instruction against each other in the classroom that they would discover "the best method" of reading instruction. The assumption underlying this "Method A versus Method B" type of research was clearly that the method rather than the materials would be the critical factor in determining any differences in effectiveness that might emerge between one program and another. In most cases such studies employed only one reading program as a representative of each method, despite the possibility that two exemplars of a given "method" might have drastically different reader content. Classroom studies comparing the same method of reading instruction, but utilizing different types of books as the children's reading material, would allow for a comparison of the relative influence of various dimensions of reader content on children's learning to read. Such studies are not in evidence in the literature of applied research on reading.

Since the early 1960s the focus of the research literature on reading has shifted away from the applied research question "What is the optimal teaching procedure?" to the basic research question "What is the process of reading?" (Levin, 1966). The goal of experimental psychologists addressing this latter question has been to elucidate the nature of the processes involved in skilled reading, their ultimate objective being to develop a comprehensive theory of reading. The specific questions examined in basic research on reading have come almost exclusively from "the laboratory," with little concern or even awareness of the practical side of reading instruction (Resnick & Beck, 1976). Thus, relatively few basic studies on reading have any immediate implications for the content of school readers.

Although it has apparently been the assumption of educators, researchers, and publishers of reading series that the method of reading instruction is the most crucial factor in determining the effectiveness of a reading program, it is our belief that since many children's first reading experiences may be restricted almost exclusively to what is contained in their school readers, the content of these books should be carefully scrutinized. Our purpose in writing this article was to bring together descriptive information about the content of current school readers with research evidence on various aspects of reader content that might affect acquisition of reading skill. Specifically, our goal was to answer the following two questions: "What is the nature of the content of school readers?" and "What is known about the effects of such content on the process of learning to read?" With these questions in mind, we conducted a comprehensive analysis of the content of the first-grade readers in four reading series and considered the results in the light of relevant research.

The content of readers has been defined very broadly in this chapter to encompass all aspects of the books that could conceivably affect a child's learning to read. Previous discussions of the content of readers have dealt with text alone, as though only the text would be expected to influence the child's beginning reading experience. It seems reasonable, however, that when the child looks at the pages of school readers any aspect of the information on a page may draw his/her attention and thus influence the process of learning to read. Characteristics of both the textual and nontextual aspects of these books may well contribute to the success of a reading program.

In view of this possibility, this article is divided into two major parts: the first dealing with the text of school readers, the second with the illustrations. Each of these is further subdivided into several sections. The text is considered in terms of vocabulary, language and readability, story content, and physical characteristics; each of these sections includes statistics describing that particular content dimension in current school readers and a review of research literature relevant to its possible effect on children's learning to read. The illustrations are discussed in terms of the amount and type of artwork in current school readers and the research evidence concerning the potential impact of this artwork on children's acquisition of reading skill.

In order to obtain a broad sample of the content of current readers we examined in some detail all of the first-grade level books of four reading series: Ginn's *Starting Points in Language Arts* (1976), Holt, Rinehart & Winston's *Language Patterns* (1976), Merrill's *The Merrill Linquistic Reading Program* (1975), and Scott Foresman's *Basics in Reading* (1978). Two of these, Ginn and Scott Foresman, serve as examples of basal reader programs; the other two, Holt and Merrill, represent current code-emphasis (i.e., "linguistic") programs. In each section of the article we include the results of our own content analysis of these four series, making comparisons within series across levels of difficulty (Levels A, B, and C), and between series across types of program (basal and code programs). Details concerning this content analysis are presented in an appendix at the end of the article. These pertain to the choice of the series, the basal and code program designations, the difficulty levels of the reading selections, and the numbers of books and words examined in each series.

I. THE TEXT

A. Vocabulary

1. Vocabulary Content of School Readers

The most striking distinction between basal and code-emphasis reading series is their choice of vocabulary in the early stages of the programs. Presented in Table I are the first 50 words in each of the four reading series included in our content analysis. Even a superficial perusal of these lists makes it clear that, in comparison with the basal programs, the vocabularies in the code-emphasis series contain a much higher proportion of words with regular spelling and words based on a limited number of symbol–sound correspondences.

These obvious differences—apparent in the word lists—are quite consistent with the contrasting approaches to vocabulary selection employed in basal and code-emphasis programs, and are also compatible with the objectives of these two approaches to reading instruction. As Beck (this volume) has pointed out, the vocabularies of basal programs are selected

TABLE I
The First 50 Words Introduced in Four Current First-Grade Reading Series

Code programs		Basal programs	
Merrill (1975)	Holt (1976)	Scott Foresman (1978)	Ginn (1976)
cat	Sam	funny	Mr.
fat	sit	face	Mugs
Nat	Tim	the	Pat
is	this	Mother	Curt
a	is	look	Mommy
sat	Matt	in	Daddy
on	it	mirror	look
mat	mitt	make	a
Pat	at	a	jet
the	bat	Father	here
hat	Jim	at	come
not	hit	lunch	it
look	Tam	girl	my
at	has	want	pet
bat	the	lemon	I
man	Tip	for	can
ran	habit	is	surprise
Dan	a	not	Tiger
fan	Pam	good	is
to	stamp	gum	dog
pan	jam	fox	love
van	mat	ate	see
lap	bath	made	thank
nap	Pat	monkey	you
cap	rat	goat	for
tap	Miss	red	on
map	Smith	boot	run
bad	ham	rain	fast
he	that	boy	get
had	bit	his	ball
Dad	trap	under	what
sad	Nan	bed	forget
mad	Tab	one	play
Sam	man	rug	Jan
in	in	has	oh
ham	snap	two	turtle
am	spit	put	the
jam	hat	on	raccoon
bag	nap	now	and
tag	mast	can	frog
and	his	go	like
wag	pants	out	this
rag	rip	seed	pretty
dig	Cam	I	fun
bit	camp	have	outdoors
fit	path	six	green
for	trap	ten	Mrs.
it	rabbit	here	White
hit	can	sun	something
tin	Nat	bean	to

to be "high frequency words and words that are likely to be in the child's experiential store," and they are not constrained by spelling–sound correspondences. On the other hand, the vocabularies of code-emphasis programs are generated almost exclusively on the basis of the particular spelling–sound correspondences taught in their reading lessons, and the availability of the words in the child's lexicon is of lesser concern. (Some linguistic programs even include nonsense "words" in their early vocabulary.) The goal of the basal programs is to capitalize on the child's well-practiced oral vocabulary to facilitate access to meanings of printed words, whereas the priority in code-emphasis programs is to focus the child's attention on the symbol–sound regularities in the language and to introduce irregularities systematically at a later stage.

Beyond these differences in the selection of their initial word lists, it seems reasonable that there should be differences on other dimensions of vocabulary use in basal and code-emphasis programs. For example, since the vocabulary in basal programs is selected with little or no concern for symbol–sound correspondences, the usefulness of "phonics cues" (irrespective of how much instructional emphasis is placed on them) will be quite limited, and the child will be forced to rely on less dependable cues such as word shapes, initial letters, and pictures. As a consequence, one might expect that in basal programs children would have to learn many words through sheer memorization of the visual form, and thus, repetition of the same words would seem to be essential for this learning to occur. In contrast, because symbol–sound correspondences are paramount in code-emphasis programs, these correspondences should require repetition rather than any particular words, the mastery of symbol–sound correspondences being better served by the use of a wide variety of words.

It also seems reasonable that the number of unique word forms introduced in first-grade basal programs would be substantially lower than in code-emphasis programs, since, in the latter, words are grouped according to phonemic patterns and thus (it is assumed) would not have to be learned individually. This difference should be reflected not only in the number of unique words in each type of program, but also in the rate at which new words are introduced.

In other words, it might be expected that on a number of different measures of vocabulary, the two code-emphasis programs in our content analysis would more closely resemble each other than they would either of the two basal reader programs. Conversely, the two basal programs would presumably be more closely matched with each other than they would be with either of the code programs.

For our analysis of vocabulary, the texts of each first-grade reader in the four series in our sample were entered into a computer. Programs were then developed to provide three different measures of vocabulary use: number of unique words, rate of introduction of words (i.e., new words per 100 running words), and number of repetitions of words. Results of these analyses are presented in Table II. The differences among the four series in the use of vocabulary are contrary to expectations and, apparently, unsystematic.

a. NUMBER OF UNIQUE WORDS

In our comparisons across series, derivative words were excluded from the lists (although some basal series include each derivative in their word lists for teachers, e.g., Ginn, 1976). The number of unique words (including proper names) appearing in the first-grade readers of the four series varies widely, from a low of 290 words in the Merrill series to a high of 1011 in the Holt series. The Ginn series was found to contain 355 unique words, while Scott Foresman includes 794. Quite unexpectedly then, one of the code-emphasis programs, Merrill, contains the fewest unique words, an even lower number than one of the basal pro-

TABLE II

Descriptive Statistics for the Vocabulary Content of All of the First-Grade Readers in Four Current Reading Series

	Code programs		Basal programs	
	Merrill (1975)	Holt (1976)	Scott Foresman (1978)	Ginn (1976)
Unique words excluding proper nouns	276	928	750	342
Proper nouns	14	83	44	13
Total unique words	290	1,011	794	355
Total running words	12,819	12,246	8,137	7,730
New words per 100 running words	2.3	8.3	9.8	4.6
Average (mean) repetitions per word	44.2	12.1	10.2	21.8

grams. Also, Scott Foresman, a basal program, presents more than double the number of unique words used in the Merrill program. Again, this finding was not anticipated, as the basal programs were expected to introduce fewer words than the code programs.

b. RATE OF INTRODUCTION OF NEW WORDS

With regard to the rate of introduction of new words, there is, once again, considerable variation. Whereas in the Scott Foresman series new words are introduced at the rate of 9.8 per 100 running words, in Ginn this rate is 4.6. The two code-emphasis series differ dramatically on this measure, as well; in Merrill new words are introduced at a rate of 2.3 per 100 running words, while in Holt, the rate is 8.3. Therefore, on both this measure and the previous one there are no consistent differences between the two types of reading programs, and the range of variation among the four series is extreme.

c. NUMBER OF REPETITIONS OF EACH WORD

Furthermore, by a large margin, Merrill is the series that presents the highest mean number of repetitions of each unique word—44.2. Next highest is the Ginn series, with an average of 21.8 repetitions per word, then Holt, with 12.1, and finally Scott Foresman, at 10.2.

In addition we grouped the number of repetitions for each word as shown in Fig. 1. In both Scott Foresman and Holt, a high proportion of the words are presented only one to five times. In Scott Foresman, 69% of the words in the first-grade readers appear five times or less, and in Holt, the figure is 68%. In comparison, in the Merrill readers, 41% of the words are presented one to five times each; in the Ginn series, 42%.

Since it would be expected that a higher number of repetitions of each word form is particularly important in basal programs in the early stages of the first grade, we compared the repetitions of words at Level A of each series, as well. The pattern of results is very similar to that shown in Fig. 1. Thus, in Scott Foresman, a basal program in which a relatively high number of words is taught, almost 70% of the words (i.e., 556 words) appear fewer than five times in the text, and 35% of them occur only once. Moreover, in the Merrill, a code-emphasis program in which very few unique words are taught, the repetition rate is quite high with 59% of the words appearing at least six times in the text.

On all of these measures of vocabulary use, then, there are no consistent differences between the two types of programs. In fact, there is great variation across the four reading series, and surprisingly, there is

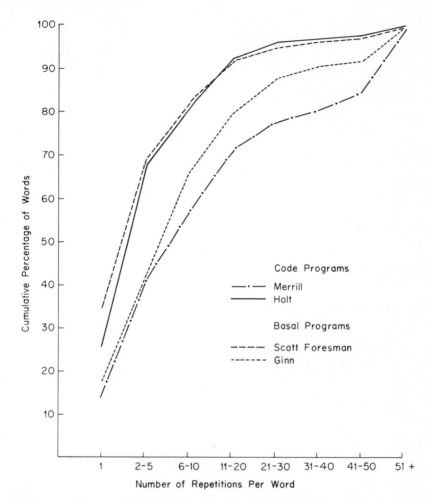

Fig. 1. Repetitions of each unique word in text in the first-grade readers in four current reading series.

more similarity on these measures between the Ginn and Merrill series, on the one hand, and the Scott Foresman and Holt series, on the other hand, than there is between reading programs of the same type.

The results of our content analysis cast some doubt on the rationales underlying vocabulary use in reading programs. If there is some reasonable basis underlying the different approaches to vocabulary selection, why is there no consistency within methods in the number of unique words presented, the rate of introduction of new words, and the number of repetitions of words? Perhaps it is safe to assume that the control of vocabulary in early readers is based more on arbitrary decisions than on theoretical principles or empirical evidence. Consistent with this assumption, we note, for example, that—on apparently no more rational grounds—the trend toward a lighter and lighter vocabulary load in Scott Foresman basal readers appears now to have reversed. In contrast to their 1962 edition, which Chall (1967) reported to contain only 153 unique words in the "first reader" (similar to Level C in this study), the 1978 Scott Foresman edition analyzed here contains substantially more—284 unique words. Given the dramatic variability on all vocabulary measures across the four series in our content analysis, there is a very clear need for research into the optimal levels of these types of measures for learning to read. These optimal levels may be expected to differ for the two types of approach discussed here and, probably, for children of differing abilities.

2. Research on the Vocabulary of School Readers

Our review of the research literature reveals that there have been no systematic examinations of any of the parameters of vocabulary included in our content analysis. Instead, the focus of most of the literature has been on the content of vocabulary—which words are included in school readers—through comparisons of the vocabulary lists of various reading series.

In three of the studies, to be reviewed in this section, the basis for comparison was the Dolch (1941) list of basic sight words. The major goal in this research was, in fact, to establish whether or not the Dolch list is still relevant rather than to answer questions about the basal readers per se. Two other studies to be reported here were concerned with historical changes in vocabulary load of basal readers. Following these studies will be discussion of one study in which two beginning reading programs, one a code-emphasis program and one a basal reader program, were evaluated on a number of vocabulary measures. Finally, an attempt by one researcher to develop a reading vocabulary based on research evidence on letter–sound correspondences will be presented.

The most common method of reading instruction continues to be some version of a basal reader approach, and the vocabulary for basal readers is supposedly selected on the basis of frequency and familiarity of words. One way to assess the vocabulary list of a reading program is to compare it to a list of words known to occur with high frequency and shown to be familiar to a majority of children. The Dolch (1941) list is purported to be such a list.

According to Johns (1970), Dolch compiled his list of basic sight words on the basis of three previous word lists compiled by other researchers. All three of these lists were constructed prior to 1930, which means that today the Dolch list is based on data obtained over 50 years ago. Eventually, Dolch arrived at a list of 220 basic sight words, words that children should learn to recognize immediately. These words had been found to occur with high frequency in children's literature and basal readers and also in children's oral language. Dolch originally excluded nouns from his list because he believed that nouns are easier to teach than other words and are less likely to retain their relevance over time; however, he subsequently added 95 nouns to his list.

In Johns' study, the goal was to determine the extent to which the Dolch list continues to be relevant. Five basal reading series, from first-grade through third-grade levels, were compared with the Dolch list. The series studied were: Allyn and Bacon, Ginn, Lippincott, Macmillan, and Scott Foresman. (Johns does not state which editions were used.) Briefly, Johns found that the 220-word Dolch list accounted for at least 50% of the running words of all of the basal reader series, with the highest proportion occurring in the grade-one level books. Note that this calculation was based on running words in a book, not on unique words, which means that every time a Dolch word occurred, it was tabulated. A different picture may have been obtained had only the unique words in a book been used. Nonetheless, Johns claims that his results are very similar to results obtained by Dolch in his original 1941 study, and concludes that the Dolch list remains of value in early reading instruction.

In a more recent study, Mangieri and Kahn (1977) also attempted to evaluate the present-day relevance of the Dolch list. They examined four basal reader series: *Holt Basic Reading Systems* (1973), *Scott Foresman Reading Systems* (1971), *Bookmark Reading Program* (1970) published by Harcourt Brace Jovanovich, and the *Read Series* (1968) published by the American Book Company. From each reader, primer to third-grade level, a sample of 3000 words was drawn, but proper nouns were excluded from the sample. Then all the words in the sample were compared with the Dolch list. The authors report that 62% of the words in their overall sample were words on the Dolch list. Also calculated was the proportion of words on the Dolch list that appeared at least once in the basal readers sampled. This proportion was 70%; thus, they conclude, because the Dolch list still accounts for a high proportion of vocabulary in basal readers, it is still useful as a guide for teachers in the elementary grades. Again, caution is necessary in interpreting these results, because a different estimate may have been obtained if the sample had consisted of unique words rather than running words.

The authors of these two studies have concluded that the Dolch list is still relevant today, even though it is based on research conducted over 50 years ago. Their conclusion rests on evidence that the words on the Dolch list continue to appear in basal readers; therefore, they argue, it may be useful to teach these words to children who are learning to read. Another interpretation of this overlap between the Dolch list and basal reader vocabulary, however, should be considered. It may be that the publishers of reading series consult the Dolch list when compiling the vocabulary for the readers and deliberately include words from that list. Therefore, this type of study does not adequately answer the question posed.

In another attempt to resolve the debate about the relevance of the Dolch list, Lowe and Follman (1974) compared the first 150 words of the Dolch list with seven other more recent word lists. They found that the most common words were "essentially the same" for all lists and concluded that the Dolch list is still useful. The reason for its continued relevance, they suggest, is that certain words occur with high frequency at all levels of reading material, including adult, and that these most common words remain fairly stable over time. While this may be true, the argument in favor of the relevance of any word list should be based on a demonstration that the words are actually in the spoken vocabulary of young children. Without this criterion of relevance, there is no way to know whether the words on a list are meaningful to children learning to read.

Johnson (reported in Johnson & Pearson, 1978) has recently developed a new list of basic sight words. In order to be included on this list, a word had to be used frequently by children in kindergarten and grade one, and also had to occur frequently in all types of reading material. The list was not derived from basal reader vocabulary. Despite this, it was found that 93% of the 180 words (out of a total of 306 on the list) that were designated as grade-one words, and 87% of the 126 grade-two words occurred in all five of the basal reader series examined. (The series are not named.) The Johnson list, or other lists that are more recent and based on the appropriate criteria, may be of more value than the Dolch list for determining the words to be included in basal reader vocabulary. But, in any case, other issues, such as those we raised earlier concerning vocabulary load, are probably of greater importance in terms of having an effect on the child's reading skills.

In addition to the research concerned with the Dolch list, there has been some investigation of changes over time in the vocabulary load of basal reader series. One such study was conducted by Rodenborn and Washburn (1974). They compared the vocabulary lists of first-grade readers from four series: Ginn, Houghton Mifflin, Macmillan, and Scott Foresman, for the editions in use in 1960 and in 1970. (No other information regarding the readers is given.) For all series, the number of words introduced in grade one had increased over the 10-year period; in one series (Scott Foresman) the number of words had doubled. Rodenborn and Washburn also report that a comparison of the vocabulary of six basal reading programs used in the 1970s revealed that there were only 134 words shared by all six programs. This means that most of the words in any given series were not common to all the other series, which could, the authors suggest, make it difficult for a child to transfer from one series to another. This is an important point. If there is very little overlap in vocabulary, the child who must switch to a new program will be faced with the task of learning a whole new set of words.

Another analysis of the vocabulary load of basal readers has been reported by Barnard and DeGracie (1976). Eight reading programs were included in the study: Harper and Row, *Design for Reading* (1972); Holt, Rinehart & Winston, *Holt Basic Reading System* (1973); Houghton Mifflin Company, *The Houghton-Mifflin Readers* (1974); Macmillan Inc., *Series r* (1975); Economy, *Keys to Reading* (1972); Allyn and Bacon, *Sheldon Basic Reading Series* (1968); Rand McNally and Co., *Young America Basic Reading Program* (1974); and Ginn, *Ginn 360* (1973). Vocabulary lists were obtained from the publishers and served as the basis for analyses. Proper nouns and derivative words were included in the lists. The cumulative total of unique words up to and including the first reader ranged widely across series, from a low of 436 in Rand McNally to a high of 811 in Economy. The mean number of words introduced was 551, which represents a large increase, according to the authors, when compared with readers used in the 1960s. They cite a study conducted by Olson (1965), in which it was found that the average number of words introduced in a series was 324; but in that study, as Barnard and DeGracie note, proper nouns and derivative words were excluded from the tally. Thus, to justify comparison of their data with Olson's, the authors reanalyzed the vocabulary lists, this time excluding proper nouns and derivative words. With this method, vocabulary load was found to average 504 words, which is 56% higher than the average reported by Olson. Unfortunately, because Barnard and DeGracie do not state whether or not any of the reading series were the same in the two studies, it is possible that some of the disparity in findings could be attributed to differences in reading series rather than to historical change.

In this same study, Barnard and DeGracie also computed the proportion of words that occurred in two or more of the eight series. Overall, this figure was 47%, which means that most of the words (53%) in a given series were unique to that series. Because of this lack of overlap, the authors recommend that a child should not be switched from one series to another.

The research discussed to this point has been concerned with the vocabulary of basal readers only. In contrast, Beck and Block (1979) have analyzed both a basal reader program, the *Ginn Reading 720* (1976) and a code-emphasis program, the *Palo Alto Reading Program* (1973). Program materials, including instruction manuals, for the first two grades were examined in order to answer questions about both phonics instruction and the teaching of sight words. Beck and Block note that both programs, in contrast to older reading series, provide earlier and more systematic teaching of letter–sound correspondences. An analysis of the sequencing and pacing of the letter–sound correspondences taught revealed that in the Palo Alto program, 69 of the 91 correspondences taught during the first two grades are taught in grade one. In the Ginn series, the correspondences are divided more evenly between the first two grades, with 52 out of 93 taught during grade one. It was found that Ginn, in comparison with Palo Alto, provides far fewer opportunities to practise the letter–sound correspondences learned. Also, in the Ginn series, there is a much lower proportion of words that are decodable, on the basis of previously learned letter–sound correspondences, than in the Palo Alto series. In the Ginn program, only 57% of the words in the grade one and two readers are decodable, while in the Palo Alto readers, 78% of the words are decodable. Furthermore, the introduction of new words in Ginn is not constrained by the learned letter–sound correspondences as is the case in the Palo Alto books.

Beck and Block also analyzed the teaching of sight words in the two series, and report that the techniques used are quite similar. The number of pairings of written word and spoken word, as implied in the instruction manuals, was calculated. Included in this calculation were pairings presented by the teacher and also those elicited from the students. In Ginn the average number of pairings of written and spoken word is 4.2 for each sight word; in the Palo Alto series, the average is 5.6. Beck and Block report that Palo Alto introduces nearly as many sight words as Ginn (534 compared to 613), but mastery of these words is not expected, nor are they maintained throughout the stories. Ginn, on the other hand, provides more continuity of vocabulary.

The approach to research on vocabulary taken by Beck and Block is potentially much more valuable than that in the other studies reported.

Both a code-emphasis and a basal reader program were analyzed and compared, and the analysis was much more thorough and detailed than the simple comparisons of vocabulary lists discussed earlier.

Another promising direction for vocabulary research has been taken by Cronnell (1973). In contrast to the other studies discussed in this section, in which the goal has been to analyze existing reading programs, Cronnell reports an attempt to **develop** a vocabulary based on orthography research. The resulting vocabulary would serve as the basis for a reading program suitable for kindergarten through grade-three level. In Cronnell's work, first a vocabulary list, appropriate for this level, was drawn up using several sources, mainly the Rinsland (1945) list of words known by elementary school students. Proper nouns and derivative words were excluded, leaving a total of about 9000 words. From this list, words of more than two syllables were eliminated, resulting in a final list of 6000 words.

Next, letter–sound correspondences were identified for the 6000 words. Cronnell reports that 166 different correspondences accounted for 97% of all the grapheme units in the words; but even so, 10% of the words contained one or more correspondences that were not accounted for by this system. Each word was analyzed in terms of its letter–sound correspondences and several other measures, and a tally was made of the frequency of occurrence of the 166 correspondences. On the basis of this frequency count, the correspondences were placed in sequence, beginning with the most frequent. Then the words on the vocabulary list were arranged according to the sequence of the letter–sound correspond-ences, so that for each correspondence, there would be one or more exemplars from the vocabulary list. Because the most frequent letter–sound correspondences would be more useful, they would be taught first. Thus, a reading program developed around this vocabulary would have the advantage of logical, empirically based phonics instruction. Further re-search into this type of program would be of value.

To reiterate, the studies reviewed here have been mainly descriptive in nature, simply comparing the vocabulary lists of reading series. Al-though such descriptive information may be useful, the questions of greater importance are those that deal with the effects, on beginning reading, of such factors as number of words taught in a reading program, rate of introduction of these words, and number of repetitions of words. Thus far, most of the research conducted in the area of vocabulary has been far too limited in scope to provide even preliminary evidence per-taining to these issues. From the single word we turn now to a more complex level of textual content, the language of the school readers.

B. Language and Readability

Possibly the most frequent criticism of first-grade school readers is that the language used is stilted or unnatural, instilling boredom, not interest, in the child who is learning to read. This criticism is not new; indeed, Huey, in 1908 commented that:

> Next to the beauty of the primers, the most striking thing about at least three-fourths of them is the inanity and disjointedness of their reading content, especially in the earlier parts. No trouble has been taken to write what the child would naturally say about the subject in hand, nor indeed, usually to say *anything* connectedly and continuously as even an adult would naturally talk about the subject. (p. 279)

Examples taken from the earliest level reading selections in current readers illustrate that this characterization may still be valid. Table III presents a reading selection from Level A of each of the four reading series in our content analysis.

As discussed by Gibson and Levin (1975), one argument in favor of the short, simple sentences and limited vocabulary of school readers is that this sort of text makes the reading task easier for the beginner. It is assumed that the use of language that is simpler than that spoken by the child is most suited to his/her slow rate of decoding. That is, the language used must be simple enough to allow the child to read to the end of a sentence without forgetting the beginning.

While it is obvious that some restrictions must be imposed on the complexity of first-grade reader text, it can be argued that in many cases the goal of maximum simplification has superseded other, perhaps equally important ideals, including coherence and interest value, that may contribute to the child's success in learning to read. Goodman (1967) argues that, contrary to popular belief, reading material that is more meaningful (and more complex) than the earliest preprimers may actually be read more successfully by young children. Although errors—or what Goodman terms miscues—will be made in reading both kinds of material, Goodman suggests that the more complex type of story provides the child with semantic and syntactic cues, which are combined with graphic cues in a "psycholinguistic guessing game." That this process occurs is inferred from the errors made by the child. According to Goodman, the child's errors in a more complex story will make sense, given the context of the story, and will be grammatically acceptable. In contrast, a story that is overly simple will give the child so few syntactic and semantic cues that reading becomes only word calling.

The controversy, in essence, consists of opposing views of the way in which young children learn to read. While proponents of a simplified text emphasize the importance of accurate decoding, i.e., identification

TABLE III

Examples of the Texts of Reading Selections in the Early Stages (Level A) of Four Current Reading Series

Code programs	
Merrill (1975)	Holt (1976)
Nat's Nap	*Mac*
Dad had bags and tags.	Babs sits.
He had maps and rags.	Babs can't skip.
Nat sat on the bags to nap.	Jan skips in the path.
Dad is mad.	Babs has Mac.
Bad Nat, to nap on the bags!	Mac hits Babs.
Nat sat on the maps.	Mac skips past Jan.
Nat, Nat, not on the maps!	Is Mac a scamp?
Nap on the rags, Nat!	Mac has a cap.
	That Mac is a scamp.
(*I Can*, p. 74)	(*Listening Letters*, pp. 51–53)

Basal programs	
Scott Foresman (1978)	Ginn (1976)
Animals in the Zoo	*A Ball*
Kangaroos are in the zoo.	Come, Mr. Mugs.
Kangaroos jump.	Here's a ball.
Kangaroos like vegetables.	Here it is.
Zebras are in the zoo.	Come on, Mr. Mugs.
Zebras run.	Get my ball.
Zebras like vegetables.	Get it!
Monkeys are in the zoo.	Run Mr. Mugs! Run!
Monkeys jump.	Run for my ball!
Monkeys like vegetables.	Come on. Get it.
Bears are in the zoo.	Get it for Pat.
Bears run.	Run, Pat! Run!
Bears like vegetables and meat.	Run fast!
	Fast, Pat! Fast!
	Mr. Mugs! Mr. Mugs!
(*Jumping Jamboree*, pp. 21–24)	(*Mr. Mugs*—A Jet-Pet, pp. 40–44)

of words, Goodman, among others, insists that reading involves more than sequential identification, that semantic and syntactic cues are also essential. At present, there is very little firm research evidence that would support either argument, and the issues are much more complex than has been indicated here.

Some critics of the simplified language of basal readers believe that the best strategy is to use language that is similar to the child's own spoken language. One of the first problems that arises is this: How can we **measure** the similarity of children's language patterns to the language of their readers? Do we measure similarity in terms of vocabulary, syntax, topics discussed, organization of discourse? What about individual differences, regional and cultural differences in language patterns? A second major issue involved here is the **effect** of similarity of oral and written language on children's acquisition of reading skill. This is a separate and important question that has been virtually unexplored. In fact, it seems that some researchers have implicitly assumed that similarity will promote reading skill, and have investigated only the first issue, that is, the degree of similarity that exists between children's oral language and the text of basal readers.

Quite aside from language similarity, there are other characteristics of text that may contribute to success and enjoyment in learning to read. One of these factors, readability, as measured by formulas, has been researched and will be discussed here. Other characteristics of language, for example, coherence, probably are important too, but because they are more nebulous and/or have not been researched (vis-à-vis basal readers), they will not be discussed here.

1. Similarity of Oral and Written Language

The first issue we will discuss is that of similarity of oral and written language patterns and the effects of such similarity on learning to read. Studies relevant to this issue include one by Ruddell (1965), a second by Tatham (1970), and a third by Glazer and Morrow (1978).

Ruddell (1965) conducted a study with 131 grade-four pupils in which he compared reading comprehension on two kinds of reading passages. Three of the passages contained "language patterns" that were defined on the basis of previous research (Strickland, 1962) as occurring with high frequency in the speech of fourth graders; the other three passages used low-frequency language patterns. To measure comprehension of the passages, Ruddell constructed cloze tests. He reports that comprehension scores were significantly greater for the high-frequency passages than for those using low-frequency patterns. This research thus offers some support for the idea that similarity of oral and written language patterns has a positive relationship with reading comprehension. Nevertheless, because this study involved only fourth-grade subjects, it is probably not advisable to generalize the findings to earlier grades.

In a study similar to Ruddell's, Tatham (1970), using subjects in grades two and four, measured reading comprehension of material written with frequent versus infrequent oral language patterns. Definition of the high-versus low-frequency patterns was also based on the results of Strick-land's (1962) study of the oral language patterns of children in grades one through six. Tatham defined "language pattern" in terms of the sequencing of syntactic elements (i.e., words, phrases, or clauses), for example, noun–verb–object. The reading material for this study consisted of two tests, each containing 37 sentences; one test contained only high-frequency patterns, and the other, only low-frequency patterns. In contrast to the material for Ruddell's study, which was comprised of passages, each on a particular topic, in Tatham's study, the sentences making up the tests were not related to each other. The same reading material was used for both grade-two and grade-four subjects. In an attempt to make the reading tests equivalent in difficulty for both groups, Tatham tried to control for a number of factors, including vocabulary, content and grammatical complexity, that she believed could bias results.

Having constructed the two tests, Tatham sought to measure comprehension of the sentences in each one. The measure of comprehension consisted of a multiple-choice task in which the subject was required to choose one of three drawings as correctly depicting a particular sentence. The three drawings for each item were identical except that one detail in each of the two incorrect pictures served as a distractor. These distractors were based on such variables as noun–verb agreement and verb tense. The two tests were administered to 163 grade-two subjects and 137 grade-four subjects.

From the results of her data analysis, Tatham concludes that sentences constructed from language patterns that occur with high frequency in children's oral language are better comprehended than are sentences constructed from low-frequency patterns. Although this study appears to have been carefully conducted, Tatham's conclusions are somewhat weakened by the presentation of the results of the study. In particular, the results are not reported in sufficient detail to be completely convincing; nonetheless, this study, when combined with that of Ruddell (1965), does offer some support for the hypothesis in question. That is, similarity between written language patterns and children's own oral language patterns may have a positive effect on reading comprehension.

Finally, in a recent study, Glazer and Morrow (1978) attempted to compare the syntactic complexity of basal readers with that of primary-grade children's oral language. Samples were taken from four reading series: *Merrill Linguistic Readers* and Workbooks (1966), *Scott Foresman Basic Reading Series* and Workbooks (1956–1962), *New Scott Foresman Reading System* (1971), and *Open Court Correlated Language Arts Program* (1970). They used the Botel, Dawkins, and Granowsky (1973) formula, the validity of which has not been established (cf. Hittleman, 1978), to analyze samples of the speech of 6-, 7-, and 8-year-old children and also to analyze the text of the four reading series. This formula is intended to calculate the difficulty of syntactic elements in a sample of language. The procedure used is unclear; nevertheless, the authors claim to have found that the language used in two of the series, the New Scott Foresman and the Open Court, was more complex than the children's oral language, as measured by the Botel *et al.* (1973) formula.

To summarize, there appears to be some evidence that children's reading comprehension is improved when the syntactic patterns of written material are similar to those of their oral language. What is now required is, first of all, more comprehensive measures of the similarity of children's oral language and the language of their school readers, and second, careful research into the effects of such similarity. The really important question is, "Does the degree of similarity between children's oral language and the language in their school readers affect their learning to read?"

2. Readability

An issue related to the one just discussed is the issue of readability. The two most important questions concerning the readability of school readers are, first, "How readable, i.e., comprehensible, are school readers?", and second, "How does reading ease affect the process of learning to read?" We do not have satisfactory answers to either of these questions as yet, primarily because of major limitations in the area of readability research. In addition, within the fairly large body of research devoted to readability, there have been very few studies of primary-grade readers.

In this section, some of the discussion will be devoted to a brief critical appraisal of the concept of readability, including various suggestions for improvement. Following this critique will be a review of two published studies of school readers. Finally, we will report the results of our own readability analyses of four reading series.

a. MEASUREMENT OF READABILITY

Although there does not appear to be any one specific definition of readability used in the literature, the general sense of the term may be stated as "ease of comprehension." Readability is usually viewed as being inherent in the text, as measured by various features such as word familiarity and sentence length. To put the concept of readability into broader perspective, one might say that readability overlaps with some aspects of writing style. Something that is highly readable (as this is usually defined) is not necessarily an example of good writing style, however.

According to Harris and Jacobson (1979), one of the earliest statements on readability is contained in an article written in 1852 by Herbert Spencer, in which he discussed some of the features of text that are often included in present-day readability formulas. Since the 1920s, an enormous amount of effort has been devoted to developing readability formulas, in an attempt to arrive at objective measures of the comprehensibility of text (Geyer, 1970). It has been the purpose of the developers of these formulas to provide writers and educators with accurate yet simple means of predicting the suitability of a given sample of written material for a particular audience (Klare, 1974–75). Bormuth (1966, p. 81) believes that "One of the great challenges to scientists of this generation is to learn how to predict and control the difficulty of language."

According to Klare (1974–75), the two most widely used readability formulas are the Flesch Reading Ease formula, and the Dale–Chall formula, both developed during the 1940s. The Flesch formula is based on two factors: word length, as measured by the number of syllables per 100 words, and sentence length, as measured by the number of words per sentence. Similarly, the Dale–Chall formula also employs just two factors: average sentence length in words, and the percentage of words not appearing on the 3000-word Dale list of frequent words (words known to 80% of children in grade four). In addition to these two most popular formulas, there have been numerous other readability formulas developed; often these have been revisions of the Flesch formula or the Dale–Chall formula (Klare, 1974–75, 1976). According to Klare (1974–75), most formulas have used the McCall–Crabbs *Standard Test Lessons in Reading* as a validation criterion, but cloze scores on passages, and sometimes judgments of readability, have also been used. Overall, the correlations between the formulas and their criterion scores have ranged from .45 to .95.

Although many of the available readability formulas are quite complex, i.e., based on many different factors, Klare (1974–75) reports that for most purposes, a simple two-factor formula that is based on word familiarity or length, and sentence length or complexity, is sufficient because these two variables are most predictive of comprehension difficulty. The addition of other variables contributes little to a formula's predictive validity. It is important to remember that no claim is made that the two factors that correlate best with readability are causally related to readability. Rather, these factors, word length/familiarity and sentence length/complexity are simply good indices of readability.

Thus far in this discussion, the validity of readability formulas has been considered in terms of their ability to predict accurately the difficulty level of a written passage. Klare (1976) points out that there is a second way to assess the validity of readability formulas; it involves what he terms production (as opposed to prediction) of readable writing. In general, the procedure in this case is to attempt to produce changes in comprehension difficulty by modifying passages according to the factors in a readability formula. This type of research is fraught with problems and has produced equivocal results (see, for example, Hansell, 1976), mainly because comprehension difficulty is based on a great many variables besides those measured by readability formulas. Indeed, Bormuth (1966) cites Chall (1958) as arguing against the use of readability formulas as guides for adjusting the difficulty level of reading materials.

There are many other problems associated with readability formulas. Perhaps the most serious limitation is that many factors that may contribute to the comprehensibility of a written passage have been ignored in the formulas, partly because they are difficult or impossible to measure. One of the most important components of the reading situation—the individual reader—is not included in the concept of readability represented in readability formulas (Geyer, 1970; Hittleman, 1978). That is, the reader's skill and motivation are not taken into account. Klare (1976) reports that these factors and others, such as the test situation, interact with readability measures.

Hittleman (1978) states that the shortcomings of readability formulas include the possibility that the formulas may not be valid when used with readers or text that are dissimilar to those used in the development of the formulas. In addition, according to Hittleman and also Geyer (1970), the formulas do not measure such factors as conceptual difficulty of the material, nor do they take account of organization of the material.

Apparently, then, readability is an extremely complex quality that is only partly assessed by the language variables that make up readability formulas. For this reason, formulas can provide only a rough estimate of the difficulty level of a sample of text (Klare, 1976). Standal (1978) suggests that "readability formulas are best thought of as guides or general indicators of a possible range of materials suited to any given child" (p. 646). Bormuth (1966) states that educators are misled in that they believe that readability formulas are more accurate than they really are.

In response to this dissatisfaction with the adequacy of present-day measurement of readability, some researchers have offered suggestions for improvement. Harris and Jacobson (1979) propose that the priorities for readability research in the future should include development of a formula that takes into account the affective response to reading material, i.e., its interest value. (In the next section, story content, we discuss some of the factors that may affect interest value.) In contrast, Bormuth (1966) has stated that the predictive accuracy of readability formulas will be improved in future through the use of new linguistic variables. He found, for example, that "the length and complexity of a sentence can be measured separately; and though length and complexity are correlated, each has an independent correlation with difficulty" (p. 129).

A number of authors (Bormuth, 1966; Geyer, 1970; Hittleman, 1978; Simons, 1971) have pointed out that cloze tests provide a more precise indication of comprehension ease than do readability formulas. Some (e.g., Hittleman, 1978) have even suggested that the cloze procedure should be used instead of readability formulas. Unlike readability formulas, which **predict** readability, cloze tests actually **measure** comprehension of text. However, the cloze procedure also has a number of disadvantages, including the need for greater time and effort on the part of the user.

Another alternative to the use of readability formulas is to obtain judgments from readers of the readability of written passages. Klare (1974–75) cites evidence that "readers can provide even more sensitive and reliable judgments of the readability of sentences than formulas can." Like the cloze procedure, judgments require more time and effort than formulas. Also, Klare raises the question of the reliability and validity of judgments with increasing task complexity.

b. READABILITY OF SCHOOL READERS

The problems associated with readability research are obviously very serious. With this in mind, we will turn now to a discussion of the literature on research investigating the readability of school readers. Unfortunately, as yet there are no definitive answers to questions concerning the readability of school readers and the resulting effect on children's progress in learning to read.

Although there have been numerous studies examining the readability of reading materials for older children and adults, there have been very few published studies of the readability of primary-grade reading materials. One such study, conducted by Kaiser, Neils, and Floriani (1975), was designed to analyze the syntactic complexity of a sample of school readers. The sample consisted of first-grade readers from four series: Ginn 360 *We Are Neighbors,* Scott Foresman *Ready to Roll,* Merrill Linguistic *Reader #3,* and SRA Basic Reading *A King on a Swing.* (The dates of the editions used are not mentioned.) The authors report that there was considerable variation of sentence complexity both within and across readers, and that there was no systematic increase in complexity from beginning to end of a given book. However, the validity of the measure of syntactic complexity used, a formula developed by Botel *et al.* (1973), has not been established. Indeed, according to Hittleman (1978), there is no good evidence that the rank ordering of sentences by this formula has any relationship to the actual order of comprehension difficulty.

In a more careful study, Bradley and Ames (1977) examined the readability of third-grade basal readers, from three different series, using the Fry Readability Graph (Fry, 1968). The validity of this measure, according to Klare (1974–75), has been established, and it correlates highly with other widely used formulas. In addition, for one series, Houghton Mifflin, a second-grade and a fourth-grade reader were analyzed. The readers examined were Houghton Mifflin, *Secrets, Panorama,* and *Kaleidoscope* (1971), Holt, Rinehart & Winston, *Never Give Up* (1973), and Macmillan, *Secret Spaces* and *Good News* (1975). One of the findings of this study was that there was substantial variation in readability—as much as several grade levels—within books and even within stories. On the other hand, there was agreement between the parameter readability means of the readers and the publishers' grade level designations. Another important finding was that it was necessary to draw at least 24 100-word samples in order to estimate accurately a book's average readability and readability variation.

Because of the almost complete lack of adequate research, it is impossible to draw any firm conclusions concerning the readability of school readers and the effect of readability on children's reading skills. Of course, this situation is partly due to serious inadequacies in readability research generally, and, as discussed above, some researchers have suggested possible ways to improve the measurement of readability.

With the limitations of readability formulas clearly in mind, we have examined the readability of the four reading series at three stages in the programs: early (Level A), middle (Level B), and late (Level C). We used the Spache formula, the details of which are described in his book (Spache, 1974). The basis for our selection of this particular formula is that it was specifically designed for use with materials at the level of grades one through three.

The Spache formula combines two measures related to text difficulty: sentence length and word familiarity. For the first component, sentence length, the total number of words in the sample is divided by the number of sentences to give the mean number of words per sentence. The second component, word familiarity, is calculated by comparing the words in the sample with the 1041-word Stone (1956) Revised Word List. Words that do not appear on this list (or are not certain specified kinds of derivatives of words on the list) are counted as unfamiliar. These two components, average number of words per sentence, and number of unfamiliar words are entered into an equation that produces an estimate of readability level in terms of number of months in a particular school grade. So, for example, an estimate of 1.4 is to be interpreted to mean that the reading material requires a level of reading ability equivalent to 4 months in grade one.

Spache recommends that three 100-word samples are taken from each book in order to estimate readability; but in our study, a computer program was used to calculate readability for the entire text of each book, thus providing a more accurate estimate than would be obtained from three samples. The results of the computations, shown in Table IV, indicate some variations across the series. In view of the differing criteria for vocabulary selection of code and basal programs—discussed in the previous section on vocabulary—we had expected that the code readers would be estimated to be more difficult. Word familiarity is a factor determining readability scores, and, in contrast to basal programs, the code programs use symbol–sound correspondences, not word familiarity, as the primary criterion for vocabulary selection. As the data show, however, once again there is more similarity between series of different types than there is between those of the same type. One code program (Merrill) and one basal program (Ginn) are similar in that there was some gradation of readability across the year, each beginning at a lower level of difficulty than it reached later in the year. The other two reading series (Holt and Scott Foresman) are quite similar to each other in that both were estimated to be at a relatively high level of difficulty throughout all of first grade. However, it appears that the latter two series were rated as difficult for different reasons. In the case of Holt, a code program, there are more unfamiliar words, while in the Scott Foresman, a basal program, it is apparently sentence length which con-

TABLE IV

Readability According to Spache's Formula of the First-Grade Readers in Four Current Reading Series

	Code programs		Basal programs	
	Merrill (1975)	Holt (1976)	Scott Foresman (1978)	Ginn (1976)
Level A	1.4	1.8	1.7	1.1
Level B	1.6	1.8	1.6	1.4
Level C	1.7	1.8	1.7	1.6

tributes more to the difficulty of the material. Sentence length in the Scott Foresman readers was quite high at all three levels (A, B, and C).

Whether longer sentences are beneficial is unknown at present because as mentioned earlier, the debate concerning the simplicity versus complexity of the language of school readers has not been subjected to empirical test. However, despite lack of evidence favoring one side or the other, it is possible that the publishers of the Scott Foresman readers have taken heed of the admonitions of psycholinguists regarding the disadvantages of using extremely short sentences. Sentence length should be investigated empirically for its effects on the child who is learning to read; and the results of such investigation, rather than theoretical speculation, should serve as the basis for publishers' decisions.

At present, readability formulas provide only a rough estimate of the reading difficulty of a sample of text. However, until better formulas are developed, it may be worthwhile to use the formulas now available to conduct further studies of the readability of school readers. The results of such research could then be used, with due caution concerning their accuracy, as guides for educators who wish to have some objective basis for curriculum planning.

Although formulas have the advantage of requiring relatively little time on the part of their users, there are alternative methods of assessing reading difficulty, as was discussed previously. These alternatives, including cloze tests of comprehension and judgments by readers, deserve further attention. Apparently such methods have not yet been used in studies of the readability of school readers. It is possible that these other methods would yield more accurate, and thus more valuable, assessments than would readability formulas.

Beyond more accurate measurement of the reading difficulty of school readers, what is clearly necessary is research into the effect of variation in readability on the process of learning to read. As discussed earlier, there are opposing views on the potential influence of using short, simple sentences and limited vocabulary in school readers. Some consider such language to be helpful, while others assert that it interferes with learning to read. If this issue is to be resolved, researchers should certainly direct their attention to the need for studies on the effects of the language and readability of school books on children's success and enjoyment of reading.

C. Story Content

Textual content is unquestionably the overriding determinant of adults' motivation to read a book or article. An enticing cover, a provocative title, or attractive pictures may serve to draw a reader to one text over another, but ultimately, whether or not the person reads it with any thoroughness is surely determined by qualitative aspects of the text itself—how interesting, amusing, or informative it is and, probably, how well written it is. Does the textual content of school readers play a role in children's motivation to learn to read? Proponents of such beginning reading approaches as Language Experience, in which children **generate** their own stories, and Individualized Reading, in which they **select** their own stories, strongly contend that it does. But, what evidence exists?

The textual content of school readers has been examined in terms of two main dimensions: themes and characters. There have been some studies concerned with describing the types of themes and characters included in major reading series, and a few others addressed to how these dimensions may affect children's motivation to learn to read.

In this section we will discuss three textual dimensions of the reading selections in current school readers that may play a role in motivating children to learn to read. Two of them, themes and characters, will be considered in the light of past research. The other, length of reading selection, has usually been overlooked in attempts to assess the motivational value of the stories in school readers, but may well be critical. Because of its potential as a modulator of both of the other factors, our discussion begins with length of selection.

1. Length of Selections

In her examination of five successive Scott Foresman editions, Chall (1967) listed the average number of running words per story in the highest level grade-one books. For the 1920, 1930, 1940, 1956, and 1962 editions, respectively, the average numbers of running words were 333, 385, 295, 305, and 230. In the 1978 Scott Foresman edition we examined, the comparable figure was only 126 words. Thus, although the reading selections in earlier editions were already very brief, those in this most recent edition were considerably briefer still.

As shown in Table V we examined the average length of the reading selections in the lowest (Level A), middle (Level B), and highest (Level C) level grade-one books in the four reading series in our content analysis. At the lowest difficulty level at the beginning of grade one, the reading selections ranged from 31 to 62 words across the four series, while even at the highest level at the end of grade one the lengths ranged from 71 to 300 words.

Just how the length of the texts might affect children's motivation to read has not been examined. There has, however, been some discussion in educational literature relevant to this aspect of school readers. As

124   Dale M. Willows et al.

TABLE V

Average Number of Running Words per "Story" in Four Current Reading Series

	Code programs		Basal programs	
	Merrill (1975)	Holt (1976)	Scott Foresman (1978)	Ginn (1976)
Level A	31 ($N=60$)[a]	38 ($N=14$)	62 ($N=36$)	48 ($N=14$)
Level B	53 ($N=58$)	82 ($N=36$)	110 ($N=20$)	82 ($N=21$)
Level C	146 ($N=54$)	183 ($N=34$)	126 ($N=21$)	300 ($N=18$)

[a] N = the number of complete stories, combining story parts in Level C of Holt and Ginn.

early as the nineteenth century, educators were debating the relative merits of "literary wholes," such as condensations of classic works of fiction, versus "literary scraps," brief selections taken from a variety of topic areas, as the content for school readers (Huey, 1908/1968). Intuitively appealing arguments have been offered on both sides. In favor of literary wholes it has been argued that a good story, well written, may serve as a powerful motivator. An exciting plot and a sense of involvement with the characters may provide the child with a reason to attempt difficult material, and to return to his/her school reader day after day with a sense of anticipation. On the other hand, brief reading selections may provide the child with a sense of accomplishment. Each reading lesson can be built around a single selection, and the child may take some satisfaction in finishing a "whole story."

In the view of the brevity of even the highest level selections in the programs we surveyed, it is apparent that the arguments for literary wholes have had little influence on the composition of current school readers. All of the selections are so short that to describe more than a few of them as "stories" is quite misleading.

In a reading selection of even 300 words the possibilities for development of a story line or plot are extremely limited. In only very rare cases did we find any thematic continuity at all from one selection to the next (15% of the stories in Ginn and 4% of those in Holt were presented in more than one part). Thus, we prefer to avoid the use of the term "story" in our discussion of themes, and refer, instead, to reading selections. Also, we found that the "characters" in the books have essentially no character. The only serious attempts at character continuity are in the Ginn (1976) and Merrill (1975) series; in these the same "characters," identifiable by their names in Merrill and by their names and pictures in Ginn, appear in many of the reading selections.

(This fact is corroborated by the vocabulary counts. The number of different proper names in Ginn and Merrill are 13 and 14, respectively, whereas in Scott Foresman and Holt the figures are 44 and 83.) No effort is made, however, to provide these "characters" with personalities or feelings. Thus, to describe them as characters is to use the term very loosely.

In the following two parts of this section, dealing with themes and characters, the very short lengths of the selections in current readers must be taken into account. The potential influences of themes and characters on children's motivation to read longer stories may bear little relation to their effects on very brief selections.

2. Themes

Critics of the thematic content of basal readers have described the reading selections as "bland" and "Pollyannish" (Blom, Waite, & Zimet, 1970), and have argued that children's motivation to read them may be adversely affected by these characteristics. The justification for these criticisms comes from research addressing three questions: "What types of thematic content appear in school readers?", "How much correspondence is there between the thematic content of their school readers and the types of material children select to read themselves?" and "Do children become more proficient in reading if the content of their school readers caters to their interests?"

Research addressed to the first two of these questions has been conducted almost exclusively by Blom, Waite, Zimet, and their co-workers (e.g., Blom, Waite, & Zimet, 1968, 1970; Blom & Wiberg, 1974; Waite, Blom, Zimet, & Edge, 1967; Wiberg & Trost, 1970; Zimet, Blom, & Waite, 1968). They examined all of the stories in the 12 major basal reader series in use in the United States during the early 1960s, and classified their content on seven dimensions including story themes. Their results on thematic content are reproduced in Table VI. As shown in the table, a very high proportion of the 1307 stories they rated had themes relating to real life events.

In order to determine the degree of correspondence between the thematic content of their readers and the types of stories children select in a free-choice situation, Wiberg and Trost (1970) conducted a library study. They coded library books using the same thematic categories as in the basal reader study of Blom et al., and inferred first graders' reading interests from the books they checked out. The most frequently selected themes were folk tales and pranks, thematic categories not well represented in their basal readers. On the basis of these results, Blom et al. (1970) concluded that "children's preferences of story content are mark-

TABLE VI

Frequency Ratings of Story Themes in 1960s Reading Programs from Blom, Waite, and Zimet (1970)

	Number of stories	%		Number of stories	%
Real life with positive			Work projects	76	6
emotions	303	23	Quiet activities	41	3
Active play	162	12	Pranks and humor	37	3
Pets	152	12	School	35	3
Outings	107	8	Parties	20	2
Imaginative play	94	7	Lessons from life	14	1
Real life with negative			Aesthetics	7	.5
emotions	93	7	Unclassified	3	.5
Nature	83	6	Religion	0	0
Folk tales	78	6			

edly discrepant from the content that is contained in first-grade reading textbooks'' (p. 212).

Because the analysis of the thematic content of basal readers by Blom *et al.* (1970) was conducted on series published about 20 years ago, we decided to rate the themes of our four recent series using the same 17 categories as they did. In this way we hoped to determine whether there have been significant changes in the thematic content of readers over the intervening years. In our attempt to do these ratings, however, we found that the categories were not mutually exclusive, and as a result, our raters were not able to achieve a satisfactory level of inter-rater agreement. Also, too high a proportion of the reading selections in our sample fell into the ''unclassified'' category.

In order to obtain reasonably reliable ratings of the thematic content in the books in our sample, we had to reduce the number of categories to four: real life, fantasy, instructive, and themeless. The real life category included all reading selections dealing with real life day-to-day events (e.g., family, school, and neighborhood activities), the fantasy category included selections about make-believe situations (e.g., folk tales, fables, etc.), instructive selections were those whose primary purpose was to convey instructive information (e.g., facts, values, etc.), and the themeless category included those selections in which the words themselves were the main focus (e.g., poetry, rhyming, etc.).

The lowest level selections (Level A) in all four series were so brief that rating their ''themes'' was meaningless. In the majority of cases, when the textual content was rated without the illustrations, the most appropriate category was "themeless." Because of this difficulty of developing any kind of theme in the earliest level books, our thematic ratings, shown in Table VII, were based on the reading selections at the middle and upper levels only (Levels B and C). Also, because our interest was in the thematic content of the text itself our ratings were based on typed transcripts of the reading selections (without pictures).

Although our ratings could not be compared with those of Blom *et al.* (1970), we could make comparisons across the reading series. As the table shows, there were substantial differences across the four series. All of the series contained a high proportion of stories based on real life, but in the Merrrill (a code program) and Ginn series (a basal program) these selections predominated—100 and 76%, respectively. In the other two series about 50% of the selections were distributed across the fantasy, instructive, and themeless categories. If, as has been assumed by Blom *et al.* (1970), there is "a relationship between the kinds of stories used to teach children to read and the development of their ability to read" (p. 109), then these series may have very different effects on children's learning. This brings us to the third question raised at the beginning of this section: Do children become more proficient in reading if the content of their school readers caters to their interests?

In a well-conceived series of studies, Asher and his colleagues have addressed this question (Asher, 1976; Asher, Hymel, & Wigfield, 1978; Asher & Markell, 1974) with fifth-grade children as subjects. Their procedure in all of the studies involved an initial phase in which children's interests were assessed by showing them a series of color slides representing various topic areas. On the basis of their individual ratings the

TABLE VII

Thematic Content of the Reading Selections (Percentages) in the Middle and Later Level Books (Levels B and C) of Four Current First-Grade Reading Series

	Code programs		Basal programs	
	Merrill (1975)	Holt (1976)	Scott Foresman (1978)	Ginn (1976)
Content categories	$N = 112^a$	$N = 65$	$N = 41$	$N = 49$
Real life	100	46	49	76
Fantasy		45	22	22
Instructive		3	17	0
Themeless		6	12	2

[a] N = number of reading selections in Levels B and C combined.

children were assigned reading selections (from the Encyclopaedia Britannica Junior) corresponding to their high and low interest areas. These passages were presented in a cloze procedure format and the children's reading comprehension was assessed from their responses. After reading the selections, as a measure of the validity of their reading preferences based on pictures children were required to indicate how interested they would be in reading more about each paragraph topic. The results in all of the studies corroborated their procedure for selecting children's high and low reading preferences and clearly showed that children's comprehension scores were affected by their interest in what they were reading. Their cloze procedure responses were more adequate on the reading selection in their high interest areas. Furthermore, these effects were consistent for high- and low-achieving students, for both black and white children, and generally, for both boys and girls.

Although these studies by Asher and his co-workers did not involve young children in the beginning stages of learning to read, their results should not be ignored. It is clear from them that the reading performance of children in the intermediate grades is affected by their interest in what they are reading. These findings are consistent with intuitions based on adults' responsiveness to qualitative aspects of text. But, because young children just learning to read may, as Huey (1908/1968) has suggested, be willing to plod through insultingly simple and boring texts "to please the beloved teacher," the influences of beginning readers' interests on their reading accuracy and understanding of texts with various thematic content should be investigated. It may be that the motivational value provided by the novelty of the reading task and a climate of enthusiasm for reading in the classroom may supersede the interest value of the text as a determinant of children's motivation to read in the beginning stages. However, such an assumption should certainly not be made without investigating the alternatives.

If it turns out that young children's motivation to read a text is largely dependent on the interest value of the thematic content of the text, school readers should be designed to cater to children's preferences. Also, if it turns out that thematic content of the text is influential in children's learning to read, it may be the case, as well, that the characters portrayed in the reading selections affect children's motivation to read the text. This possibility is discussed in the next section.

3. Characters

The Women's Movement in the early 1970s drew attention to the underrepresentation of females and minority groups among the characters in school readers, and also to the presence of sex-role and ethnic stereotyping in the characters portrayed. Although the methodological adequacy of some of these studies has been justifiably criticized by Kingston and Lovelace (1977–78), who reviewed 78 studies investigating sexism in basal readers, textbooks, and children's literature, the weight of evidence is, nevertheless, overwhelming. In a wide range of studies examining the content of school textbooks (e.g., Britton, 1975; Frasher & Walker, 1972; Graebner, 1972; Saario, Jacklin, & Tittle, 1973; Women on Words & Images, 1972), the evidence has consistently shown that females and minority groups are grossly underrepresented among the major characters, that they appear in a small fraction of the careers and roles available to the white male characters, and that the image projected of them is often an uncomplimentary or stereotyped one.

In response to these criticisms, the publishers of major reading series issued guidelines for improving the image of minority groups and females in their textbooks (e.g., Ginn, 1973; Holt, Rinehart & Winston, 1975; Houghton-Mifflin, 1975; Macmillan, 1975; McGraw-Hill, 1974; Scott Foresman, 1972). Studies of the textbooks published after the guidelines indicate, however, that their effectiveness has been quite limited (Britton & Lumpkin, 1977; Marten & Matlin, 1976; Women on Words & Images, 1975). The numbers of females and minority group members depicted as major characters, and the variety of roles and careers in which they are presented are still disproportionately low.

Because there has already been so much attention in the literature to the distribution of characters in school readers, we did not obtain statistics on the characters in the reading series included in our content analysis. Whether or not they reflect the same biases and stereotypes that have been documented in the vast majority of previous series is of no great importance. Although there may be far-reaching social consequences (yet undocumented) of sex-role and minority group stereotypes in school textbooks, our concern here is with their potential influence on children's learning to read. Do the characters portrayed in school readers affect children's motivation to read the text?

Zimet (1976) stated that:

> One of the basic assumptions in investigating the influence of textbook content on behavior is that learning to read will be motivated by presenting characters in the textbook stories who are clearly identifiable as similar to the children reading them and who are carrying out activities that are considered interesting and prestigious. (p. 760)

The introduction of multiethnic readers in the 1960s, and criticism by the Women's Movement of the inadequate representation and uncomplimentary treatment of female characters in the texts in the 1970s, both arose, in part, out of a belief in this assumption.

Although it seems a very reasonable assumption that children would read with more enthusiasm if they could identify with the characters in their readers, the extent to which children of both sexes and of various ethnic backgrounds can and do identify with characters in their school readers has not been investigated. And, given the brevity of the reading selections and the failure to provide the "characters" in school readers with feelings and personalities (noted in our previous discussion of the length of reading selections), it may be that the only way in which young children could conceivably identify with the "characters" would be on the basis of superficial physical characteristics depicted in the illustrations—such as their sex and skin color, for example.

Evidence concerning the role of story characters in children's motivation to read a text is very limited and relates almost exclusively to the sex of the characters. It has been a common research finding that girls outperform boys on tests of reading achievement (Dwyer, 1973), and because these sex differences have not been consistent across all cultures (Johnson, 1973–74; Preston, 1962) researchers have sought an explanation of the differences in environmental factors related to reading that might differentially affect boys and girls. In this context, it has been suggested that whereas boys are sex-stereotyped in their reading **preferences**, avoiding stories with female main characters or involving themes that are stereotypically feminine, girls show less sex bias in their reading preferences (Frasher & Frasher, 1978; Tibbetts, 1974). Also, it has been argued that "sex appropriateness" of themes and characters may affect the reading **comprehension** of boys but not of girls (Zimet, 1976), citing as evidence a study seeming to show that boys' reading comprehension is lower on materials that represents nonpreferred topics while that of girls is not (Asher & Markell, 1974). On both reading preferences and comprehension, however, the evidence is very weak.

Jennings (1975) told stories to preschool boys and girls where the main character engaged in either sex-appropriate or sex-inappropriate activities. During the story sessions pictures were displayed to illustrate information in the story. The boys and girls in the study heard stories with a child of the same sex as the main character. The results showed that although children in general preferred the stories in which the main character displayed sex-appropriate behavior, both boys and girls recalled more from the stories where the main character's role was atypical.

In another study involving reading to children, Frasher (1977) read *Pippi Longstocking* to third graders over a number of days. Pippi, the main character in the book is characterized as "super-strong, super-brave, super-clever, and super-independent" (p. 861)—not at all like the female characters in the vast majority of children's books. Two other characters who figure strongly in Pippi's adventures, a boy, Tommy, and a girl, Annika, are presented in sex-stereotyped roles. Frasher found that on a preference measure, boys and girls both selected Pippi over either of the other characters. Thus, it may be that previous evidence indicating that boys reject stories with female main characters may be a result of the fact that the female characters in most children's books are depicted as weak, passive, dull, and dependent, and boys prefer more interesting and exciting main characters. Evidence that girls like stories with either boys or girls as main characters may simply show that girls, too, like stories with strong interesting characters, but defer to social expectations and show an interest in stories that are "sex-role appropriate" as well.

Finally, the study by Asher and Markell (1974), described in the previous section on themes, reported a sex difference in the effect of interest value of reading material on children's comprehension of the text, such that boys' performance was affected by interest value but girls' was not. The later research of Asher *et al.* (1978), however, failed to corroborate their earlier finding. In their later studies both girls' and boys' comprehension was superior on high interest reading selections.

In sum then, despite a relatively large body of research evidence concerned with the themes and characters in school readers very little is, in fact, known about how these dimensions affect children's learning to read. The usefulness of further studies describing these aspects of reader content is questionable, unless a serious effort is also made to determine their impact on children's acquisition of skill in reading. It is important, in such studies, that length of reading selection be included as a variable, since it is clear from our content analysis that the "stories" in first-grade readers may be substantially shorter than other children's literature in which a story line and characters are usually more fully developed. The motivational value of themes and characters in very brief reading selections may be minimal.

Thus far in our discussion we have been mainly concerned with the more abstract aspects of the text of school readers. In the following section we turn to the more concrete aspects of reader content, typography, and the presentation of the text.

D. Physical Characteristics of Text

Almost no research has been done to study the physical characteristics of the text of school readers, and yet, this is an area that certainly deserves attention. Without any experimental evidence, it is impossible to know how best to design primary readers in a way that will promote reading skills. This point deserves emphasis, and in this section, a number of recommendations for future research are made. The bases of these recommendations are first, a descriptive survey of the physical characteristics of our sample of readers, and second, a review of the literature relevant to this topic.

Presented here is a preliminary survey of the four reading series in our content analysis (see Table VIII). The text of the readers is described according to several physical characteristics including: type size, form of typeface, line width and leading, and brightness contrast between print and page. The rationale for examining these particular factors is derived from suggestions made by Tinker (1965), who is the leading figure in typography research. His suggestions concern several factors that may be important in the design of reading material for children. In the following subsections, each characteristic listed in Table VIII will be described, and then the four series will be compared on that dimension.

As stated previously, there is a dearth of research concerning physical attributes of the text in beginning readers; however, some scholars have investigated reading material suitable for older children and adults. [It is pertinent to note here that 10–13 years has been suggested as the age span in which children's level of mechanical skill in reading no longer differs from that of adults (Tinker, 1963).] A discussion of such research

TABLE VIII

Physical Characteristics of the Texts in the First-Grade Books in Four Current Reading Series[a]

Physical characteristic	Book level	Code programs		Basal programs	
		Merrill (1975)	Holt (1976)	Scott Foresman (1978)	Ginn (1976)
Type size	A	1	1	2	1
	B	1	1	2	1
	C	1	1	2	1
Style, form, and	A	1	1	3	1
color of	B	1	2	3	1
typeface	C	1	2	3	1
Line width and	A	2	2	3	2
leading	B	2	2	3	2
	C	2	3	3	2
Brightness	A	1	2	2	2
contrast	B	1	2	2	3
	C	1	3	2	3

[a] Ratings: 1, highly consistent; 2, slightly variable; 3, highly variable.

findings is included within the description of our sample of basal readers whenever relevant.

1. Typography

a. TYPE SIZE

The first characteristic listed in Table VIII, type size, refers to the height of the letters. Type size is normally measured in points, one point being approximately equal to 1/72 of an inch. Information on type size in the readers surveyed was not readily available, and because of the difficulty of measuring type size accurately, the sizes were simply compared across levels within each series, and across series. It was found that the Merrill program uses the largest print and Ginn the smallest; and all four of the series use much larger type than that normally used in material for older children and adults. On the surface, this practice may appear to be based on an assumption that younger children are unable to read small print. In fact, there is no research evidence that would support this belief and it is possible that larger type size is used simply to cover more space, thus increasing the apparent length of the readers.

Perhaps the origin of the belief that larger type size should be used in primary grade reading material is to be found in the early twentieth century concern with what was termed "hygiene." In his chapter on the Hygiene of Reading, Huey (1908/1968) reported that

> from fifty to eighty-five percent of the [European] books come short of hygienic requirements. American books are somewhat better, but include many that are very bad. Even when the principal part of the book is in good type, there will often be large sections printed in a type so small as to be very injurious. (p. 417)

Although researchers no longer express Huey's fears about the damaging effects of small print, they have shown an interest in type size for other reasons, particularly for its effects on visual discriminability and reading rate. For example, McNamara, Paterson, and Tinker (1953) studied the effect of variations in the size of type on the reading speed of children in grades one, two, and three. The range of type size used in their test materials was 8 to 24 point type. Their most important finding was that size of type does not affect speed of reading for children in grades one and two. By grade three, speed of reading was fastest for 10, 12, and 14 point type, which, the authors note, is consistent with adult data.

Whatever other implications these findings may have, the authors caution against the use of reading rate as a criterion for determining the size of type to be used in primary grade books. Easy visual discrimination, rather than reading speed, is the important issue at this level, they claim. Tinker (1965) concurs with this conclusion. Unfortunately, it seems that there has been no research reported that deals with this particular issue.

Another aspect of type size used in school readers that has not been investigated is the effect, on reading, of switching type size within one reader. As noted in Table VIII, three of the reading series in our sample employ one type size consistently throughout each level, while Scott Foresman is somewhat variable on this dimension. It may be that such inconsistency in type size causes confusion for beginning readers, but at the moment there is no research reported that would provide answers to this question.

b. STYLE, FORM, AND COLOR OF TYPEFACE

Other characteristics of typography we examined were the style, form, and color of typeface (see Table VIII). Form of typeface refers to uppercase versus lowercase letters, as well as italics and boldface, and is not the same as style of typeface. In the Ginn and Merrill readers, these aspects of typography were very consistent; however, in the Holt readers, there was some variability—a few words were printed in all capitals, and others were deliberately distorted (presumably to add interest). Finally, we found that the Scott Foresman readers were highly variable on these dimensions, with frequent switches from one style or form of typeface to another, and with titles printed in a variety of colors.

Again, very little is know about the effects of such inconsistencies. In a small-scale study conducted by McNinch (1973), grade-two children had more difficulty in identifying words printed in a mixture of uppercase and lowercase letters than words printed conventionally. Also, the poor readers, but not the good readers, found words printed in all uppercase letters more difficult than conventionally printed words. Unfortunately, this study has a number of limitations; even the author advised caution in interpreting his results. On the other hand, McNinch's results are consistent with research involving older children and adults, which indicates that lowercase print is more legible than all-capitals. Tinker (1965) attributes this finding to the lack of clues to word form in uppercase print, and suggests that this finding is relevant to primary grade children.

In another study involving form of typeface, Smith, Lott, and Cronnell (1969), using college students as subjects, investigated the effect on legibility of distortions of word form. These distortions consisted of mixing upper- and lowercase type within words, and mixing the sizes of individual letters within words. Although a combination of these two kinds of distortion did cause some disruption of word legibility, the most important conclusion reached was that experienced readers adapt easily to distortions of type, much as they adapt, with little difficulty, to reading various handwriting styles. Because of the age of the subjects in this study, however, it is most inadvisable to assume that these results can be generalized to young children just beginning to read. Instead, similar studies with primary-grade subjects should certainly be carried out.

2. Presentation of Text

a. LINE WIDTH AND LEADING

In Table VIII, there are two other typographical factors that were compared across reading series: line width, and leading, which is the amount of space between lines. There is no research evidence concerning either of these aspects of primary-grade reader text; however, Tinker (1965) makes some recommendations which may be worth investigating experimentally. He suggests that it would be advantageous to use one line width consistently in any given book. In addition, he states that ''generous'' leading will promote more accurate return eye movements from one line to the next.

With regard to line width and leading, all of the readers vary on this dimension depending mostly on the size and spacing of illustrations; but the Scott Foresman readers were rated as highly variable because the lines of text were printed in many different locations on the page, and were often inconsistent even within reading selections.

b. QUALITY OF PAPER AND BRIGHTNESS CONTRAST

In addition to typographical factors, two other physical characteristics of the four reading series were examined. One of these characteristics is the quality of paper used; that is, whether or not the paper is thick enough to prevent print from showing through on the other side of the page, and whether or not the paper is rough enough to prevent reflected glare. Both of these qualities are suggested by Tinker (1965) to be important for discriminability. All four of the readers are constructed of fairly opaque paper, and, except for the Ginn series, in which the paper is noticeably shiny, the paper used is sufficiently rough to prevent glare.

The final characteristic surveyed was the brightness contrast between the color of paper and the color of ink. Black ink on white paper provides maximal contrast, and Tinker suggests that for adequate legibility, brightness contrast should not fall below 65%. Only the Merrill Linguistic Program uses black ink on white paper throughout, whereas the others, especially Ginn, often use black print on top of color illustrations. It is possible that such practice has a deleterious effect on legibility; certainly this is a question worth exploring experimentally.

On the basis of our preliminary survey of a small sample of school readers, combined with a review of studies of typography—most of which employed adult subjects and reading materials—we have discussed several factors that seem worthy of experimental investigation. As yet there has been practically no research examining the effects physical characteristics of the text have on the performance of children in the beginning stages of learning to read. Generalizations from research involving older children and adults seem entirely inappropriate in this area. Beginning readers are undoubtedly more "stimulus bound" than are more experienced readers. It is well known that young children in the initial stages of learning to read make errors based on confusable aspects of the visual stimulus, such as orientation of letters (Gibson & Levin, 1975), but that after a year or two of reading instruction such errors diminish dramatically (Shankweiler & Liberman, 1972). Thus, it seems probable that other physical characteristics of the text, such as size, style, and form of typeface, affect beginning readers quite differently than they do children more experienced in reading, and adult skilled readers who have had many years of experience with print.

At workshops and teacher training courses, it is a popular practice to "teach" new primary-grade teachers to read using an artificial or unfamiliar (foreign) alphabet. Although we recognize that a literate adult "learning to read" using an artificial alphabet is likely to employ qualitatively different strategies from those of a young child who has little or no familiarity with print, the exercise of having adults attempt to put themselves into the shoes of the child just learning to read probably serves a very useful function. Indeed, we believe that researchers, educators, authors, and publishers of children's early readers should subject themselves regularly to such an exercise as a reminder of the complexity of the visual stimulus with which the child is confronted. For the child any information on the page may appear to be relevant to the reading task.

In view of the variability we found across reading series in the physical aspects of text, it is quite conceivable to us that the ease or difficulty a child has in learning to read with a particular reading series may be due in large part to irrelevant variations in the typography, and to other physical attributes of the books, such as those discussed in the next part of this article—the illustrations.

II. THE ILLUSTRATIONS

The most obvious feature of the content of school readers is not the text itself, but the illustrations that accompany it. This was apparently true as early as the turn of the century when Huey (1908/1968) wrote of the pervasiveness of artwork in school readers:

> Concerning texts, manuals, and specific systems for teaching children to read, the writer has recently examined with some care more than a hundred, representing the best that could be found in the modern literature of the subject. . . . In working over the primers and first readers, one is impressed with the fact that the artistic side has had far more attention and far greater development than has the side of method and reading content. The books are often superbly illustrated, in colors or with fine photographs, and the covers and typography are most attractive. Of course these are the features which sell the books when, as too often occurs, the selection of texts is in the hands of persons who have no familiarity with the methods and needs of the subject concerned. Competition has therefore forced the publishers to give attention to the art side. (p. 276)

Chall (1967), in her comparison of five successive editions of Scott Foresman's basal reader series, also examined the use of illustrations. Her statistics showed that more and more space was allotted to artwork in each edition. As the vocabulary load decreased there was a systematic increase in the number of pictures. There were .9 pictures per 100 running words in 1920, 1.3 in 1930, 1.4 in 1940, 1.6 in 1956, and 1.7 in 1962. And, when we examined the 1978 edition of a Scott Foresman basal reader series as part of our content analysis, we found that the number of pictures per 100 running words is now 6.5, almost four times what it was in 1962.

No one would dispute that the major function of school readers is to teach children to read **text.** The question is, "What contribution do the illustrations make toward achieving this objective?" In the first part of this section on illustrations, we present descriptive statistics on the artwork content of the same four reading series included in our content analysis throughout this article. Then, in the latter part of the section, we review the research on pictures and reading in the light of the assumptions made about the value of the artwork content of school readers. Finally, in a concluding section, we offer suggestions for future research directions and for educational practice.

A. The Artwork Content of School Readers

In attempting to derive a pictures-per-100 running words statistic for each of the illustrated reading series, we found that pictures are not as easily countable as one might expect, and that simple picture counts do not adequately reflect the amount and salience of the artwork in current school readers. Whereas, in reading series published during the 1960s and earlier, the pictures were usually set off from the text with a picture being placed above or below the text on every page or two, in the 1970s editions, pictures are less clearly defined. These more recent books have pictures and text intermixed, with pictures often overlapping, surrounding, and even serving as the background for the text.

Our preliminary examination of the books also revealed that picture counts alone do not provide a meaningful index of the potential impact of artwork in today's readers. The salience of the pictures—in terms of size, brightness, placement, information content, artwork style, and so on—is undoubtedly a significant factor in the influence of artwork on reading. Picture-counting statistics entirely overlook qualitative aspects of the artwork.

In an effort to generate some meaningful descriptive statistics concerning the use of artwork in current school readers, we examined the illustrations on both quantitative and qualitative dimensions. The quantitative measures include the number of pictures per page, the number of pictures per 100 running words, and the area of each page covered by artwork. The qualitative measures include the types of pictures used, the placement of the pictures, the vividness of the pictures, the complexity of the pictures, and the overall eye-catching appeal of the pictures.

Although our content analysis was performed on the same reading series included in the previous sections, of the four series, only three contain pictures; the Merrill readers (1975) have no illustrations at the primary level. Of the three illustrated series—Ginn (1976), Holt (1976), and Scott Foresman (1978)—we examined only the highest level (Level C) readers. Since the highest level books in each series have substantially more running words per page than the lower level books, the quantitative statistics we generated underestimate the amount of artwork in the series as wholes. The qualitative aspects of the artwork are very similar in all of the books within each series, however, so the statistics on them reflect all of the first-grade books reasonably well. All of the quantitative and qualitative judgments were done by two independent raters.

1. Quantity of Artwork

In our effort to quantify artwork we found that any criterion we set for defining **one picture** was somewhat arbitrary, and could result in the production of misleading statistics. To avoid this pitfall we adopted multiple measures (the three just mentioned) of the quantity of artwork in the readers: the number of pictures per page, number of pictures per 100 running words, and the approximate area of each page covered by artwork. Table IX summarizes our findings.

TABLE IX

Quantitative Measures of the Artwork Contained in the Highest Level First-Grade Books (Level C) in Four Current Reading Series

	Code programs		Basal programs	
	Merrill (1975)	Holt (1976)	Scott Foresman (1978)	Ginn (1976)
Measure	$N = 65^a$	$N = 121$	$N = 100$	$N = 129$
Average number of pictures per page	0	1.0	1.5	1.1
Average number of pictures per 100 running words	0	3.7	6.5	2.7
Percentage of pages with artwork covering				
1–25%	0	1	2	1
26–50%	0	16	8	26
51–75%	0	40	61	55
76–100%	0	43	29	18

[a] N = number of pages rated.

a. NUMBER OF PICTURES

Although a picture-counting statistic might seem to be a very objective one, we found a certain amount of ambiguity in it. Some of the pictures in all three reading series extend across two adjacent pages. Technically it could be argued that only .5 of these pictures appear on each page, but we decided that it is most reasonable to count 1.0 picture per page in such situations. Also, in a few instances the picture elements on a page are physically or thematically separate and independent. In such cases, individual judgments had to be made whether to count each element as one picture or as part of the whole. Despite the necessity of such judgments and arbitrary criterion setting, the two independent raters who scored all of the books agreed 100% on the picture counts.

In summary of the number-of-pictures-per-page data, there is a picture on virtually every page of all three series, but, as the table shows, the Scott Foresman series has 1.5 pictures per page while the other two series have just over 1.0 picture per page.

b. NUMBER OF PICTURES PER 100 RUNNING WORDS

As another measure of the quantity of artwork in the readers, it is revealing to examine the number of pictures with respect to the rate of presentation of textual information. As indicated earlier, a comparison of this statistic for the Scott Foresman series shows that the proportion of pictures to words almost quadrupled between 1962 and 1978. We also calculated this statistic for the Ginn series comparing their 1968 edition (*The Ginn Integrated Language Program*) with the 1976 revision. In that series, as well, the number of pictures per 100 running words has substantially increased—from 1.3 in 1968 to 2.7 in 1976.

As our table shows, the results on this measure were consistent with the pictures-per-page findings. In comparing across series, the Scott Foresman program has considerably more pictures per 100 running words than do the other two series.

c. AREA COVERED BY PICTURES

Without taking picture size into account, the number-of-pictures statistics may distort the amount-of-artwork measures to some extent. One series might have more artwork in terms of numbers of pictures, but might, in fact, have less artwork in terms of the amount of area covered by the pictures.

Although these judgments of the area covered by artwork are not precise, they are nevertheless quite reliable; inter-rater agreement by two independent judges was 99%. As the table shows, the average page-area covered by artwork in all three series is very great: in the Scott Foresman series 90% of the pages have pictures that cover more' than half of the area of the page, while the comparable figure is 83% for Holt and 73% for Ginn. Thus, this quantitative measure, too, indicates that the amount of artwork in the Scott Foresman series is greater than in the other two series. But, as the table also shows, the Holt series has a somewhat greater proportion of pages with illustrations in the largest picture category.

In sum then, from the descriptive statistics on the quantity of artwork in the three illustrated series, all are highly illustrated. There are from 1 to 1.5 pictures on every page, and a very high proportion of these pictures cover more than half of the area of the page (many cover more than three-quarters of the area of the page). Moreover, comparisons of the number of pictures per 100 running words with earlier editions indicate that in the newer editions the proportion of artwork relative to text has dramatically increased.

2. Qualitative Dimensions of Artwork

The qualitative measures of artwork were considerably more subjective than the quantitative ones; however, the inter-rater agreements on these, as well, were very high, ranging from 97 to 99%. There are several ways in which the qualitative aspects of pictures can be classified. The five qualitative categories we employed were types of pictures, locations of pictures, vividness of pictures, complexity of pictures, and overall eye-catching appeal of each picture. The results of these measures are summarized in Table X.

a. TYPES OF ILLUSTRATIONS

As the data in the table reveal, there are basically two types of illustrations in the books we examined: colored photographs and colored

TABLE X

Qualitative Measures of the Artwork Contained in the Highest Level First-Grade Books (Level C) in Four Current Reading Series

	Code programs		Basal programs	
	Merrill (1975)	Holt (1976)	Scott Foresman (1978)	Ginn (1976)
Measure	$N = 65^a$	$N = 121$	$N = 100$	$N = 129$
Picture type				
Color photo	0	9	23	0
Color drawing				
Realistic	0	9	18	0
Stylized	0	82	59	97
Combination of				
photo and drawing	0	0	0	3
Picture placement				
With respect to text				
Above	0	43	49	68
Below	0	72	61	67
Beside	0	34	36	37
With respect to page				
Center (by measurement)	0	92	72	64
Vividness of colors				
Dull	0	1	13	1
Medium	0	20	37	10
Bright	0	79	50	89
Complexity of picture				
Low	0	8	5	2
Moderate	0	61	44	56
High	0	31	51	42
Eye-catching quality				
Minimum	0	0	4	0
Moderate	0	21	39	22
Maximum	0	79	57	78

[a] N = number of pages rated. Scores in the table are percentages.

drawings, with the vast majority being of the latter type. In a few instances, colored photographs and drawings are integrated into the same picture. There is considerable variability in the color drawings along a realistic-stylized dimension. On the whole the color drawings in all three series range from moderately to highly stylized, and the artwork style varies considerably across stories. The major difference between the series in terms of the types of illustrations is in the extent to which colored photographs are used—Scott Foresman includes a large number, Ginn includes a few, and Holt even fewer.

b. LOCATION OF PICTURES

The common practice in older reading series was to place one picture above or below the text. As mentioned earlier, in the 1970s editions that we examined, there is more variability in the placement of pictures: they appear above, below, to the side, surrounding, or as the background with respect to the text. The ratings in Table X describing picture locations indicate the proportion of pages on which there is artwork above, below, and/or to the side of the text. Since a single picture could be rated in two or more of these, the categories are not mutually exclusive and the percentages total more than 100%. In addition to judging the location of the artwork with respect to the text, we also determined by measurement of each page whether there was artwork in the center of the page.

As the table shows, with respect to the text, the pictures are in all possible locations, frequently both above and below, or above and to the side on a single page; and, with respect to the page, a very large proportion of the pages (64 to 92% of them) has a picture that is centrally located. The only noteworthy differences across series in terms of picture placement are that the Holt series has more artwork that is centrally located and to the side of the text relative to both Ginn and Scott Foresman.

c. VIVIDNESS OF PICTURES

Although all of the pictures in the books we examined are in color, there is quite a range among them in terms of the vividness of the hues. As Table X indicates, the largest proportion of the illustrations in all three series were rated as being of maximal brightness, and very few were rated as dull. There are, however, quite marked differences across series: nearly 90% of the pictures in Ginn were rated as very bright, about 80% in Holt and only 50% in Scott Foresman.

d. PICTURE COMPLEXITY

The vast majority of the pictures, both drawings and photographs, are very complex in all three illustrated series. Our ratings of picture complexity reflect judgments of two main components: amount of content and amount of detail. Some of the pictures provide a considerable amount of information in terms of the number of words represented. (In fact, many of the illustrations depict considerably more words than actually appear in the accompanying text.) Others of the pictures although relatively low in information content, include a large amount of detail. Some of the photographs, for example, represent only one or two objects but were rated as very complex because of the detail shown.

e. EYE-CATCHING QUALITY

The extent to which a given illustration attracts a reader's attention is undoubtedly a function of many attributes; location, vividness, and complexity are but a few. In an attempt to capture overall eye-catching quality, we simply made subjective judgments. As with the other qualitative dimensions, however, we found that our judgments were remarkably reliable, in this case, 97%. As the statistics in Table X show, a very high proportion of the illustrations in both Ginn and Holt were rated as maximally eye catching, while, on the whole, those in the Scott Foresman were somewhat less so.

Taken together, the qualitative measures present a very consistent pattern. In all three series the pictures were generally rated as bright, complex, and centrally located on the page—in other words, very salient. There is some variability within series, with the artwork characteristics changing from one story to another; and across series, Ginn and Holt were rated as very similar, with both surpassing Scott Foresman on almost every measure reflecting picture salience.

In conclusion, concerning the artwork content of current school reading series, our descriptive statistics show that both the sheer numbers of pictures, and the variety and salience of the artwork in all three illustrated series are considerably greater than previous series with which we are familiar. Although there were no statistics available from previous editions of these and other series with which to compare some of our measures of the quantitative and qualitative dimensions of today's school readers, we conducted an informal rating of several series for which we had 1960s and 1970s editions. In making these subjective comparisons we found that the differences in the artwork between the 1970s editions and their 1960s counterparts are very striking—the illustrations in the later editions are consistently larger, brighter, more complex, more numerous, and generally, more salient. These differences were so obvious as to make statistical comparisons superfluous. To demonstrate this point—"a picture is worth a thousand words"—see Fig. 2.

3. Rationale for the Use of Artwork

In the early stages of learning to read, in order for the child to do any independent reading it is essential that he/she be able to utilize word-recognition "cues" (or, "clues"). As explained in the vocabulary section, code-emphasis (i.e., "linguistic") programs are very "regular" in terms of letter–sound correspondences, at least in the initial stages. Thus, the most reliable word-recognition cues in such programs are phonics cues. Basal reader programs, on the other hand, do not select their vocabulary on the basis of symbol–sound correspondences; and, as Beck (this volume) has shown, the vocabulary in such series is substantially less "decodable" than that in code-emphasis programs. In basal programs, therefore, phonics cues alone (whether they are emphasized or not) fail to serve as reliable aids to word recognition; and so, for the child to decode words without the teacher's help, he/she must depend on other types of information on the page. The guidebooks of basal reader programs suggest a variety of additional word identification cues that can be taught, the most common of which are context cues, word shape cues, initial letter cues, and picture cues. The usefulness of some of these cues has never been demonstrated; some of them may, in fact, be of little value to the child attempting to identify an unknown word. Pictures, for example, have long been included in basal reader programs, but the range of opinion about their value among the authors of basal readers is considerable, with some being convinced of their beneficial effects while others express strong doubts about their worth (Chall, 1967).

As our descriptive statistics demonstrated, three of the reading programs included in our content analysis contain a large amount of very salient artwork; the fourth has no pictures at all. Merrill (1975), the nonillustrated series, is a code-emphasis program, and the exclusion of pictures is consistent with the instructional philosophy of such programs. On the other hand, in the Holt (1976) series, also a code-emphasis program, the use of artwork is very similar to that in the basal programs (particularly to Ginn).

In order to determine more specifically the rationales underlying the publishers' use of artwork in the three illustrated series, we examined the teachers' guidebooks accompanying the first-grade readers. From these we inferred the assumptions the publishers seem to be making about the value of pictures in learning to read.

Cathy led the pig down to the pen.
"Don't jump in the mud," she said.
But a pig is a pig.
It jumped in the mud.
Now it was a brown pig.

Magic Letters (Holt et al., 1976, pp. 78-79)

A park bench is not a horse.
If I ride on it, it is my horse.

"Did you see a big sheep dog like this?"

"No, just little dogs have come
to this place."

Calico Capers
(Scott Foresman, 1978, p. 51)

Mr. Mugs is Lost
(Ginn, 1976, p. 47)

Fig. 2. Examples of illustrations in the highest level first-grade books (Level C) in three current reading series.

The three primary assumptions appear to be that (a) pictures aid in learning new words out of context (e.g., Scott Foresman, 1978), (b) pictures serve as cues to word recognition for words in context (e.g., Scott Foresman, 1978), and (c) the presence of illustrated information will stimulate interest in reading the text and promote a better under- standing of textual information (e.g., Ginn, 1976; Holt, 1976; Scott Fores- man, 1978). The last of these three assumptions is far more prevalent than the other two in the series we sampled. Only in the Scott Foresman series is there clear evidence of all three assumptions. In Ginn and Holt the only explicit instructions to teachers about picture use concern draw- ing the child's attention to pictures in preparation for reading the text, and clearly the intent of these instructions is to motivate the child to read the text and to aid his/her comprehension of it. Virtually every reading lesson in all three illustrated series includes instructions of this type. Thus, although one publisher, Scott Foresman, encourages the use of pictures as cues to the identification of words both in and out of context, far more widespread are suggestions for using pictures to "pro- vide a purpose for reading" and to promote better reading comprehension.

In sharp contrast to the assumptions made by the publishers of the illustrated series, the Merrill program's lack of pictures is based on the assumption that "Pictures constitute a distracting element in the process of learning to read, and they furnish only superficial cues to word rec- ognition." The program authors also claim that "pictures lead pupils to **guess** at words rather than read them."

In the next section we examine the validity of these various assump- tions about the value of pictures in school readers on the basis of the available research evidence.

B. Research on Pictures and Reading

Despite the long history of artwork as an integral part of school readers and the dramatic increase in the number and salience of illustrations during the last decade, this aspect of the content of readers was, until quite recently, largely overlooked in the research literature. In a review of the "Effects of pictures on learning to read, comprehension and at- titudes," Samuels (1970) observed:

> If fish were to become scientists, the last thing they might discover would be water. Similarly, researchers have too often failed to investigate important aspects of their environment because being immersed in it, they fail to notice certain components of it; or, having noticed a component, they simply assume that it must be that way. One such example from reading is the ubiquitous use of illustrations in books for beginning reading instruction. Today nearly all children are taught to read from

books containing pictures. In this country this practice goes back at least to 1729 when the New England Primer incorporated pictures with the text. In Europe during the 1650's, Comenius used pictures in his Orbis Pictus to teach reading. Only occasionally does one find a writer (Dechant, 1964) questioning the use of pictures or a published reading series, such as the Bloomfield and Barnhard (1963) readers, attempting to teach reading without pictures. Teachers usually accept the fact that beginning reading texts have pictures without wondering what effect pictures have on learning to read. (p. 397)

There has, however, been a recent upsurge of interest in this topic, and there is now a fairly extensive body of research literature relevant to the role of pictures in learning to read. Our presentation of the research evidence is organized around the assumptions most commonly made about how pictures affect children's learning to read.

1. Effects of Pictures on Learning Words Out of Context

The first assumption to be considered states that:

If only one object—such as an animal, person, or thing—is represented in a picture, that object may serve as a clue to a written word form. For example, if a picture consisting only of a dog appears with a single word form (dog), readers may assume the word form represents the word *dog*. (Ives, Bursuk, & Ives, 1979, p. 33)

Although only one of the two basal reader series in our content analysis (i.e., Scott Foresman, 1978) advocates it, the practice of presenting an identifying picture along with each new sight word used to be very common in basal reader programs. The assumption is essentially that the picture–word pairing procedure will cause paired-associate learning to take place. That is, by looking at the sight word along with an identifying picture the child will learn to associate the picture with the word. Then, when the child encounters the word on its own, he/she will remember the picture that went with it and, through that association, be able to identify the word. This intuitively appealing assumption was, however, challenged by Samuels (1967) in a paper that has been widely cited. In that paper, Samuels raised the possibility that when a picture and a word are presented together, the picture may actually distract the child's attention away from the word and interfere with learning it.

Samuels' study involved teaching kindergarten children to read four new words (*boy, bed, man, car*) either with or without pictures. There were three conditions: in a no-picture condition each of the words was printed on an individual index card; in a simple-picture condition, a black-and-white drawing portraying the word appeared above it on the index card; and in a complex-picture condition, a colorful illustration in which the word on the card was only one element was placed above each word. For the children in all three conditions (10 children in each), the task was simply to learn to read the words. Learning and test trials were alternated. On learning trials, each of the four words was individually presented (word alone or word + picture) and verbal feedback was provided if a child failed to give the correct oral response within a time limit (4 seconds). On test trials the four words were each presented without pictures and with no feedback.

The results of Samuels' study showed that the children in both picture conditions made significantly more correct responses on the learning trials, but fewer on the test trials than did the children who never had pictures with the words. These results were interpreted as evidence that during acquisition trials the children in the picture conditions responded on the basis of the pictures and were less attentive to the words. The pictures were, therefore, considered as distractors rather than as facilitators of learning. In the literature this interpretation has become known as "the focal attention hypothesis."

Since the appearance of Samuels' (1967) original study, four others using quite similar procedures have confirmed and extended his findings (viz., Braun, 1967, 1969; Harris, 1967; Harzem, Lee, & Miles, 1976; Singer, Samuels, & Spiroff, 1973–74). Nevertheless, Samuels' (1967) findings and his interpretation of them have not been without their detractors, as will be explained later. Because the controversy surrounding "the focal attention hypothesis" rests primarily on misinformation about the methodologies of some of the studies, our review of the studies places particular emphasis on the methodological details.

The most crucial study was that of Braun (1967, 1969). Braun conducted his dissertation research on kindergarten children's learning of sight words, with or without pictures. The paradigm was essentially the same as Samuels', involving learning and test cycles; but, there was one noteworthy procedural difference. Whereas Samuels had employed a paired-associate learning approach, using the anticipation method (such that on training trials verbal feedback was provided only if a child failed to respond within the anticipation interval of four seconds), Braun employed a training procedure in which the experimenter always said the word aloud after presenting the visual stimulus (word alone or word + picture), and the child "echoed" the experimenter's response.

The research design was a $2 \times 2 \times 2 \times 2$ between-groups comparison (15 subjects per group) that included the following variables: ability level (high, low), sex of subject, sex-typing of word list (boy-interest-words, girl-interest-words), and stimulus presentation condition (word alone, word + picture). Three measures of learning were employed: mean number of words learned, mean number of trials to criterion (two successive correct test trials), and total number of words correct on a retention test (24 hours after training). There were numerous significant effects favoring the word alone over the word + picture condition for both ability groups, for boys and for girls, and on all three dependent measures. Every significant comparison contrasting learning in the word alone and word + picture condition favored the word alone condition.

At the same university and at about the same time, Harris (1967) conducted a dissertation study that was very similar in design and procedure to Braun's; but the subjects in Harris' study were from a lower socioeconomic background. Harris' study, like Braun's, was well-controlled, and of major proportions (240 kindergarten children served as subjects). Harris' results paralleled those of Braun, but in Harris' study less learning took place overall. Comparisons of sight word learning with and without pictures consistently favored the word only condition on the acquisition measures, although fewer comparisons were statistically significant because of the generally low level of learning among the lower SES kindergarten children tested in Harris' experiment.

More recently in Britain, Harzem et al. (1976) conducted a study that, although much less extensive than the two just described, corroborated the findings of these other researchers. Using a within-subjects research design, Harzem et al. taught 6-year-olds to read words under each of four conditions: without pictures, with nonsense pictures not resembling any object, with inappropriate pictures unrelated to the words, and with appropriate pictures. (The pictures in all cases were brightly colored.) Four words were taught under each of these conditions, for a total of 16 words. The study also included a between-groups (10 children per group) comparison of learning under conditions of massed and distributed practice. Each learning cycle (i.e., presentation of 16 words with feedback) was alternated with a test cycle. As in Samuels' (1967) study, the anticipation method was employed such that a child received feedback on acquisition trials only when he/she did not respond within a time limit (20 seconds). Like Samuels, too, Harzem et al. had a total of 20 sessions (10 acquisition and 10 test) in their study. Overall, there were no significant differences between the massed and distributed practice conditions; and the numbers of correct responses on the test trials indicated that significantly fewer words were learned in both the appropriate-picture and nonsense-picture conditions than in the no-picture condition. Moreover, the results of a retention test 1 month later suggested that these differences persisted over time.

Finally, a fourth study corroborating Samuels' (1967) original findings was conducted by Singer et al. (1973–74). In a well-designed study, these researchers investigated the effects of contextual conditions, as well as pictures, on learning responses to printed words. Their research subjects were first- and second-graders who already had experience in reading. There were four treatment conditions in which four "words" (printed in an artificial alphabet) were taught: a word-alone condition, a word-picture condition, a sentence-alone condition, and a sentence-picture condition. A between-groups design was employed with approximately 20 first- and 20 second-graders tested in each condition. Under each condition the four "words" (representing *cup, cat, bat,* and *bed*) were presented in a study-test cycle like that used by Samuels (1967). In the word-picture and sentence-picture conditions, a picture of the word appeared above it on the card; in the sentence-alone and sentence-picture conditions, a sentence in standard English alphabet, except for the target word, was printed on the card. On study trials the child was asked to look at the word, point to it, and say it. As in Samuels' (1967) original procedure an anticipation method was used, such that verbal feedback was provided only if the child failed to correctly identify the word during a delay interval (7 seconds).

Test trials involved presenting each of the four words alone and having the child look at the word, point to it, and say it (with no feedback). Study–test cycles were continued for 12 trials or until 2 successive trials were completely correct. The pattern of results on both trials to criterion and number correct was consistent: the word-no-picture condition resulted in significantly fewer trials to criterion and in more correct responses than the other three conditions. The only additional difference between the treatments was that the children in the word-picture condition learned in fewer trials to criterion than did children in the sentence-picture condition. On both measures the order of the means from most to least efficient learning was word-no-picture, word-picture, sentence-no-picture, sentence-picture. All of the effects were consistent across the two grade levels.

Taken together, the evidence from the four studies just reviewed overwhelmingly supports Samuels' (1967) original conclusion "that when pictures and words are presented together the pictures . . . retard the acquisition of reading responses" (p. 339). Moreover, Samuels' results were corroborated under a variety of different training conditions, with much larger samples of subjects, for children of high and low ability, for both boys and girls, for lower SES children, and for British children under conditions of massed and distributed practice, and for older children already experienced in reading.

As mentioned earlier, despite the remarkable consistency of the evidence subsequent to his original research, Samuels' (1967) findings and his interpretation of them have been disputed. In two recently published articles Montare, Elman, and Cohen (1977) and Arlin, Scott, and Webster

(1978–79) have presented research evidence seemingly contradictory to "the focal attention hypothesis." Both articles are based on misconceptions about the procedures used in the previous studies.

In the case of Montare *et al.* the researchers claimed to have replicated Samuels' (1967) procedures but to have obtained different results. In fact, however, Montare *et al.* misunderstood Samuels' procedures, and changed them in a critical way. Whereas Samuels had alternated training trials on the four words with test trials on the four words, Montare *et al.* alternated each acquisition trial with a test trial on the same word. That is, each word was presented twice in a row, the first presentation being a training trial on which feedback was given, the second presentation being a test trial to see if the child had "learned" the word. To be correct, all the child had to do was repeat the word that had just been said. The article of Montare *et al.* has been seriously criticized on a number of other counts, as well (e.g., Samuels, 1977; Willows, 1979b); but the procedural error just mentioned is sufficient to explain their findings and their study does not warrant further attention here.

The problems with the second article challenging "the focal attention hypothesis," the paper by Arlin *et al.* (1978–79), are far more complex and far more serious than the simple-minded error of Montare *et al.* The nature and seriousness of the problems surrounding the paper by Arlin *et al.* have already been discussed elsewhere (see Singer, 1980 and Willows, 1979b), and only one major point will be mentioned here.

In presenting the rationale for conducting their study, Arlin *et al.* briefly alluded to the studies just reviewed and claimed that they were "seriously flawed" because "the medium of presentation (picture or no-picture) and voice feedback have been confounded" (p. 649). Taking their cue from a statement in the paper of Montare *et al.*, Arlin *et al.* argued that in the previous studies subjects in the no-picture condition received substantially more voice feedback from the experimenter than did children in the picture condition—since, in the picture condition, children could almost always respond correctly on the basis of the picture prompt and would, therefore, not have received nearly as much voice feedback. However, as Willows (1979b) has pointed out, although this is undoubtedly true of those studies that employed the anticipation method, neither Braun's (1969) nor Harris' (1967) research employed the anticipation method. As explained in our review of the methodology of these studies, both Braun and Harris used a training procedure in which, under all conditions, the experimenter-teacher said the word aloud and the child **echoed** it. Therefore, the data from their studies would not be subject to the criticism of Arlin *et al.* about differential amounts of voice feedback in the picture and no-picture conditions. Thus, the major "methodological flaw" that Arlin *et al.* presented as a justification for conducting their research was ill-founded.

The research of Arlin *et al.* attempting to examine "the effects of pictures on rate of learning sight words" was so seriously flawed that it does not merit consideration in its own right. Moreover, since the publication of their article Arlin has reported having obtained results **supporting** the focal attention hypothesis (see Arlin, 1980).

Returning to the original question underlying these studies then, "Do pictures facilitate children's learning of individually presented sight words?" the answer is clearly, "No. In fact, they interfere with learning." But, as is so often the case with research, a qualifying statement must be added: "At least, not under the conditions tested." On the basis of the results of one other study, by Hartley (1970–71), employing somewhat similar procedures, it has been suggested that the amount of visual similarity between the words being taught may interact with presentation conditions. In that study, however, there were three cue conditions, viz., word alone, word + picture, and word + verbal word context; and the significant interaction resulted from the fact that minimal contrast lists (e.g., *hen, ten, pen, men*) were learned best when the word was presented alone, and maximal contrast lists (e.g., *king, ten, show, rake*) were learned best when a verbal context was provided. With both types of word lists, the word + picture condition was about midway between the word-alone and the verbal-context conditions in terms of effectiveness; and there is no evidence presented in the paper that the word + picture condition differed significantly from either of the other two.

2. Effects of Pictures on Learning Words in Text

A second assumption underlying the use of illustrations in beginning readers is that when a child comes to an unknown word in the text, he/she can consult the picture accompanying the text and may be able to identify the word on the basis of pictured information.

> For example, a dog may be pictured eating from a dish on the kitchen floor, while a kitten watches him and a family group sits eating at a nearby table. Any of the objects ["details of the pictured objects", "actions portrayed by pictured objects", "relationships between pictured objects", or "attributes of pictured objects"] included in the picture might be the clue to an unfamiliar word form. (Ives *et al.*, 1979, p. 34)

It is a fairly common classroom practice to encourage children to search the picture for "clues" when they come to an unknown word in the text; although, only the Scott Foresman program, of the three illustrated series we surveyed, is clearly designed to promote this use of pictures.

On this assumption concerning the value of pictures accompanying text there have been only two studies of any importance. The first was reported by Samuels (1967). In the same paper in which he presented his influential research on children's learning of sight words out of context, Samuels also described a classroom study in which first-graders (with 7 months of reading instruction) read a "story" (106 running words in length) either with or without a color illustration (representing objects and activities in the story) on the adjacent page. Then their learning of the 50 different words in the text was assessed. The procedure in the study was designed to parallel a "typical" classroom reading lesson:

> Instruction consisted of motivating and building background for the story, reading for a purpose, silent reading, and then oral reading. The subjects were instructed to raise their hands during silent reading if they were unable to read any word. The experimenter went about whispering the words to the children who requested help. (Samuels, 1967, p. 341)

On the basis of a pretest in which the children's ability to decode the 50 different words was assessed, subjects were grouped into those above and below the median on word recognition. After their reading lesson— either with or without a picture—the children were posttested on the same 50 words. The results showed that the children above the median on word recognition were unaffected by the picture accompanying the text (mean numbers of words correct were 42.08 and 43.15 for the no-picture and picture groups respectively); but for the children lower in word recognition, more words were correctly identified on the posttest in the no-picture condition (26.23), compared to the picture condition (23.69).

The results of this study by Samuels were very weak and should certainly be replicated before they are taken very seriously. Although the picture and no-picture treatment groups (13 good and 13 poor readers in each) were described as being "matched on pretest scores," no pretest data were provided in the article. The difference between the no-picture and picture groups for the children classed as low in word recognition was a very small one and might be due to measurement error on the pretest. There were no data presented in the paper to demonstrate that word learning did, in fact, occur under either treatment condition. So, although Samuels interpreted his findings as an indication that the word learning of poor readers is adversely affected by pictures accompanying the text, his evidence is not very compelling.

In his review of the research on pictures, Samuels (1970) added a detail about his 1967 study that was not in the original paper. He indicated that for the first 5 months of reading instruction the teachers of the children in the study had encouraged them to use pictures as cues to word identification, and then for the 2 months just prior to the study they had instructed their students to ignore pictures. Such a change in teaching approaches could well have played a role in the outcome of the study.

Montare *et al.* (1977) attempted and failed to "replicate" this classroom study by Samuels, as well. Their results showed no differences between the picture and no-picture conditions. Because of the serious weaknesses in their paper (discussed in Samuels, 1977 and Willows, 1979b) their findings do not justify rejecting Samuels'. But, it is noteworthy that Montare *et al.*, despite using more pictures and more new words, found no facilitation of word learning by pictures.

Another study relevant to the second assumption about the effects of pictures on identification and learning of words in context was conducted by Denburg (1976–77). This study was a major one involving complex procedures, and its results have been misunderstood. It is, therefore, worthwhile to examine some of its methodological details. The approach in Denburg's research differed substantially from that taken in Samuels'. Denburg's study involved an individually administered laboratory task quite unlike any classroom learning situation. In her study, first-graders (in the final months of the grade) were exposed to 48 unfamiliar nouns (words they could not visually identify but could understand), first in a sentence task and then in a word list task. There were 24 sentences, each containing an actor noun and an object noun. For example, the nouns *donkey* and *wagon* would appear in a sentence such as *The donkey pulls the wagon*. Six sentences were presented in each of the following four treatment conditions: with no picture, with a full picture including both the actor and the object nouns, with a partial picture showing the actor noun with part of the object noun picture deleted, and with a partial picture showing the object noun with part of the actor noun picture deleted. The child's task was simply to read the 24 sentences aloud without verbal feedback (in a 15-minute experimental session). Then, a word list containing the 48 nouns was presented, and the child's task was to identify each noun in isolation. (It should be noted that the children were exposed to approximately ⅙ as many new words in a 15-minute period in this study as they would encounter in an entire year in two of the reading programs we analyzed. The external validity of such a procedure is certainly questionable.)

Children's utilization of contextual and pictorial information under the four conditions was assessed by comparing the number of words correctly identified in the sentence task, on a second administration 5 days after the first. The results showed that all of the picture conditions resulted in more accurate word identification than did the no-picture condition. That is, when children were unable to identify a word in a sentence they looked at the illustration, and figured it out from there. Since no feedback was given in the no-picture condition and the illustrations in the picture conditions were specifically designed to provide unknown words, the higher word identification rate in the picture conditions is essentially trivial. Even the fact that partial pictures resulted in higher word identification accuracy in the sentence reading task may well be due to the fact that children could guess the missing information from the partial picture alone. Without a control condition assessing the "guessability" of words from the partial pictures, this possibility cannot be assessed.

The critical test of the differential effectiveness of the various treatment conditions is provided by the number of words correct on the word list task. Since the learning rate, as evidenced by the second administration of the word list task, was very low (a mean of approximately 8 out of 48 nouns were learned), the differences between the treatment conditions were extremely small. Although the author indicates that picture conditions resulted in better learning than the no-picture conditions, statistics are not provided in the paper, and the graph shows a mean difference of less than ½ of a word between the no-picture condition and any of the picture conditions. Moreover, since, in the no-picture condition, at least two of the five words in the sentences were unknown, and no verbal feedback was given, it is very surprising that any of the words in this condition were learned. The pictures in the other conditions may simply have served as a form of feedback, so any minimal picture-no-picture differences in word learning may be attributable to the greater availability of cues of any sort in these conditions. Had a more extensive context of known words been provided in the no-picture condition, undoubtedly word learning would have been facilitated by it.

So far then, the research addressing the question, "Do pictures accompanying text facilitate children's learning of sight words in the text?" has provided no convincing answers.

3. Effects of Pictures on Comprehension of Text

On the basis of the findings from studies of sight word learning such as those reviewed in the last two sections, the possibility has been raised that the illustrations in their early readers may have a detrimental rather than a beneficial effect on children's learning to read. It has been argued by educators and publishers, however, that the primary function of the illustrations in school readers is not to aid in the decoding of single words but to stimulate interest in the text and to promote a better understanding of it. The impact of such influences would be more adequately reflected in measures of children's reading comprehension than in measures of their decoding skills.

Our examination of the guidebooks of the three illustrated reading series included in our content analysis confirms that by far the most common teaching technique involving illustrations is directing the children's attention to the pictures and asking questions about them. These questions, which precede the reading of almost every part of every reading selection, follow a standard formula in which the children are asked some variation of: "What is going on in the picture?" or "What do you think will happen next?" Then, the children are instructed to read the text to verify their answers to the questions. It is clearly the intent of this exercise to use the illustrations as a means of stimulating the children's interest in the text and of promoting a better understanding of it. Presumably, also, the children are expected to transfer the use of this approach to independent reading situations, in which case children would be expected to use the pictures to provide "a purpose for reading."

In view of the prevalence of this teaching technique, there has been amazingly little research examining its effectiveness. It appears that both educators and researchers have been so persuaded by the intuitive appeal of this use of illustrations that they have rarely questioned it. Only three researchers have conducted major, programmatic research efforts of relevance to this question (viz. Peeck, 1974; Vernon, 1953, 1954; Willows, 1979a), and none of the studies have involved first-grade children.

Vernon (1953, 1954) undertook a series of four studies examining the value of pictorial illustration in the acquisition of knowledge from text and orally presented prose. In the first two studies, teenagers (15 to 18 years of age) studied relatively long reading passages (700 to 800 words) under pictorial and nonpictorial conditions. In both experiments, a within-subjects design was employed, with passages counterbalanced across conditions. After a 10-minute study session with each passage, knowledge of the major points and details was assessed from the subjects' oral recall.

In the first study, the "pictorial" condition involved passages written in popular style and illustrated, while the "nonpictorial" condition consisted of stories written in formal style and accompanied by graphs. In the second study, the "pictorial" condition was the same as in the first study, but the "nonpictorial" condition included only stories written in popular style and with no accompanying pictures or graphs. The patterns of results in the two studies were essentially the same. There was no overall difference in accuracy of recall of information between the pictorial and nonpictorial conditions. Differences were, however, apparent in precisely which points from the text were recalled. A comparison of the accuracy of recall of main points across the pictorial and nonpictorial versions of the text indicated that points directly illustrated in the pictorial condition were recalled more accurately than in the nonpictorial condition; but, there appeared to be a trade-off, such that points appearing in the text alone in the pictorial condition were recalled less accurately than in the nonpictorial condition. On the basis of these findings, Vernon suggested that, "Perhaps the pictures laid undue emphasis on certain points, and therefore, distracted attention from the rest of the text" (p. 183).

The second set of two studies by Vernon (1954) involved somewhat younger children (ranging in age from 10–5 to 12–10). The first experiment of the two examined the influence of pictures on children's recall of information in the text. As in the earlier studies, the task was one of silently studying a relatively long passage (755 to 940 words). In the "pictorial" condition, color illustrations appeared on the pages opposite the text, while in the "nonpictorial" condition small black and white drawings of some of the objects mentioned in the text were used in place of pictures. (These provided much less information than the original illustrations.) A within-subjects design was again employed, picture conditions being counterbalanced across stories. After studying the text freely for 10 minutes, children's recall of points mentioned in the text was assessed with general questions designed to elicit specific information. This procedure differed from the totally free recall approach used in the earlier studies. Results from this experiment indicated that the presence of text-relevant pictures had no effect on children's recall of story content.

In discussing the implications of these findings, Vernon (1954) raised the possibility that the children might have been concentrating so hard on memorizing the text that they paid little or no attention to the illustrations. To assess this possibility, Vernon conducted a second study with children in the same age range. This time stories were read aloud to the children and pictorial material was presented in three different ways. In one of the conditions, pictures mounted on cards were shown at appropriate points in the text to illustrate specific information and sequence of events. The other two conditions involved the presentation of less informative pictures, with little or no emphasis on sequence of events in the text. The orally presented texts were considerably shorter than in the previous studies (about 300 words). Recall was assessed with both free recall and questions to assess knowledge of the most essential general points in the text. Consistent with the previous studies, the pictures did not affect overall recall of textual information. But, as in two of the previous studies, isolated items specifically presented in pictures tended to be recalled more accurately at the cost of nonillustrated textual information.

Based on Vernon's (1953, 1954) findings from her well-documented series of studies, it is evident that for older children the value of pictorial illustration is very questionable in facilitating acquisition of knowledge from the text. Indeed, a reasonable interpretation of children's tendency toward differential recall of pictured and nonpictured information is that the presence of pictures may have drawn children's attention away from the text itself. In their recall of the stories they may have relied to a large extent on what they remembered from the picture rather than the text.

More recently in the Netherlands, Peeck (1974) conducted an elegant experiment in which he examined younger children's (fourth-graders') retention of pictorial and verbal content of text with illustrations. The task was one of silently ''reading for pleasure'' a lengthy children's story (aproximately 3000 words), either with or without pictures. In the experimental condition the text was presented in a cartoon strip, while in the control condition the text was unillustrated. Retention of the story was assessed (unexpectedly) at three different intervals with different groups—one group of children was tested immediately after they finished reading; another, 1 day later; and a third, 1 week later. The retention test was in a multiple-choice format with items tapping information that had appeared in the text alone and information that had been illustrated. The questions concerned with illustrated information (in the experimental condition) were of three types: some dealt with information that had appeared only in the picture, others with information presented in both the picture and text, and others with textual information that had been incongruously illustrated.

Multiple-choice reading comprehension questions tapping information that had appeared in the text alone were answered equally well by both groups of children; items concerned with information in the pictures alone were, not surprisingly, answered more accurately by children in the illustrated condition; items dealing with information presented both in the text and the illustration were also more accurately answered by children in the picture condition; but, items concerned with textual information that was incongruously represented in the illustration were less accurately answered by children who read the illustrated stories. ''Taken together these results indicate that the exposure of subjects in the experimental condition to both pictures and text had a powerful effect on behavior on the retention test: They chose the alternative corresponding to the pictorial information far more frequently than subjects who had only seen the text'' (p. 885). This was true even when the picture was, in fact, incongruous with the text.

In relating his findings to educational practice, Peeck (1974) pointed out that the effects of pictures in his study may have been somewhat inflated because the learning material used in the study was ''probably more conducive to pictorial retention than illustrated text books used in education generally are''; indicating further that although the text of the strip cartoon carried the actual story, ''the pictures continuously provided the reader with some visualization of its contents, thus reinforcing the tendency, already natural in reading strip cartoons, to pay attention to the illustrations.'' (p. 886).

Effects similar to those observed by Peeck (1974) have, however, been reported for test materials much more like those in beginning readers. In a series of three closely related studies, Willows (1979a) examined the influence of pictures on second-, third-, and fourth-graders' retention of illustrated and nonillustrated aspects of text. The children in these studies (matched groups of good and poor readers) silently read a set of nine brief passages (ranging from approximately 50 to 100 words) and completed multiple-choice reading comprehension questions after each. The reading materials included three stories at each of three levels of difficulty; and, at each difficulty level, one of the stories was not illustrated, one had an illustration that was consistent with the text, and one had an illustration that was contradictory to details of the text. The illustrations were realistic and colorful, quite similar to those found in 1960s school readers. The multiple-choice questions accompanying each story included equal proportions of two types of items: items that were relevant to illustrated aspects of the text (under the two illustrated conditions), and items that were never illustrated. The child's task was simply to read each story silently ''just like you do in class'' and to be prepared to answer some questions about it afterward. The instructions indicated that there would be ''some different kinds of stories,'' but no mention was made of illustrations. The child was also assured ''If you come to any words you don't know, you can ask me for help.''

The pattern of results on the reading comprehension measure was very clear and consistent. The presence of illustrations always affected children's responses to the multiple-choice questions, but this influence was restricted to those aspects of the text which were illustrated. If the illustrated information was consistent with the text, response accuracy went up; if it conflicted with the text, response accuracy went down. In other words, children relied on illustrated information to answer questions about the text. There was, however, no influence of illustrations on response accuracy to the questions about nonillustrated textual information. Even in the situation where the illustrations accurately depicted story details, there was no evidence of improved reading comprehension of textual information. These findings were consistent across grade, sex, reading ability, and text difficulty.

The reading time data corroborated the reading comprehension measure. When children were reading illustrated stories to themselves, they took more time to "read" than when they were silently reading other stories of similar difficulty without illustrations, or than when they were reading the same stories aloud without illustrations. It thus seems clear that although instructed to read the text to themselves and remember the information in it, children spontaneously paid attention to illustrated information in addition to the text.

These results confirmed and extended the findings of Vernon (1953, 1954) and Peeck (1974). Children at several grade levels, under a variety of experimental conditions, appear to give illustrated information priority over textual information when they are responding to comprehension questions about the text. And, contrary to widely held views, it appears that the presence of illustrations does not stimulate greater interest in and attention to the text itself. In none of the studies was there any evidence to suggest that nonillustrated textual information was remembered more accurately when the text was accompanied by illustrations. Although none of the studies have involved first-graders just beginning to read, the consistency of results across all of these studies with children ranging from second grade to high school suggests that similar effects probably occur among younger children, as well. But, in view of the prevalence of the assumption that the presence of illustrations will improve children's motivation to read the text and comprehension of textual information, further research involving first-grade children should certainly be undertaken.

4. Future Research Directions

It should now be clear that the question, "What effects do the pictures in their readers have on children's acquisition of skill in reading?", is far from simple to answer. There has been a tendency among researchers concerned with the issue to conduct one or two laboratory studies and then to draw conclusions far more general than are warranted by their findings. The ultimate answer to the question will undoubtedly be conditional on a whole range of factors including subject variables, text variables, picture variables, teaching method variables, and the types of measures used to assess reading performance or skill. Conclusions from studies that fail to consider some of these potentially relevant influences must be suitably qualified. Some of the possible effects of these variables are briefly discussed on the following pages.

a. SUBJECT VARIABLES

It seems most unlikely that all children are affected in the same way and to the same degree by the pictures in their readers. Factors related to grade, level of reading skill, and personality characteristics probably all play a role in determining the extent to which pictures affect children's learning to read.

Long before entering school most children have considerable experience with books and magazines, and for most children that experience almost exclusively involves looking at and responding to illustrations. Upon first entering school the child's concept of books may well be that the illustrations are the important part and that the text simply "tells about the pictures." Given such a view, children in the early grades of school may focus most of their attention on the pictures in their readers simply as a result of a carry-over from preschool picturebook experiences. Also, as mentioned earlier, teachers' guidebooks usually promote and encourage attention to pictures at the early grade levels. Thus, both a predisposition to define school readers as picturebooks, and an early instructional emphasis on illustrations might well result in greater attention to pictures in the early grade levels than in more advanced grades.

Even within grade levels there may be considerable variation among children in their attention to pictures in reading situations. There is, for example, some evidence to suggest that relatively stable individual differences in selective attention may exist, and that such differences may predispose some children to be easily distracted by superfluous visual information (Willows, 1978a, 1978b). For such children the pictures in their school readers could serve as a compelling source of visual distraction, and could play a direct role in retarding their acquisition of skill in reading. Other children whose capacity for selective attention is more highly developed may be affected quite differently by the pictures in their school readers.

Alternatively, differences in reading ability could be a causal factor in differences among children in attention to pictures. Children who are relatively skilled readers may have confidence in their ability to process text, and so may not feel compelled to seek "clues" to the meaning of the text from accompanying illustrations. As well, skilled readers may find text intrinsically interesting and may not require additional motivation to stimulate their interest in reading. Children lower in reading skill, however, may lack confidence in their ability to decode the text accurately without regularly checking the illustrations. Also, less skilled readers who can read only very simple texts may require additional external motivators, such as pictures, to arouse their interest in reading text at all.

b. TEXT VARIABLES

As discussed in our sections on language and motivational content, the types of reading selections included in school readers are quite varied. The extent to which the content of the text determines the influences of pictures has not been investigated, but it seems likely that it plays an important role. If the text is **redundant** with the illustration or contains less information than the picture the child may find the text disappointing and the presence of pictures may actually detract from rather than stimulate interest in the text. The child may examine the illustration and then read the text only to discover that the text is bland in comparison with the picture. If, on the other hand, the text is **complementary** or **supplementary** to the pictures, then the presence of pictures may serve to encourage reading of the accompanying text. The influences of the relation between textual content and picture content on children's attention to the text should certainly be examined.

Other factors such as length of selection and text difficulty probably also determine the extent to which the illustrations influence children's reading. Indeed, when text difficulty has been included as a variable in studies examining the influences of pictures on reading (e.g., Willows, 1979a), it was demonstrated that children paid more attention to the pictures when the text was more difficult.

c. PICTURE VARIABLES

Our analyses of the quantitative and qualitative aspects of the illustrations in school readers indicate that there are numerous pictures in all of the series, and most of them are large, complex, brightly colored, and centrally located on the page. From story to story, and from one series to another, there is, however, drastic variability among pictures, particularly along the qualitative dimensions. Nevertheless, as Willows (1980) has pointed out, researchers examining the effects of pictures on reading have almost invariably used the term *picture* as though "a picture is a picture is a picture."

Studies concerning the influences of pictures on reading have usually employed only one style of illustration; and, from study to study, there has been little consistency in the type of illustration selected. Moreover, examples of the pictures used in studies have very rarely been reproduced in journals, so it has been left to the reader to visualize the characteristics of the artwork on the basis of verbal descriptions such as "a simple colored picture" (Hartley, 1970–71, p. 107), "rather striking photographs" (Vernon, 1953, p. 181), "black and white drawings" (Koenke & Otto, 1969, p. 299), or "a simple black line drawing" (King & Muehl, 1965, p. 164).

The discussion sections of research articles concerned with pictures and reading almost invariably make some mention of the implications of the findings for educational practice. In other words, researchers generalize the results of their studies to the illustrations used in school readers. But, is such generalization justified? Can one type or style of illustration be selected as representative of those included in school readers? Our systematic examination of the first grade readers in the most recent editions of three major readings series revealed that although all three series have an illustration on virtually every page, there is not a single "line drawing" among them, and only a very small proportion of the illustrations could be described as "simple."

At an intuitive level it seems reasonable to expect that qualitative aspects of illustrations may affect reading, but few researchers have been concerned with this possibility. Research specifically designed to assess the influence of one dimension of picture salience—color—on reading comprehension of illustrated and nonillustrated aspects of text, has shown, however, that colored illustrations have a more compelling influence than black-and-white line drawings; and that the influence of picture salience is greater among less-skilled readers (Willows, 1980). Further studies examining the influences of picture size, picture placement, picture complexity, and other dimensions of picture salience should certainly be conducted.

III. OVERVIEW AND CONCLUSIONS

Problems in learning to read are usually assumed to originate with the pupil, the teacher, or the method of reading instruction; one potentially crucial factor—reader content—is seldom considered. In this article we have analyzed several aspects of the content of school readers and have found that, on every dimension examined, there is considerable variability among series; but, the variability across types of programs (basal versus code) is no greater than that within types. Indeed, beyond the differences in the decodability of the words, demonstrated in Beck's article in this volume, the differences in the content of the first-grade readers in basal and code-emphasis programs do not appear to be theory-based or systematic. Rather, it appears that the selection of first-grade reader content has been largely based on intuition, and the range of intuitions in the areas of vocabulary, language, story content, typography, and illustrations is very broad. In each of these areas, it is possible that the choices made by some publishers **adversely** affect the acquisition of reading skill. In an effort to determine the probable effects of publishers' decisions concerning various aspects of reader content, we have considered the findings of our content analysis in the light of research evidence in each area.

A. Overview

Our analysis of the vocabularies of four current reading series has demonstrated that the range of differences in vocabulary load in terms of number of unique words taught in first grade is extreme, with the heaviest load being more than triple the lightest. Also, the rate of introduction of new words and the number of repetitions of each word in text vary dramatically across series and these variations seem to bear no logical relationship to the type of reading program. Research on vocabulary has focused primarily on comparing the vocabulary lists of school readers and offers no guidance concerning appropriate levels for the vocabulary measures considered here.

In the beginning stages of learning to read, undoubtedly the type of words selected (whether based on considerations of phonics or of familiarity) plays a role in children's acquisition of reading skill, but probably even more important are the size of the vocabulary load, the rate at which new words are introduced, and the number of opportunities there are in the text for reading these words. Systematic research into the optimal levels of these variables, for both basal and code-emphasis programs, is much needed.

Although few would deny the necessity of imposing some restrictions on the difficulty of children's first-grade readers, the simple language of school readers has long been a target of ridicule. This is particularly true in the case of the early parts of first-grade reading programs when the number of word forms (in basal programs) and the number of letter–sound correspondences (in code-emphasis programs) are both very limited. The criticism is that the stilted and unnatural language, which has typified these books for so long, may reduce children's interest in reading. Beyond this intuitive argument about motivation, more theoretical concerns have also been raised. For example, psycholinguists have contended that the simple and redundant texts that usually characterize early first-grade readers are impoverished in terms of semantic and syntactic information that provides important cues to word identification. As yet, however, the simplicity-versus-complexity debate remains unresolved, partly because the issues are difficult to delineate, and partly because there has been so little research into the effects on children's reading of variations in text complexity.

In response to the need for some objective measure of the complexity of written language, numerous readability formulas have been developed. Unfortunately, these formulas can provide only a crude estimate of the difficulty level of reading material because they do not take into account certain factors, such as the reader's interest, that probably affect comprehensibility. Nevertheless, such formulas may offer some guidance to those who must select reading materials for children.

In our comparisons of the readability levels of the first-grade readers in our sample, we have found that, contrary to expectations, there is no apparent relationship between the type of reading program and the estimated difficulty of the readers. Furthermore, in only two of the four series is there evidence of some gradation of readability over the first year of reading instruction.

As yet, the research on the language and readability of school readers has been very limited and the research questions of greatest concern have not been addressed. What we need to know is how the various facets of written language influence the process of learning to read.

The story content of first-grade readers, like the language, has long been maligned. Basal readers of 20 years ago have been described as "bland" and "Pollyannish." Our content analysis of current school readers has revealed that there is now considerable variability across series in terms of both themes and characters. In two of the series examined (one basal and one code program) most of the reading selections deal with "real life" events, and the same characters recur from one selection to the next. In the other two series (one of each type of program), there is more variety in themes and characters, with quite a few selections being classified as "fantasy" and "instructive," and new characters being introduced in almost every selection.

Research on the story content of school readers has been primarily descriptive, cataloguing the themes and characters. Much less attention has been given to the potential effects of different types of story content on children's learning to read. Also, none of the research has considered a possibly crucial factor—length of selection. The reading selections in all of the books in our sample are very brief with few even in the highest level books exceeding 300 words, the vast majority being much shorter.

The physical characteristics of the text of first-grade readers have been almost totally ignored by researchers. But, here too, current reading series are quite variable. Three of the series in our content analysis were found to be relatively consistent in their use of typography; there is a decrease in type size across the text levels, but typestyle and form of typeface remain fairly uniform. The fourth series was found to be more variable on all aspects of typography, changing size, form, and style of typeface from one selection to another, and using different colored type for story titles. From an adult's perspective such variations might seem a trivial matter, but intuitions based on mature reading are probably inappropriate. For the naive reader, less experienced with the critical features of print, variations in typography and other physical character-istics of text might be quite confusing. In any case, research in this area is essential.

Although some physical characteristics pertaining to the text may go unnoticed, the artwork in these books is another matter. The typical reaction of an adult glancing through the pages of present-day readers is that they are far more "attractive" than they were "when we were in school." An objective analysis of the artwork in three current reading series, on both quantitative and qualitative dimensions, has corroborated this informal observation. The quantitative measures showed that there is at least one picture on virtually every page, and a very high proportion of the pages in all three of the illustrated series have artwork covering more than half of the page. Also, the amount of artwork relative to presentation of textual information (i.e., number of pictures per 100 running words) is very great. Our content analysis of the artwork involved only the highest level books in each series (Level C), the books con-taining, by far, the largest number of words per page. Yet, even in these books, the proportion of artwork to text is very high. A comparison of these current series with some earlier editions shows that there has been a dramatic increase in the amount of artwork in school readers during the last decade.

Our qualitative measures of the artwork in current readers included the type of illustrations, the placement of the illustrations, the vividness of the colors, the complexity of the pictures, and the overall eye-catching appeal of the pictures. Clearly the artwork in all three illustrated series is very salient; most of the pictures are complex, brightly colored, cen-trally located on the page, and very eye-catching. On these dimensions, too, informal comparisons with earlier editions indicate a substantial increase over the past 10 years.

The use of artwork in school readers is not new; indeed, it goes back more than 300 years. Nevertheless, the recent increase in its use is quite striking. In view of its longstanding inclusion in first-grade readers and the changes that have occurred during the last decade, it is certainly reasonable to ask "What role does this artwork play in teaching children to read?" Our examination of the teachers' guidebooks accompanying the illustrated reading series has indicated that three main assumptions have been made about the value of pictures in teaching reading. The first is that pictures aid in learning new words out of context; the second is that pictures serve as a cue to word recognition for words in context; and the third, and most widespread, assumption is that the presence of pictures stimulates an interest in the text and promotes a better understanding of textual information.

A review of a fairly large body of research evidence relevant to these three assumptions shows that there is no support for any of them. There is, in fact, evidence that in some situations pictures have an interfering effect rather than a facilitative one. The question of how the presence of pictures in their first-grade readers affects children's learning to read is, however, not a simple one. Much is yet to be investigated concerning the influences of subject variables, text variables, and picture variables before conclusions should be drawn about the use of artwork in school readers.

B. Conclusions

The findings from our content analysis of current school readers and from our survey of the available research literature on a number of dimensions of particular relevance to the content of school readers have shown that both publishers of reading series and researchers conducting studies of reading have failed to address some very important questions. This failure should not be interpreted as an indictment of either publishers or researchers, but rather should be viewed as a symptom of a serious problem: Communication is clearly inadequate between publishers of beginning reader series and researchers investigating the process of learning to read.

It is evident from our content analysis that publishers' decisions about the vocabulary, language, story content, physical characteristics of text, and the very pervasive artwork contained in current school readers must be largely based on intuitions, arbitrary decisions, and marketing considerations. Without careful research on all aspects of reader content, the design of school readers will continue to be based on such inappropriate criteria. In many of these areas there has been very little adequate research on which to base more reasoned decisions. In a few areas, however, research relevant to the content of school readers has been conducted, but publishers of school books are apparently unaware of it. For example, although there is now considerable research evidence that pictures do not facilitate learning to read, there has recently been a dramatic increase in the amount and salience of the artwork in school readers. If publishers were to take account of research results when designing primary-grade readers, the task of learning to read would, perhaps, be made easier.

For their part, reading researchers have failed to address many potentially crucial questions concerning the content of school readers. This failure probably stems, in part, from the longstanding bias that the method of reading instruction is all-important. The dramatic variability we found on almost every dimension of reader content—between reading series that are superficially similar as far as "method" is concerned (i.e., basal programs or code-emphasis programs)—demonstrates that factors other than method should be investigated. Further applied research based on the "Method A versus Method B" model is unlikely to provide many useful insights. Since, as our content analysis has shown, two exemplars of "Method A" or "Method B" may differ substantially on any or all of the dimensions of reader content examined, the outcome of particular "Method A versus Method B" comparisons may be attributable to aspects of the reader content alone and have very little to do with method.

Several more productive research directions have been suggested throughout this article, and they will not be reiterated here. Suffice it to say that research on the potential impact of reader content on children's acquisition of reading skill is much needed. At present this issue is often ignored and, indeed, in reviewing the relevant research literature we found that many of the studies focused on merely measuring and describing reader content; few addressed the more difficult issues related to how the various aspects of reader content might affect children's learning to read. Furthermore, even when such attempts have been made, the researchers have sometimes failed to take account of the practical constraints on classroom learning and have designed studies lacking in external validity. For example, most of the research on the effects of pictures on children's learning of new words out of context has involved a one-to-one teaching situation. In the "real world" of education in the schools, such a situation is usually impractical if not impossible to achieve. Thus the outcome of many of these studies may be of little or no value to educators and publishers of reading programs; similar studies involving group instruction should certainly be conducted before the results are generalized to the classroom. Researchers need to familiarize themselves with current educational materials and classroom practices and be mindful of these when formulating their research questions.

Reading researchers and publishers of school readers have been working in apparent isolation from each other, even though an exchange of ideas and information would be of benefit to both. Such an exchange could contribute much toward the child's mastery of reading skills through improved design of primary-grade readers.

IV. APPENDIX

Throughout this article we present statistics to describe the content of the first-grade readers in four current series. Two of them, *Starting Points in Language Arts* (Ginn, 1976) and *Basics in Reading* (Scott Foresman, 1978) will be referred to as "basal programs." The other two, *Language Patterns* (Holt, Rinehart & Winston, 1976) and *The Merrill Linguistic Reading Program* (Merrill, 1975), both examples of "linguistic" programs, will be referred to as "code programs." Both of these designations have been borrowed from Beck (this volume) to avoid confusion in making comparisons across articles. The primary defining characteristic used in our assignment of these designations is the vocabulary taught in the early stages of the program. The "basal programs" clearly reflect an emphasis on word frequency and familiarity rather than on regularity of letter–sound correspondences. In contrast, the "code programs" generate their initial vocabulary almost exclusively on the basis of the letter–sound correspondences taught, including only enough "sight words" to be able to construct meaningful sentences.

Our choice of the particular series was arbitrary. Two of them, Ginn (1976) and Holt (1976), were selected because they are widely used in our area. The Scott Foresman (1978) series was chosen so that we would be able to compare a recent Scott Foresman edition with the data presented by Chall (1967) on five earlier ones. Merrill (1975) was included because it is a clear-cut example of a "linguistic" program, in contrast to Holt which is somewhat more eclectic.

The difficulty levels of the four series are not explicitly stated in the guidebooks. But, it is indicated in the Scott Foresman guidebook that the series is designed for the "average" child, with special options for "below average" and "above average" children; the Merrill guidebook indicates that the series is particularly well suited to pupils "who might have difficulty getting meaning and satisfaction from reading." We found no indication of the presumed relative difficulty of the other two series in the teachers' manuals, but, from discussions with publishers' representatives, we concluded that both seem to be aimed at the "average" child. In the cases where some suggestion is made about the suitability of the program for different ability groups (in Scott Foresman and Merrill) there is, however, no indication of how this was determined. So we must assume that the difficulty estimates are based on informal feedback from classes where the programs were pilot tested, rather than from systematic analysis of the programs.

In order to examine the content of the readers at various stages in the programs, we divided each series into three levels (A, B, and C) for some of our analyses. These levels are based, in part, on the publishers' own divisions and since the programs vary considerably, these units are not equal in absolute size. They do, however, permit comparisons across early, middle, and late stages of the first-grade content. For Ginn, Merrill, and Scott Foresman the three levels simply correspond to the three teachers' guidebooks. (The "readiness" level of Scott Foresman is not included.) For Holt there are four readers and only one guidebook. The previous Holt edition (the 1967 version of the same series) had only three readers. A fourth was added when the series was revised. Hence, we assumed that the three original books represent three levels in the program, and we combined the newly added book with the previous highest level book. (Our content analysis revealed the two top level books to be quite similar in difficulty, thus confirming our decision to combine them.) Because there was considerable variability in overall length of the series and in the levels (A, B, and C), we used percentage scores rather than frequencies for most of our descriptive statistics (see Table XI).

TABLE XI

Books Included in the Analysis of First-Grade Reader Content in Four Current Series

Series	Level	Book title	Number of running words per level
Merrill	A	I Can	1837
(1975)	B	Dig In	3074
	C	Catch On	7908
Holt	A	Listening Letters	2951
(1976)	B	Laughing Letters	3069
	C	Magic Letters	6226
		Rainbow Letters	
Scott Foresman	A	Puppy Paws	3281
(1978)		Jumping Jamboree	
		No Cages, Please	
	B	Dragon Wings	2193
	C	Calico Capers	2663
Ginn	A	Mr. Mugs	671
(1976)		Mr. Mugs—A Jet-Pet	
	B	Mr. Mugs Plays Ball	1724
		Mr. Mugs and the Blue Whale	
	C	First Prize for Mr. Mugs	5335
		Mr. Mugs is Lost	

The reader content of two of the series was not restricted to reading selections for pupils. The Ginn (1976) program includes 25 selections labeled "Teacher Read." These are typed in smaller print than the children's text, and include many vocabulary words that the children would not be expected to know. We excluded these "Teacher Read" selections from our content analysis. The Scott Foresman (1978) series includes far more than standard reading selections in the readers. It also includes teaching and assessment components, and some workbook-type activities. In our examination of the "reader content" in the Scott Foresman series, we included only the reading selections (those designated "Apply" and "Bonus" selections).

REFERENCES

Arlin, M., Scott, M., & Webster, J. The effects of pictures on rate of learning sight words: A critique of the focal attention hypothesis. *Reading Research Quarterly*, 1978–79, **14**, 645–660.

Arlin, M. Commentary: A response to Singer. *Reading Research Quarterly*, 1980, **15**, 550–558.

Asher, S. R. *The effect of interest on reading comprehension for black children and white children.* Unpublished manuscript, University of Illinois, 1976.

Asher, S. R., Hymel, S., & Wigfield, A. Influence of topic interest on children's reading comprehension. *Journal of Reading Behavior*, 1978, **10**, 35–47.

Asher, S. R., & Markell, R. A. Sex differences in comprehension of high- and low-interest reading material. *Journal of Educational Psychology*, 1974, **66**, 680–687.

Barnard, D. P., & DeGracie, J. Vocabulary analysis of new primary reading series. *The Reading Teacher*, 1976, **30**, 177–180.

Beck, I. L., & Block, K. K. An analysis of two beginning reading programs: Some facts and some opinions. In L. B. Resnick & P. A. Weaver (Eds.), *Theory and practice of early reading* (Vol. 1). New Jersey: Erlbaum, 1979.

Bernstein, J. The changing roles of females in books for young children. *The Reading Teacher*, 1974, **27**, 546–549.

Blom, G. E., Waite, R. W., & Zimet, S. G. Content of first grade reading books. *The Reading Teacher*, 1968, **21**, 317–323.

Blom, G. E., Waite, R. W., & Zimet, S. G. A motivational content analysis of children's primers. In H. Levin & J. P. Williams (Eds.), *Basic studies on reading*. New York: Basic Books, 1970.

Blom, G. E., & Wiberg, J. L. Attitude contents in reading primers. In J. Downing (Ed.), *Comparative reading: Cross-national studies of behavior and processes in reading and writing*. New York: Macmillan, 1973.

Bormuth, J. Readability: A new approach. *Reading Research Quarterly*, 1966, **1**, 79–132.

Botel, M., Dawkins, J., & Granowsky, A. A syntactic complexity formula. In W. H. MacGinitie (Ed.), *Assessment problems in reading*. Newark, Delaware: International Reading Association, 1973.

Bradley, J. M., & Ames, W. S. Readability parameters of basal readers, *Journal of Reading Behavior*, 1977, **9**, 175–183.

Braun, C. *The efficacy of selected stimulus modalities in acquisition and retention of sex-typed textual responses of kindergarten children.* Unpublished doctoral dissertation, University of Minnesota, 1967.

Braun, C. Interest-loading and modality effects on textual response acquisition. *Reading Research Quarterly*, 1969, **4**, 428–444.

Britton, G. E. Danger: State adopted texts may be hazardous to our future. *The Reading Teacher*, 1975, **29**, 52–58.

Britton, G. E., & Lumpkin, M. C. For sale: Subliminal bias in textbooks. *The Reading Teacher*, 1977, **31**, 40–45.

Chall, J. S. Readability: An appraisal of research and application. *Ohio State University Educational Research Monograph*, 1958, No. 34.

Chall, J. *Learning to read: The great debate*. New York: McGraw-Hill, 1967.

Cronnell, B. Designing a reading program based on research findings in orthography. *Elementary English*, 1973, **50**, 27–34.

Denburg, S. D. The interaction of picture and print in reading instruction (abstracted report). *Reading Research Quarterly*, 1976–77, **12**, 176–189.

Dolch, E. W. *Teaching primary reading*. Champaign: The Garrard Press, 1941.

Dwyer, C. A. Sex differences in reading: An evaluation and a critique of current theories. *Review of Educational Research*, 1973, **43**, 455–467.

Frasher, R. Boys, girls and *Pippi Longstocking*. *The Reading Teacher*, 1977, **30**, 860–863.

Frasher, R., & Frasher, J. M. Influence of story characters' roles on comprehension. *The Reading Teacher*, 1978, **32**, 160–164.

Frasher, R., & Walker, A. Sex roles in early reading textbooks. *The Reading Teacher*, 1972, **25**, 741–749.

Fry, E. A readability formula that saves time. *Journal of Reading*, 1968, **11**, 513–516, 575–578.

Geyer, J. R. Evaluation of readability—prediction of comprehension? *Journal of the Reading Specialist*, 1970, **10**, 83–86.

Gibson, E. J., & Levin, H. *The psychology of reading*. Cambridge, Massachusetts: M.I.T. Press, 1975.

Ginn. *The Ginn integrated language program*. New York: Ginn, 1967.

Ginn. *Treatment of minority groups and women*. New York: Ginn, 1973.

Ginn. *Starting points in language arts*. New York: Ginn, 1976.

Glazer, S. M., & Morrow, L. M. The syntactic complexity of primary grade children's oral language and primary grade reading materials: A comparative analysis. *Journal of Reading Behavior*, 1978, **10**, 200–203.

Goodman, K. S. Reading: A psycholinguistic guessing game. *Journal of the Reading Specialist*, 1967, **6**, 126–135.

Graebner, D. B. A decade of sexism in readers. *The Reading Teacher*, 1972, **26**, 52–58.

Hansell, T. S. Readability, syntactic transformations, and generative semantics. *Journal of Reading*, 1976, **19**, 557–562.

Harris, A. J., & Jacobson, M. D. A framework for readability research: Moving beyond Herbert Spencer. *Journal of Reading*, 1979, **22**, 390–398.

Harris, L. A. *A study of the rate of acquisition and retention of interest-loaded words by low socioeconomic children*. Unpublished doctoral dissertation, University of Minnesota, 1967.

Hartley, R. N. Effects of list types and cues on the learning of word lists. *Reading Research Quarterly*, 1970–71, **6**, 97–121.

Harzem, P., Lee, I., & Miles, T. R. The effects of pictures on learning to read. *British Journal of Educational Psychology*, 1976, **46**, 318–322.

Hittleman, D. R. Readability, readability formulas, and cloze: Selecting instructional materials. *Journal of Reading*, 1978, **22**, 117–122.

Holt. *Language patterns*. New York: Holt, 1967.

Holt. *Guidelines for the development of elementary and secondary instructinal materials: The treatment of sex roles.* New York: Holt, 1975.

Holt. *Language Patterns* (revised). New York: Holt, 1976.

Houghton Mifflin. *Avoiding stereotypes.* Boston: Houghton, 1975.

Huey, E. B. *The psychology and pedagogy of reading.* New York: Macmillan, 1908. Republished by MIT Press, Cambridge, Massachusetts, 1968.

Ives, J. P., Bursuk, L. Z., & Ives, S. A. *Word identification techniques.* Chicago: Rand McNally, 1979.

Jennings, S. A. Effects of sex typing in children's stories on preference and recall. *Child Development,* 1975, **46,** 220–223.

Johns, J. L. The Dolch Basic Word List—then and now. *Journal of Reading Behavior,* 1970–71, **3,** 35–40.

Johnson, D. Sex differences in reading across cultures. *Reading Research Quarterly,* 1973–74, **9,** 67–86.

Johnson, D. D., & Pearson, P. D. *Teaching reading vocabulary.* New York: Holt, 1978.

Kaiser, R. A., Neils, C. F., & Floriani, B. P. Syntactic complexity of primary grade reading materials: A preliminary look. *The Reading Teacher,* 1975, **29,** 262–266.

King, E. M., & Muehl, S. Different sensory cues as aids in beginning reading. *The Reading Teacher,* 1965, **19,** 163–168.

Kingston, A. J., & Lovelace, T. Sexism and reading: A critical review of the literature. *Reading Research Quarterly,* 1977–78, **13,** 134–161.

Klare, G. R. Assessing readability. *Reading Research Quarterly,* 1974–75, **10,** 62–102.

Klare, G. R. A second look at the validity of readability formulas. *Journal of Reading Behavior,* 1976, **8,** 129–152.

Koenke, K., & Otto, W. Contribution of pictures to children's comprehension of the main idea in reading. *Psychology in the Schools,* 1969, **6,** 298–302.

Levin, H. Reading research: What, why, and for whom? *Elementary English,* 1966, **43,** 138–147.

Lowe, A. J., & Follman, J. Comparison of the Dolch List with other word lists. *The Reading Teacher,* 1974, **28,** 40–44.

McGraw-Hill. *Guidelines for equal treatment of the sexes in McGraw-Hill Book Company publications.* New York: McGraw-Hill, 1974.

McNamara, W. J., Paterson, D. G., & Tinker, M. A. The influence of size of type on speed of reading in the primary grades. *The Sight-Saving Review,* 1953, **23,** 28–33.

McNinch, G. Graphic constraints on children's ability to read words. In P. L. Nacke (Ed.), Diversity in mature reading: Theory and research. *22nd Yearbook of the National Reading Conference* (Vol. 1). Boone, North Carolina: The National Reading Conference, Inc., 1973.

Macmillan. *Guidelines for creating positive sexual and racial images.* New York: Macmillan, 1975.

Mangieri, J. N., & Kahn, M. S. Is the Dolch list of 220 basic sight words irrelevant? *The Reading Teacher,* 1977, **30,** 649–651.

Marten, L. A., & Matlin, M. W. Does sexism in elementary readers still exist? *The Reading Teacher,* 1976, **29,** 764–767.

Merrill. *The Merrill Linguistic Reading Program.* Columbus, Ohio: Charles E. Merrill, 1975.

Montare, A., Elman, E., & Cohen, J. Words and pictures: A test of Samuels' findings. *Journal of Reading Behavior,* 1977, **9,** 269–285.

Olson, A. V. An analysis of the vocabulary of seven primary reading series. *Elementary English,* 1965, **43,** 261–264.

Peeck, J. Retention of pictorial and verbal content of a text with illustrations. *Journal of Educational Psychology*, 1974, **66**, 880–888.

Preston, R. C. Reading achievement of German and American children. *School and Society*, 1962, **90**, 350–354.

Resnick, L. B., & Beck, I. L. Designing instruction in reading: Interaction of theory and practice. In J. T. Guthrie (Ed.), *Aspects of reading acquisition*. Baltimore: Johns Hopkins Univ. Press, 1976.

Rinsland, H. D. *A basic vocabulary of elementary school children*. New York: Macmillan, 1945.

Rodenborn, L. V., & Washburn, E. Some implications of the new basal readers. *Elementary English*, 1974, **51**, 885–888.

Ruddell, R. B. The effect of oral and written patterns of language structure on reading comprehension. *The Reading Teacher*, 1965, **18**, 271–275.

Saario, T. N., Jacklin, C. N., & Tittle, C. K. Sex role stereotyping in the public schools. *Harvard Educational Review*, 1973, **43**, 386–416.

Samuels, S. J. Attentional process in reading: The effect of pictures in the acquisition of reading responses. *Journal of Educational Psychology*, 1967, **58**, 337–342.

Samuels, S. J. Effects of pictures on learning to read, comprehension and attitudes. *Review of Educational Research*, 1970, **40**, 397–407.

Samuels, S. J. Can pictures distract students from the printed word: A rebuttal. *Journal of Reading Behavior*, 1977, **9**, 361–364.

Scott Foresman. *Guidelines for improving the image of women in textbooks*. Glenview, Illinois: Scott Foresman, 1972.

Scott Foresman. *Basics in Reading*. Glenview, Illinois: Scott Foresman, 1978.

Shankweiler, D., & Liberman, I. Y. Misreading: A search for causes. In J. F. Kavanagh & I. G. Mattingly (Eds.), *Language by ear and by eye: The relationships between speech and reading*. Cambridge, Massachusetts: M.I.T. Press, 1972.

Simons, H. D. Reading comprehension: The need for a new perspective. *Reading Research Quarterly*, 1971, **6**, 338–363.

Singer, H. Commentary: Sight word learning with and without pictures: A critique of Arlin, Scott and Webster's research. *Reading Research Quarterly*, 1980, **15**, 290–298.

Singer, H., Samuels, S. J., & Spiroff, J. The effect of pictures and contextual conditions on learning responses to printed words. *Reading Research Quarterly*, 1973–74, **9**, 555–567.

Smith, F. S., Lott, D., & Cronnell, B. The effect of type size and case alternation on word identification. *American Journal of Psychology*, 1969, **82**, 248–253.

Spache, G. D. *Good reading for poor readers*. (Revised 9th Edition) Champaign, Illinois: Garrard, 1974.

Standal, T. C. Readability formulas: What's out, what's in? *The Reading Teacher*, 1978, **31**, 642–646.

Stone, C. R. Measuring difficulty of primary reading material: A constructive criticism of Spache's measure. *Elementary School Journal*, 1956, **51**, 36–41.

Strickland, R. G. The language of elementary school children: Its relationship to the language of reading textbooks and the quality of reading of selected children. *Bulletin of the School of Education*, 1962, **38**, (7).

Tatham, S. M. Reading comprehension of materials written with select oral language patterns: A study at grades two and four. *Reading Research Quarterly*, 1970, **5**, 402–426.

Tibbetts, S. L. Sex differences in children's reading preferences. *The Reading Teacher*, 1974, **28**, 279–281.

Tinker, M. A. *Legibility of print*. Ames, Iowa: Iowa State Univ. Press, 1963.

Tinker, M. A. *Bases for effective reading.* Minneapolis: Univ. of Minnesota Press, 1965.

Venezky, R. L. Research on reading processes: A historical perspective. *American Psychologist,* 1977, **32,** 339–345.

Vernon, M. D. The value of pictorial illustration. *British Journal of Educational Psychology,* 1953, **23,** 180–187.

Vernon, M. D. The instruction of children by pictorial illustration. *British Journal of Educational Psychology,* 1954, **24,** 171–179.

Waite, R. R., Blom, G. E., Zimet, S. G., & Edge, S. First-grade reading text-books. *Elementary School Journal,* 1967, **67,** 366–374.

Wiberg, J. L., & Trost, M. Comparison of content of first-grade primers and free choice library selections, *Elementary English,* 1970, **47,** 792–798.

Willows, D. M. A picture is not always worth a thousand words: Pictures as distractors in reading. *Journal of Educational Psychology,* 1978, **70,** 255–262. (a)

Willows, D. M. Individual differences in distraction by pictures in a reading situation. *Journal of Educational Psychology,* 1978, **70,** 837–847. (b)

Willows, D. M. *Reading comprehension of illustrated and nonillustrated aspects of text.* Paper presented at the annual meeting of the American Educational Research Association, San Francisco, 1979. (a)

Willows, D. M. *A distorted picture of "The effects of pictures on rate of learning sight words."* Unpublished manuscript, University of Waterloo, Waterloo, Ontario, 1979. (b)

Willows, D. M. *Effects of picture salience on reading comprehension of illustrated and nonillustrated aspects of text.* Paper presented at the annual meeting of the American Educational Research Association, Boston, 1980.

Women on Words and Images. *Dick and Jane as victims: Sex stereotyping in children's readers.* Princeton, New Jersey: Women on Words and Images, 1972.

Women on Words and Images. *Dick and Jane as victims: Sex stereotyping in children's readers* (revised ed.). Princeton, New Jersey: Women on Words and Images, 1975.

Zimet, S. G. Reader content and sex differences in achievement. *The Reading Teacher,* 1976, **29,** 758–763.

Zimet, S. G., Blom, G. E. & Waite, R. R. *A teacher's guide for selecting stories for children: The content of first-grade reading textbooks.* Detroit: Wayne State Univ. Press, 1968.

AN EDUCATIONAL EXPERIMENT STATION FOR READING: HOW CAN LEARNING TO READ BE FACILITATED?[1]

EDMUND B. COLEMAN

University of Texas at El Paso
El Paso, Texas

[1] Some of this research was conducted under National Science Foundation Grant GB-3535 and under OEG-7-9-530279-0122-010, a grant awarded by the Committee on Basic Research in Education of the National Academy of Sciences. Five universities supported the work, and some of the more significant contributions were made by Judith Goggin, Milagro Aquino, Dennis Brown, Barbara Morgan, Murray Newman, James Ranson, Andrew Chitwood, and Glenn Takken.

The purpose of this article is to suggest how learning to read can be facilitated (1) to the extent that we can teach reading more effectively, and (2) to the extent that we can teach it to much younger children.

I. WHY SHOULD READING BE TAUGHT AT A YOUNGER AGE?

Reading should be taught at a younger age because there is good evidence that early enrichment can increase intelligence, and because casual observation suggests that the infant brain has a built-in genius for learning language, but that it begins to lose it at an accelerated rate at about 4–7 years.

A. Language—Spoken and Printed

Language is the basic tool of human intelligence. This may be so because man learns to talk during the critical years of infancy; there is mounting physiological evidence that learning during infancy forms a neural circuitry that differs in critical aspects from the circuitry formed by learning in later years. Spoken language, learned during infancy, is engrained into the neural bedrock of the cerebral cortex.

The thesis of this article is that it may be possible to engrain into the next generation a similar genius for printed language. It may be possible to teach printed language during the critical years when the child is forming the interconnections among cerebral neurons that lay the foundations of his intelligence. Coming generations might reach school age thinking with printed language in the same automatic unconscious fashion that children now think with spoken language.

The child learns spoken language, not by formal instruction, but by being immersed in a sea of talk. By using animation plus television, any industrialized nation now has the means to immerse its next generation in a sea of animated printed language. Television already exposes children to animated print, but it is too haphazard to have any great teaching efficiency. Most of the ink expended in this article will deal with a program of R & D that can multiply the teaching efficiency of animated print. First, however, let me develop the argument that early enrichment may increase the synaptic interconnections that appear to be the basis of an organism's intelligence (see Coleman & Morton, 1976).

B. Evidence That Intelligence Can Be Raised by Early Enrichment

Considerable research—ranging from anecdotal case histories to microscopic analysis of individual cerebral neurons—has shown the possibility of increasing learning capacity by training in infancy. A long series of experiments, carried out in different laboratories by scientists from different disciplines, has studied the effects of raising infant animals in enriched environments. In the typical experiment, the litters are separated at weaning, and the animals are raised in three or four different levels of enrichment.

Easily measured differences have been found in animals raised under the different levels. Psychologists have reported behavioral differences (e.g., adult animals who had been raised from infancy in the enriched environments learn mazes and concept formation tasks more easily; they are also more playful and curious). Chemists have reported differences in the chemistry of the brain (e.g., the ratio of RNA to DNA is higher in animals raised in the enriched environments). Physiologists have reported that the cortex of the brain is thicker and heavier in the animals raised in the enriched environments. Not only is the cortex as a whole larger, but microscopic study shows that the cell bodies of individual neurons are higher. Even more suggestive, study with the electron microscope shows that individual neurons have more interconnections with nearby cerebral neurons (Greenough, 1975).

By using the electron microscope at high magnification, it is possible to count the hundreds of "spine growths" on a single neuron. Each spine shows where the neuron synapses with another neuron. New spines form as neurons grow together during periods of learning. For example, a number of new spines form in neurons of the visual cortex as soon as infant mice open their eyes and expose the visual system to light. If the animals are kept in the dark at this time, there is a severe reduction in the number of new spines. Furthermore, if these mice are exposed to light in adult life, a few new spines form, but the number never reaches that of the infant raised in normal light (Valverde, 1971).

Of course, changes in biochemistry and neural structure also occur in the brains of older animals placed in enriched environments, but the differences are smaller, and more important, of a different nature. In older animals, the new spines form more on the apex of the dendrite, and these apical spines are more likely to be connections to sensory and motor neurons coming in from the periphery. In younger animals, on the other hand, the new spines form nearer the cell body, and these are more likely to be connections to other cerebral neurons. This suggests that the changes occurring in older animals are the kind that animals might form when learning specific tasks rather than developing a generalized problem-solving ability.

Experiments such as the above are carried out on animals, but there is a considerable record of supporting evidence showing that level of enrichment also affects the neural structure of the human infant's brain. For example, almost a century ago, Donaldson (1890) studied the brain of Laura Bridgman, who became blind and deaf when she was 2 years old because of scarlet fever, and he found that both the visual and auditory parts of her cortex were abnormally thin and had fewer and smaller cells.

C. What Should Be Taught to Have the Greatest Effect on Intelligence?

Arguments could be advanced in favor of social skills, motor skills, perceptual skills, general problem-solving strategies, art, music, sandboxing, and what have you. For four reasons, I am going to argue for beginning infant enrichment with printed language (with mathematics being a close second). First, the concepts of printed language are basic problem-solving skills; second, we already know a fair amount about teaching them; third, a systematic program of R & D could multiply that amount by several magnitudes in short order; and fourth, there is every indication that during infancy, the brain has a built-in genius for learning language that it does not have in later years.

Much of the remainder of this article will be an attempt to show that we know enough about printed language skills to select and order the most appropriate subskills—the ones that will get the child off to the fastest start—the ones that will work the most immediate and substantial increase in his intelligence. Moreover, we can start a program of infant enrichment with feasible expenditures of R & D competence, money, and entrepreneursmanship. The next section will address three questions.

II. THE PHILOSOPHY OF SCIENCE OF EXPERIMENT STATIONS

1. How can we simplify materials to the extent that printed language can be taught during the period of explosive neuron growth? By progressing from the techniques of craftsmanship to the techniques of engineering. Craftsmen who build houses, for example, must assemble their wood, stone, thatch, etc. into a finished product before they can tell how well that particular assemblage of materials will work. Engineers, on the other hand, can manipulate numbers instead of manipulating the actual materials. They have measures on the various characteristics of their materials. This enables them to precalculate the probable strengths of 100 different assemblages and discard the weaker 99. The history of science shows that there tends to be a rapid spurt in efficiency as soon as a craft advances to an engineernig science.

2. Why is engineering not possible in the applied fields of the behavioral sciences? Because the necessary measures on the materials do not exist. The behavioral sciences have modeled themselves after the physical sciences such as physics and chemistry. Frequently, the physical sciences can apply straightforward mathematics to the findings of laboratory experiments and transform them into tables that technicians can use. But there are no mathematics for transforming findings on proactive transfer, for example, into a set of tables that will tell a first-grade teacher which words, phonic rules, grammatical rules, etc. can be assembled into the most effective instructional program.

3. What is a better model for the behavioral sciences? Perhaps agriculture, at least for the applied behavioral sciences like education. Education is at about the same stage as agriculture in the 1840s when the first agricultural experiment stations were being established. Although great advances had been made in the chemistry and biology of plant

nutrition, an academic chemist would have known less than a shrewd peasant about which particular chemical fertilizer would give best results on a particular crop in a particular soil.

A. Agricultural Experiment Stations

This section will expand the answers to the above three questions by arguing that agricultural experiment stations provide a promising model for building an applied science of education. Educational research is patterned after the theory-building strategy of the physical sciences, but the detailed analysis and measurement practiced at agricultural stations may be more appropriate for certain educational problems. In reading, for example, there are conspicuous parallels between the current state of affairs and those of agriculture before the establishment of the first experiment station in 1843. Until that time, basic sciences such as chemistry had exerted little effect upon crop production. Dalton had presented his theory of atomic structure almost 40 years before, but a chemist interested in increasing crop production would have had no knowledge of such agricultural phenomena as nitrogen fixation, nor would he have had systematic knowledge in the form of tables giving the effect of particular fertilizers upon particular crops. His scientific insights were so far removed from the farm that he could have improved few of the calculated guesses that a shrewd peasant could make.

His potential contribution depended upon his methods for analyzing and measuring the materials that affect plant nutrition. By applying these methods, chemists at agricultural experiment stations began collecting systematic data that soon laid the foundation for scientific agriculture. In the milieu of an educational experiment station, an experimental psychologist might begin building the foundation for an applied science of reading by following the same strategy followed by Sir Joseph Henry Gilbert in his position as chemist at the first agricultural experiment station. Like chemistry, psychology has methods for making precise measures that can transmute crafts into applied sciences. This article will describe a few tables of measures that are needed to convert the craft of developing educational programs into a science.

B. Raising a Craft to an Applied Science

At present, an educational programmer who tries to choose the most effective words or sounds to assemble into a reading program has nothing better than calculated guesses about the characteristics of potential materials. To return to the agricultural analogy, he is in much the position of a farmer several hundred years ago. The farmer had practical knowledge about the gross effects of manure and silt, but he had no understanding of the constituents of fertilizers and soils that were actually responsible for plant nutrition. He did not even have tables that gave the increase to be expected when a particular fertilizer was applied to a particular crop, although thoughtful farmers could have appreciated the value of such tables. George Washington's diary of April 14, 1760 described a controlled experiment he attempted at Mount Vernon.

He tested the increase to be expected from marl, black mold, mud, clay, sand, and manure from cows, sheep, and horses. Each was placed in a separate box with two pecks of earth and "mixed in the most effectual manner by reducing the whole to a tolerable degree of fineness and ju[m]bling them well together in a Cloth. In each of the divisions was planted three grains of Wheat, 3 of Oats and as many of Barley." On May 1, the diary related that "The two Grains in No. 8 were I think rather the strongest, but upon the whole No. 9 was the best." No. 8 had contained sheep manure and No. 9 black mold (Washington, 1925).

In the 1830s and 1840s, such modest field experiments were raised to the required level of precision by applying the measurement and analytic techniques of chemistry. On his farm in Alsace, Jean Baptiste Joseph Dieudonne Boussingault developed methods for field experiments that are still followed. He weighed and analyzed the soil, the manures, and the crop. Among his first results was the discovery that there was far more carbon in the crop than had been supplied by the manure, thus confirming de Saussure's conclusion that the carbon came from the air. Such straightforward methods soon answered many basic questions of plant nutrition. The publication of Justus von Liebig's *Die Chemie in ihrer Anwendung auf Agricultur und Physiologie* systematized the techniques into an academic science. In this influential volume, von Liebig also suggested that the mineral constituents could be more conveniently supplied as simple salts, an idea already being tested from the applied standpoint by Sir John Bennet Lawes.

In 1843, field experiments began to be conducted on the required scale with the establishment of the first agricultural experiment station at Rothamsted by Sir John. He had just patented a process for treating mineral phosphates with acid, thereby founding the synthetic fertilizer industry. Wishing to study the effects of his synthetic fertilizer in a systematic manner, he induced one of von Liebig's PH.D.s, Joseph Henry Gilbert, to join him. The two initiated the continuous field treatment in which a crop is grown on the same plot year after year, each plot always receiving the same fertilizer. Over the years, the difference between good and poor treatments steadily increases, and the simplest farmboy can understand the dramatic visual difference between adjacent plots (Hall, 1905).

The methods of linguistics and experimental psychology, applied in studies as straightforward as those of Lawes and Gilbert or Boussingault or even George Washington, can calibrate the language units that constitute a reading program. If an Educational Experiment Station in Reading were to collect such measures on the scale that field studies are performed at agricultural experiment stations, a set of tables would quickly accumulate that would permit reading programs to be designed in the sense that an engineer designs—rather than fashions—a taller skyscraper.

To design a reading program in the engineering sense, an elemental prerequisite is a systematic set of measures on the letters, morphemes, phonic rules, grammatical rules, and other language units that will be assembled into the program. With measures, the educational programmer could operate as an engineer, precalculating the probable effectiveness of hundreds of tentative assemblages at inconsequential time and expense. Without them, he must operate as at present, as a craftsman, carefully fashioning materials into a single physical program which is then tested in the classroom.

For the benefit of those who reason from the viewpoint of the physical sciences, it may be worthwhile to elaborate on the implications of not having systematic tables. One of the purposes of a highschool course in general science is to show that basic knowledge from the physical sciences can be transformed into useful tables with straightforward mathematical formulas. This pattern of reasoning may have obscured the obvious; the basic knowledge of the behavioral sciences is usually restricted by some limiting condition such as the use of nonsense syllables or albino rats and it is seldom possible to use mathematics to transform it into applied knowledge—for example, into tables that calibrate the letters, phonic rules, etc. that are important to reading. (See Section X for a nontechnical mathematical statement of why this is so.)

As a consequence, before reading can be raised to an applied science, each pertinent unit will have to be calibrated by direct experimentation much as Boussingault analyzed and weighed the particular elements important to plant nutrition.

C. Analyzing Printed Language into Constituent Skills: A First Approximation

The first step for an experiment station would be to analyze printed language into a set of constituent skills. Then, using young children as calipers, the station would calibrate the appropriate language units according to the several skills. Since linguistics and the psychology of verbal learning, the sciences that underlie printed language, have developed techniques capable of handling only the simplest reading processes, the complex behavior that constitutes reading must be analyzed into skills each of which is simple enough to yield to the experimental techniques these sciences have developed. Table I presents an incomplete first approximation to an analysis; it is restricted to the first year of reading only; its only purpose is to suggest the first calibration experiments.

The constituent skills of Table I are forms of concept induction or paired associate learning. Ever since Ebbinghaus published *Über das Gedächtnis* in 1885, psychologists have been developing techniques for studying these learning processes. They have techniques for analyzing them into still simpler subprocesses (Battig, 1968), and they have a considerable collection of studies that have measured the variables that affect the subprocesses.

As might be expected, however, studies performed by theoretically inclined psychologists used language and learner populations that are of

TABLE I

Partial List of Skills Involved in Early Printed language[a]

Stimulus	Response
Skill 1. Child perceived printed word as a whole	He says word; he recognizes whole word-shape
Skill 2. Child sees letter	He says phoneme
Skill 3. Child hears phoneme	He gives letter
Skill 4. Child hears phoneme	He prints letter
Sounding out a word	
Skill 5. Child sees printed word	He segments into sequence of letters, and/or syllables, and/or morphemes
Skill 6. Sequence of letters, and/or syllables, and/or morphemes	He maps into sequence of phonemes, sylllables, morphemes
Skill 7. Child hears sequence of isolated sounds (that he says himself)	He blends into word
Spelling a word	
Skill 8. Child hears word	He segments into sequence of phonemes
Skill 9. Sequence of phonemes (that he says himself)	He maps into sequence of letters

[a] For simplicity of explanation, Table I has assumed a regularized English.

scant importance to reading, and therefore, in order to calibrate pertinent units, similar studies must be performed on relevant populations. A systematic strategy for collecting this extensive hierarchy of calibrations might start at the most general level with broadband studies of the gross skills, and then, as soon as a coherent pattern began to emerge, narrowband studies could be conducted that plot the variables that affect the subprocesses.

III. BROADBAND STUDIES

A broadband study is one that calibrates pertinent language units according to one of the broad skills of Table I.

The broadband studies can be outlined by summarizing a sample of exploratory studies carried out over the past 10 years for the express purpose of formulating an efficient research strategy for an experiment station in reading. The return from agricultural research can be expressed as increase in yield per acre; the return from reading research might be expressed as increase in the efficiency of getting the child to a functional level of reading. He achieves a functional level in Skill 1 as soon as he masters a sufficient number of words to read meaningful stories. The number of words required to get a child to this level might be substantially reduced by systematic selection, since, like seed varieties, some words are more productive than others, i.e., some sets of them combine with one another to yield larger numbers of sentences. Systematic selection might also reduce the difficulty of learning the set since some words are learned with only a small fraction of the effort required to learn others. It follows that it would be worthwhile to conduct broadband studies that calibrate each language unit for (1) productivity and (2) ease of learning. Broadband studies will be illustrated with calibrations of the units pertinent for Skills 1, 2, and 7 of Table I.

A. Skill 1: Calibrating Words for Productivity

Skill 1 is look–say learning of whole words. Measures of productivity are not only necessary for designing programs that will get the child to functional levels with maximum dispatch; they serve a methodological purpose as well. An educational experiment station cannot restrict itself to studying small samples of language units; it must scale entire populations, or, if the population is too large to be treated exhaustively, it must at least focus its effort on the most important members. In scaling words, this means that the core to be studied should be selected according to productivity or, as a first approximation, according to frequency of usage with the caveat that it may be necessary to add subsets selected by other criteria. A number of investigators have tallied the frequency with which the words of English are used. Rinsland (1945), for example, provides a count based on 353,874 words of conversation by the appropriate age group, 5- and 6-year-olds. Horn (1927) provides another count for this age group based on 489,555 words. The frequency of occurrence of each word in both counts was summed and transformed to a percentage, and then the words were rank-ordered according to that percentage.

Table II, an excerpt from the top and bottom of the rank-ordering, provides several insights about children's usage of words. Note the words that lie in the upper regions of Table II, and note the percentages in the next to last column. These individual percentages might be accepted as, or transformed into, an index of the importance of particular words. Note also the last column which gives cumulative percentage. For example, out of 1000 words of conversation by the average 6-year-old, 250 of them will be repetitions of the first 10 words on the list. Similarly, the first 20 account for 34% of the 6-year-old's verbal behavior, the first 100 account for 61%, and so on. The message of the percentages is inescapable. They show how to study the population as exhaustively as is economically feasible—the 500 words that account for 84% of the child's verbal behavior, the 1000 that account for 92%, or whatever degree of exhaustiveness is desired.

B. Skill 1: Calibrating Words for Ease of Learning

Calibrations have been reported elsewhere (e.g., Coleman, 1970) that scale the most frequently used words for learnability. A paired-associate technique was used to teach the child to read the words, the printed word being the stimulus and pronouncing it being the response. Each word was then scaled by averaging the errors the children made in learning to read it. The sort of data that were collected is depicted in simplified fashion by Skill 1 of Fig. 1. The important point is that some words are many times as hard to learn as others. Other experimenters have scaled the words using other measures (e.g., Ranson, 1970, used free recall) and found much the same magnitude of differences. An educational programmer could use the tables in choosing items for initial instruction since they show which words are easiest to learn, the ones to use when the child is struggling with the base concept of reading, and they also show which words are difficult and will necessitate extra effort. Straightforward analysis of the words into categories suggests narrow-

TABLE II

Words Ranked as to Frequency of Usage by 6-Year-Olds

Rank Word	Frequency in 353,874 (Rinsland)	Frequency in 489,555 (Horn)	Total Frequency in 843,429	Percentages	Cumulative percentage
1. *I*	18740	21893	40633	4.8176	4.8176
2. *a*	14830	20582	35412	4.1986	9.0162
3. *the*	10126	15734	25860	3.0661	12.0822
4. *to*	9469	12611	22080	2.6179	14.7001
5. *and*	8360	11737	20097	2.3828	17.0829
6. *it*	7611	10025	17636	2.0910	19.1739
7. *is*	7601	7755	15356	1.8207	20.9945
8. *you*	5929	7129	13058	1.5482	22.5427
9. *my*	4805	6714	11519	1.3657	23.9085
10. *in*	3940	6016	9956	1.1804	25.0889
11. *we*	3897	5078	8975	1.0641	26.1530
12. *have*	4362	4496	8858	1.0502	27.2032
13. *that*	3146	4839	7985	.9467	28.1500
14. *on*	2593	4885	7478	.8866	29.0366
15. *this*	2618	4371	6989	.8286	29.8652
16. *me*	3744	3083	6827	.8094	30.6747
17. *going*	2177	4537	6714	.7960	31.4707
18. *he*	2961	3452	6413	.7603	32.2310
19. *one*	2498	3748	6246	.7405	32.9716
20. *of*	2135	3803	5938	.7040	33.6756
.					
.					
.					
.					
.					
984. *Valentines*	39	?	92	.0110	92.1175
985. *dead*	30	62	92	.0109	92.1284
986. *skip*	31	61	92	.0109	92.1393
987. *stuff*	21	71	92	.0109	92.1502
988. *woman*	43	49	92	.0109	92.1611
989. *bank*	34	57	91	.0108	92.1719
990. *Jesus*	?	53	91	.0108	92.1827
991. *anyway*	46	44	90	.0107	92.1934
992. *brings*	38	?	90	.0107	92.2041
993. *calf*	38	?	90	.0107	92.2149
994. *chalk*	38	?	90	.0107	92.2256
995. *curls*	38	?	90	.0107	92.2364
996. *either*	44	46	90	.0107	92.2470
997. *nurse*	38	?	90	.0107	92.2578
998. *planted*	42	48	90	.0107	92.2684
999. *sentences*	38	?	90	.0107	92.2792
1000. *shirt*	38	?	90	.0107	92.2899

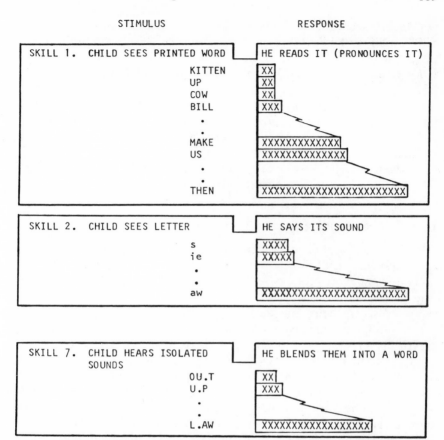

Fig. 1. A sample of the broadband tables to be collected by an experiment station. The bar diagrams, which give the difficulty of learning each unit to criterion, were derived by averaging together several studies. Each X represents one error to criterion.

band studies that will isolate variables that determine why the words rank-order as they do. For example, nouns of high image-evoking potential appear easy to learn and verbs that combine with particles (*get up, take up*) appear difficult.

C. Skill 2: Calibrating Letter–Sound Associations for Ease of Learning

Using a similar paired-associate task except that a letter was the stimulus and pronouncing its sound was the response, an experiment reported by Rentel (1969) rank-orders 35 letters and letter-combinations (*sh, th, ch*) according to the ease with which children learn their sounds. Skill 2 of Fig. 1 illustrates the kind of results that he and others have collected (e.g., Coleman, 1970, p. 11). As with words, grouping the letter–sounds into categories suggests narrowband studies of characteristics that may determine relative difficulty. For example, the characteristic that accounts for most of the variance in learnability appears to be the manner of articulation of the sound. For example, sibilants (a mean of 2.33 errors to criterion) were easier to learn than long vowels (3.28 errors) which were easier than stops (5.30 errors) which were easier than short vowels (5.94 errors). [See Coleman (1970, p. 12) for a more detailed discussion of promising narrowband studies.]

D. Skill 7: Calibrating Isolated Sounds for Ease of Blending

Skill 7, an essential component of phonics, is blending isolated sounds (*u.p*) into the word (*up*). Laumbach (1968) used 4-year-olds to calibrate all two-sound words for ease of blending their constituents into the word. She pronounced the two isolated sounds (*ou . . . t*) with a 1 second pause between them, and the child's task was to pronounce the word (*out*). Using the same task, Coleman (1970, p. 14) scaled all combinations of vowels and consonants that form CV and VC syllables.

In a more extensive study of blending, I calibrated the blendability of six consonant–vowel combinations: C.V/t.oo/, V.C /i.t/, C.CV~ /s.tu~/, CC.V~ /st.u~/, ~VC.C /~an.k/, and ~V.CC /~a.nk/. The ~ stands for varying numbers of phonemes so that there were 24 different types of blends. The word frequency data illustrated by Table II show that 6-year-olds use 23 initial CCs and 35 final CCs; each of them was calibrated, thereby exhausting the population of consonants I want to generalize to.

Ten preschool children were used as subjects. Each of them was given 24 blends (one for each blend type) each day for 10 days. By giving each child a different sample of 240 words, I was able to come close to exhausting the population of words I want to generalize to—namely, the population most likely to be taught in a beginning reading program.

One general finding of all these studies was that phonic blending is a concept; after trying a dozen or so blends, 4-year-olds began successfully blending larger and larger percentages of isolated pairs they had never heard before. Thus, a specific result of the studies were 24 concept induction curves showing which of the different blend types were most quickly mastered. The data were also grouped into a table rank-ordering each of the 23 initial and 35 final CCs as to blendability. Other arrangements of the data suggest a number of hypotheses for testing in narrowband studies. For example, in a V.C blend, it appears to be easier to blend an unvoiced /a.t/ than a voiced consonant /a.d/. For example, longer blends are easier: /rabbi.t/ is easier than /spi.t/ which in turn is easier than /i.t/.

More generally, as with Skills 1 and 2, some blends (*maca.roni, tele.phone*) were 10 to 20 times easier than others (*l.aw, t.ea*). To sum up the message of the broadband studies, Fig. 1 shows that the difference in language units is at least as great as say the difference in rice varieties that more than doubled crop yields in Asia after World War II.

IV. FIRST-LEVEL NARROWBAND STUDIES

A narrowband study is a finegrained study that calibrates the same units as a broadband study, but according to a subprocess of a reading skill.

Broadband studies were illustrated by scaling the language units of Skills 1, 2, and 7. But most of the skills of Table I can be analyzed into at least three subprocesses: (a) discriminating the stimulus units from one another, (b) mastering the response, and (c) pairing the stimuli and responses correctly. Scaling a set of language units according to one of these subprocesses will be called a first-level narrowband study. Let us consider narrowband studies for two subprocesses of Skill 2.

A. Scaling the Stimulus Units of Letter–Sound Associations for Discriminability

In Skill 2, learning the sounds of the letters, the child must first be able to discriminate the letter stimuli from one another. A number of investigators have studied which letters cause most problems at the stimulus discrimination stage. For example, Popp (1964) used nonreading kindergarteners as subjects to compare each letter with every other letter. She projected one letter, and then asked the child to pick it out from a pair of letters. Table III is a confusion matrix giving a rearrangement of her data to show how often the child confused each letter with every other.

As will be demonstrated in more detail for the next narrowband calibrations, one can use such a confusion matrix to pinpoint which letters cause trouble, why they cause it, and what might be done to reduce it. In passing, simply note that the largest number of confusions occur with mirror images: *d–b* with 9 confusions and *p–q* with 10 (why not join *q* to *u* and always print them as a ligature qu?). It is interesting to refer

TABLE III
Confusion Matrix Showing Which Letters Are Confused with Others

Total number of errors		u	q	d	h	p	v	b	e	f	i	k	t	r	y	x	j	m	z	n	o	s	c	l	a	g	w
65	u		3	3	6	4	4	1	4	1	1	4	6	1	3	1	0	2	4	5	3	2	1	1	3	0	2
63	q	3		4	4	10	3	7	2	4	2	1	0	0	0	1	1	3	4	2	2	2	1	2	1	3	1
58	d	3	4		5	7	2	9	2	2	0	0	0	1	0	3	1	2	2	1	3	3	0	3	0	1	4
57	h	6	4	5		0	1	3	2	1	3	4	1	0	5	1	3	2	0	5	1	1	2	2	3	2	0
57	p	4	10	7	0		2	6	1	1	2	1	1	1	0	1	3	0	3	3	1	1	0	0	3	4	2
52	v	4	3	2	1	2		1	1	2	3	1	3	4	4	3	1	4	1	1	2	2	1	1	3	1	1
51	b	1	7	9	3	6	1		1	2	2	1	1	1	0	1	2	3	3	0	2	0	3	0	1	1	0
50	e	4	2	2	2	1	1	1		3	2	2	3	2	0	2	0	1	2	2	1	4	5	1	3	1	3
49	f	1	4	2	1	1	2	2	3		2	1	3	3	1	2	3	3	1	2	0	3	1	1	3	2	2
49	i	1	2	0	3	2	3	2	2	2		2	1	3	3	0	3	3	2	2	2	1	2	6	0	2	0
49	k	4	1	0	4	1	1	1	2	1	2		3	3	6	3	5	2	1	3	1	0	1	0	0	2	2
47	t	6	0	0	1	1	3	1	3	3	1	3		3	4	4	2	1	2	2	1	1	1	2	2	0	0
44	r	1	0	1	0	1	4	1	2	3	3	3	3		4	1	1	2	2	0	2	2	2	3	0	1	2
43	y	3	0	0	5	0	4	0	0	1	3	6	4	4		1	1	0	2	1	1	1	0	3	1	1	1
42	x	1	1	3	1	1	3	1	2	2	0	3	4	1	1		1	1	2	1	2	1	3	1	2	2	2
41	j	0	1	1	3	3	1	2	0	3	3	5	2	1	1	1		1	2	1	0	1	4	3	1	1	0
41	m	2	3	2	2	0	4	3	1	3	3	2	1	2	0	1	1		0	2	3	2	0	3	0	1	0
41	z	4	4	2	0	3	1	3	2	1	2	1	2	2	2	2	0	0		1	1	3	0	1	0	1	1
39	n	5	2	1	5	3	1	0	2	2	2	3	2	0	1	1	1	2	1		2	1	0	1	0	0	1
38	o	3	2	3	1	1	2	2	1	0	2	1	1	2	1	2	0	3	1	2		1	2	0	1	3	1
37	s	2	2	3	1	1	2	0	4	3	1	0	1	2	1	1	1	2	3	1	1		2	0	2	0	1
36	c	1	1	0	2	0	1	3	5	1	2	1	1	2	0	3	4	0	0	0	2	2		0	2	1	2
36	l	1	2	3	2	0	1	0	1	1	6	0	2	3	3	1	3	3	1	1	0	0	0		0	1	1
35	a	3	1	0	3	3	3	1	3	3	0	0	2	0	1	2	1	0	0	0	1	2	2	0		3	1
35	g	0	3	1	2	4	1	1	1	2	2	2	0	1	1	2	1	1	1	0	3	0	1	1	3		1
31	w	2	1	4	0	2	1	0	3	2	0	2	0	2	1	2	0	0	1	1	1	1	2	1	1	1	

to Taylor's article, Section IV (this volume) and note that the letters of the Korean alphabet do not suffer from such problems of stimulus discrimination. Moreover, the letters were designed to make it easy to discriminate the consonants as a group from the vowels as a group.

B. Scaling the Response Units of Letter–Sound Associations According to Level of Mastery

In learning the sounds of the letters, the second subprocess is that the child must be able to make the response; in the skill under discussion, he must be able to enunciate the sound.

One can assemble studies that give a crude indication of which sounds give young children the most difficulty. Normative studies that measure the age at which the child first uses each sound meaningfully have been conducted by Wellman, Chase, Mengert, and Bradbury (1931), by Poole (1934), and by Templin (1957).

Another way to rank the isolated sounds as to level of mastery is to ask the child to repeat the sound after it is pronounced in isolation—in other words, to echo it. Marsh and Sherman (1971) have rank ordered the sounds according to the echoing task. A reanalysis of the data—casting them into the confusion matrix of Table IV—shows that children make almost all the errors when attempting to echo a handful of sounds.

TABLE IV

Confusion Matrix Showing Which Incorrect Responses Children Gave to 23 Stimulus Sounds

Child's response											Stimulus presented to child													Total errors
	h	t	p	y	k	d	w	s	b	z	sh	r	g	j	m	n	ch	v	f	ng	l	*th*	th	
v	—	—	—	—	—	—	1ª	—	3	—	—	—	—	—	2	2	—	—	2	—	—	103	1	114
s	—	—	—	—	1	—	—	—	—	—	5	2	—	—	—	—	2	1	—	43	—	—	54	108
m	—	—	—	—	—	—	—	—	—	—	—	—	—	—	—	33	—	—	—	65	—	2	—	100
f	—	—	—	—	—	—	—	—	3	—	—	—	—	—	—	—	—	2	—	—	—	8	82	95
n	—	—	—	—	—	—	—	—	—	1	—	—	—	—	29	—	—	—	—	24	—	—	1	57
z	—	—	—	—	—	—	3	—	—	—	—	—	4	2	—	—	29	1	—	—	—	13	—	52
sh	—	—	—	—	—	—	—	—	—	—	—	—	—	32	—	8	—	—	—	—	—	1	2	43
ch	—	—	—	1	—	—	—	—	—	8	—	—	17	—	—	—	—	1	—	—	—	—	—	27
th	—	—	—	—	—	—	—	—	1	—	—	—	—	—	—	—	11	2	—	—	—	—	1	15
th	—	—	—	—	—	—	4	—	1	—	—	—	—	—	—	—	2	8	—	—	—	—	—	15
w	—	—	—	—	—	—	—	—	—	—	10	—	—	—	—	—	—	—	—	—	—	—	1	11
d	—	—	—	—	—	—	—	2	—	—	1	5	—	—	—	—	1	—	—	—	1	—	—	10
g	—	—	—	—	3	—	—	—	—	—	—	5	—	—	—	—	—	—	—	—	—	—	—	8
j	—	—	—	—	—	—	—	—	—	1	—	—	—	—	—	3	—	1	—	—	—	—	—	5
t	—	—	—	—	1	—	—	—	—	—	2	—	—	—	—	—	—	—	—	—	—	—	2	5
k	—	—	—	—	—	—	—	—	—	5	—	—	—	—	—	—	—	—	—	—	—	—	—	5
p	—	—	—	—	—	—	—	—	—	—	—	—	—	—	—	4	—	—	—	—	—	—	—	4
b	—	—	—	—	—	—	—	—	—	—	—	—	1	—	1	—	—	—	—	1	—	—	—	3
r	—	—	—	—	—	2	—	—	—	—	—	—	1	—	—	—	—	—	—	—	—	—	—	3
y	—	—	—	—	—	—	—	—	—	—	—	—	1	—	—	—	—	1	—	—	—	—	—	2
h	—	—	—	—	—	—	—	—	—	—	—	—	—	—	—	—	—	—	—	—	—	—	—	
ng	—	—	—	—	—	—	—	—	—	—	—	—	—	—	—	—	—	—	—	—	—	—	—	
l	—	—	—	—	—	—	—	—	—	—	—	—	—	—	—	—	—	—	—	—	—	—	—	
Total errors					3	3	3	7	8	9	10	11	12	27	34	38	40	47	66	89		131	144	682

275 (bracket under *th* th)

ª Values represent child's incorrect response.

Note that five sounds, those for v, f, ng, and the two th sounds account for 477 out of the total of 682 errors. In fact, errors for th alone account for 275, or 40%, or the errors. A reanalysis of a similar experiment by Bricker (1967) shows similar percentages. Because the stimulus as well as the response is changed, the echoing technique is admittedly imperfect as a measure of response mastery. But since accurate auditory perception precedes accurate speech production, Table IV probably reflects response mastery well enough for preliminary work.

The point is that this table of calibrations shows that in the response mastery subprocess, most children have difficulty with only four or five sounds (*th*, **th**, *l*, *f*, *v*). The analysis tells a person designing instructional materials that when he is concerned with response mastery, he should concentrate on this handful of units rather than dissipating his effort, as is current practice, in an equal distribution across all sounds. Study the percentages and mentally compute the percentage of effort that the child might be spared by a more efficient distribution.

Further analysis will enable the designer to pinpoint his instruction still more effectively. Even a casual study of the matrix in Table IV will show anyone having a nodding acquaintance with linguistics that most of the confusions (some 90%) were due to errors in **place** of articulation (note the confusions to /v/, for example), not to errors in manner of articulation or errors in voicing. So multiply your above mental computation of probable savings by 5 or 10 magnitudes. By way of summary, this table of calibrations shows that most children had most difficulty with the th sounds and the difficulty lay in misplacing their tongue, teeth, and other articulators. The learning aids of Fig. 2 show how an as yet nonexistent education engineer could use such information to focus upon the particular subprocess and the particular problem within the subprocess that causes most of the difficulty in learning the association [the reader should also refer to Taylor's article, Section IV (this volume) and her Table VII to see how Korean scholars of the fifteenth century built the same kind of learning aid directly into their alphabet].

Summary. First-level narrowband studies were illustrated by scaling the pertinent language units for two subprocesses of a single skill, learning the sounds of the letters. Further, one of the scalings was analyzed to illustrate the massive savings that result from pinpointing which units cause difficulty and pinpointing why they are difficult. It is not unreasonable to assume that the full set of narrowband studies of all the skills of the Table I would pinpoint other sources of difficulty and suggest their solutions. The suggested solutions suggest in turn more finegrained narrowband studies which will be called second-level narrowband studies.

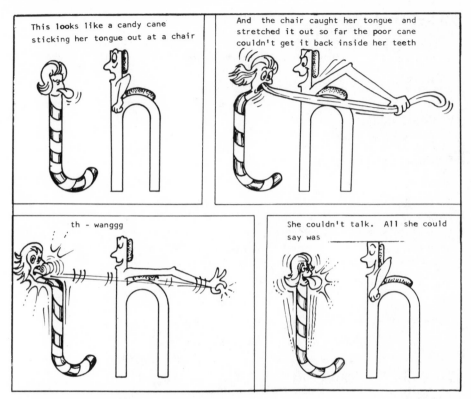

Fig. 2. Studying the errors in the *th* columns of Table IV will explain the reasoning behind the story and why it focuses upon the position of the articulators.

V. SECOND-LEVEL NARROWBAND STUDIES

A second-level narrowband study is a still more finegrained study that calibrates pertinent language units according to some single characteristic that influences ease of learning.

Imagery is an example of a characteristic that promises handsome rewards for second-level scaling studies because it probably facilitates all three subprocesses of paired associate learning. The present section will discuss the effects of imagery on a single skill, the same skill of the previous section, learning the sounds of the letters. Introspectively described images will be collected to each letter (the stimuli) and cast into a habit hierarchy. Then analogous images will be collected to each letter's sound (the responses) and cast into a matching hierarchy.

A. Collecting Images to the Printed Shapes

The images to the printed shapes were collected from 40 undergraduates in a group. The subjects were asked to look at a letter, close their eyes, and form a visual image incorporating the letter shape. They were cautioned to ensure that they were visualizing images to the shape of the letter, not to its name or to its sound. Multiple images were reported by some subjects.

B. Collecting Images to the Sounds

A similar technique was employed to elicit images to the sounds from a new group of 40 subjects. Each subject recorded his responses in a booklet as the experimenter enunciated the letter sounds. To guard against perseveration effects, only eight responses were obtained from each subject on four successive days. Again, the subjects were frequently reminded to be sure that their images were being visualized to the sound, not to its name or its shape.

C. Pairs of Image Hierarchies

I grouped similar images together to yield habit hierarchies such as Fig. 3. There was considerable subjective judgment in this categorization. For example, reports such as:

"Surprise!"
"Child being surprised"

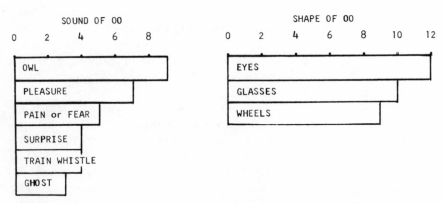

Fig. 3. Pair of image hierarchies to the sound and shape of "OO." The measure is the number of subjects (out of 40) who reported the image.

"Someone surprising me"
"Somebody jumping out at me"

were grouped into one category (surprise); other categorizers might have grouped them differently. More reliable hierarchies could be obtained by using a large number of categorizers, but the present hierarchies will serve to demonstrate the value of the general methodology for working with imagery.

VI. REVIEW AND PREVIEW

A. Review: Collecting Calibrations

I have argued that the findings of basic research in learning are so hemmed in by fixed-effect restrictions that it is impossible to transform them into the sorts of tables necessary to raise the design of educational programs to an applied science (also see Section X). A possible answer is suggested by agricultural experiment stations; namely, use the particular subjects of interest to calibrate the particular units of interest according to the particular skill of interest. (1) First, the collection of brandband tables was illustrated by experiments that calibrated the language units pertinent to look–say learning, phonics, and phonic blending. (2) Then more finegrained calibrations were illustrated by scaling the letters and sounds according to two of the subprocesses of paired-associate learning, namely, according to the ease of discriminating the letter stimuli from one another and according to the ease of echoing the phoneme responses. (3) Finally, still more finegrained calibrations were illustrated by collecting a pair of image hierarchies to each letter–sound association.

B. Other Calibrations

It should be made clear that the above is only a small sample of broadband and narrowband calibrations. A fairly complete set exists on printing skills, for example. Coleman (1970) and Karagouris (1969) have conducted broadband studies which scale each letter according to the ease of 4-year-old's learning to print it. Himelstein (1971) did a narrowband study which scaled each of the constituent strokes that comprise the letters. She also scaled the different ways of combining the strokes. Both Karagouris and Himelstein plotted learning curves on 11 errors that children make when they are learning to print (e.g., printing a mirror image of the stimulus).

These 11 error curves are particularly useful; they tell an instructional designer which mistakes justify little concern because they disappear almost automatically with a little casual practice (for example, making circles instead of dots, making 90-degree rotations, perseverative errors, and closure errors). Equally important, the curves tell the designer that certain mistakes are so refractory that it might be prudent to bypass them in an introductory program. Mirror images, for example, are important to discriminating a few letters only, but the curves suggest that a massive expenditure of time and frustration would be required to eliminate this error. The value received is probably not worth the cost. In other words, some mistakes are so formidable that they are best ignored temporarily like redoubts bypassed by an army, trusting that later strategies such as use of context will reduce them to insignificance.

C. Preview: A Mix of Engineering and Craftsmanship

A good bit of engineering rests on the truism that it is more economical to manipulate numbers than things. An engineer does not build a better bridge by putting in, taking out, and rearranging steel and concrete until he gets a structure that works; he does his putting in, taking out, and rearranging with numbers that describe characteristics of these materials. In the same way, a plausible way to derive a more effective instructional program is to start by manipulating numbers (or measures) that describe relevant characteristics of each unit that will go into the program.

The crude calibrations that currently exist will not lead to a design that has the same degree of preordination as say a civil engineer's design for a bridge. The civil engineer can turn his design over to a contractor, confident in the final product, while he goes on to other problems. The first design for an instructional program, on the other hand, is more like the first model for a wind tunnel. Using the usual craftsmanship of product development, the designer himself must further shape the program by running it through a number of test-refine–test-refine iterations. Calculations based on the measures, however, will save him from many false starts and blind alleys. They will also enable him to design a more effective beginning product and to make greater gains in each test-refine cycle.

The next step in this article will be to describe a little of this halfway engineering and show that, crude as it is, it can still lead to reasonably substantial improvements.

VII. A FIRST ATTEMPT AT ENGINEERING: USING IMAGE HIERARCHIES TO DESIGN PHONICS PROGRAMS

In this article "engineering" is defined as exploratory, cut-and-fit techniques. The only thing that qualifies them as engineering is that they are based on a primitive, rank-order mathematics. What is impressive about the techniques is not great sophistication, but how much they accomplish without any.

Some of the engineering—putting the image hierarchies to use, for example—may be enhanced by preliminary experiments designed to answer relatively abstract questions.

A. Experiment 1: Stimulus versus Response versus Overlapping Elaborators

Characteristics of image hierarchies (such as those illustrated in Fig. 3) suggest a number of independent variables crucial to using the images to facilitate learning. Preliminary experiments have been conducted on several obvious variables.

Coleman and Morris (1979) used these hierarchies to facilitate the teaching of the sounds of the letters to preschool children, the printed letter being the stimulus (OO) and the child's pronunciation of its sound /oo/ being the response. We had an artist paint elaborators (learning aids) based on an image from the hierarchies, resulting in four treatments, (a) paired associates with no elaborators, (b) with elaborators painted from response images (i.e., images to sounds), (c) with elaborators painted from stimulus images (i.e., images to the letter shape), and (d) overlapping elaborators painted from a compound of stimulus plus response images. In teaching the sound /oo/, for example, the overlapping elaborator was an owl with huge eyes like OO hooting /oo . . . oo/. If the reader will study the pair of hierarchies in Fig. 3, he can probably think of other overlapping elaborators. Average errors to learning the sound were 5.3 for stimulus elaborators and 3.2 for response elaborators.[2] As might be expected, the paired associates with no elaborators had the

---

[2] Note that elaborators painted from an image to the letter, which concerns stimulus imagery, were less effective than elaborators painted from an image to the sound, which concerns response imagery. Anyone familiar with the imagery research will recognize that this is a complete reversal of a massive body of laboratory findings. Thus, it is a good illustration of the main refrain of this article; there are usually unsuspected problems when one tries to generalize contemporary psychological research beyond the fixed-effect restrictions of the laboratory.

highest number of errors (5.8), and the pairs with overlapping elaborators had the least, only 2.3.

It is hardly surprising that overlapping elaborators should facilitate learning. Consider paired-associate learning to be the building of a mental bridge between the stimulus and response, and consider overlapping elaborators to be a way to build such a bridge. Image hierarchies such as Fig. 3 are crude indicators of analogous hierarchies in the mind, and so overlapping elaborators build the bridge out of building blocks that already exist in the mind.

B. Experiment 2: One versus Two versus Three Overlapping Elaborators

Without pairs of hierarchies such as Fig. 3, it is extraordinarily difficult to think of even a single overlapping elaborator for teaching a child the sound of some of the letters. With pairs of hierarchies, it is relatively simple. So simple, in fact, that a moderately creative cartoonist can think of three or four that associate each letter with its sound. An obvious extension of the Coleman–Morris experiment, therefore, is to compare the relative facilitative effects of one versus several overlapping elaborators.

One plausible interpretation of most learning theories would argue that the single strongest overlapping elaborator presented three times would be more facilitative than three different elaborators, since the second and third elaborators are weaker by necessity. But an equally plausible argument could be made that the strongest elaborator would lose some of its facilitative potential with every repetition. Or, to repeat the refrain of this article, learning theory is not sufficiently quantitative to permit engineering. An experiment using representative boundary conditions must decide between the two alternatives. The experiment (Coleman & Morton, 1976) compared the relative facilitative effects of 0, 1, 2, or 3 overlapping elaborators.

Each of 12 preschool children was taught four letter–sound associates each day for 8 days. In brief, the 0-elaborator pair was presented three times with no elaborator, the 1-elaborator pair was presented three times with the same elaborator, the 2-elaborator pair was presented three times with one of its elaborators shown once and the other twice, and the 3-elaborator pair was presented three times, each time with a different elaborator.

The children were tested by using delayed recall following a 24-hour lag. Each child was tested by shuffling the letters for the four pairs which he had learned the day before, presenting a letter, and asking him to give its sound. The measure of learning was the percentage of correct sounds recalled. The mean percentages for the 0-, 1-, 2-, and 3-elaborator treatments were 21, 37, 50, and 73% respectively. In short, there was massive facilitation—over three to one—in progressing from the 0- to the 3-elaborator treatment. The following points suggest that the facilitation might be increased even more:

1. The picture elaborators were crudely drawn; substantial improvements could be made.

2. Elaborators were presented as line drawings; significant improvement could be made by presenting them in animation.

3. The verbal component of each elaborator was a simple story. There is good reason to suspect that facilitation could be increased by employing such devices as rhyme, alliteration, and song.

C. Experiment 3: Prose versus Rhyme versus Song

Marilynn Deutch (1975) followed up the third point. She used the 3-elaborator technique to teach the letter–sound correspondences to trainable retardates. Her independent variable was having the verbal component of the elaborational story in prose, or in rhyme, or in song. As expected, there were significant differences in favor of rhyme over prose and in favor of song over rhyme. In other words, rhyme and song further improved the 3-to-1 improvement of the preceding experiment.

Clearly, there is little point in teaching children as incapacitated as trainable retardates a skill as abstract as phonics. It would be more practical to apply the same technique to teach them a handful of useful words such as *stop, go, men, women,* and the like. The point is simply that by accumulating facilitation effects, the most abstract concepts of printed language can be brought within the competence of extremely restricted intellects. And there are quite a few more improvements still in the wings, waiting to be added to Deutch's improvement of the Coleman–Morton treatment. Several of the more obvious ones are professional art work, color, and animation.

The improvement with greatest potential, however, would be based on little dramas like the one in Fig. 4. Specifically, a reasonably creative cartoonist could tie each letter's overlapping images into a coherent story like the one for OO. Then he could work and rework these 30 some odd little stories until they could be strung together into a single narrative plot, or perhaps into three or four related narratives. And finally, these longer narratives would be produced as animated songs, each lasting about four or five minutes.

Summary. Calibrations on the language units to be assembled into an enrichment program can lead to massive gains in the program's instruc-

Fig. 4. Three overlapping images tied into a little story. With**out** pairs of image hierarchies, it is almost impossible to think of overlapping images for most of the letters; **with** them, it is surprisingly easy. If you will study the pair of hierarchies in Fig. 3, you can probably add more overlapping images to the above story: a little boy goggle-eyed in fear of the ghost; then changing to wide-eyed pleasure when offered a ride, and on and on. To appreciate the full potential of the image hierarchies, imagine a little drama like this for each of the letters, and then imagine them strung together into a coherent narrative, and presented in animation and song.

tional efficiency. Given pairs of image hierarchies, creative cartoonists will sooner or later reduce the basic concepts of phonics to a single animated song that ties 30 some odd little dramas like Fig. 4 into a single plot. It does not seem unduly extravagant to hope that such a song would be within the mental competence of a 2-year-old, or to hope that televised public service spots could distribute such a song so widely that the next generation would grow up never remembering a time when they were not masters of the phonic concept. A more speculative hope is that because the concept was learned so young, it would involve a larger amount of growth in basal dendrites and a larger number of synaptic interconnections among cerebral neurons than is the case for the present generation.

VIII. A SECOND EXAMPLE OF ENGINEERING: CONVERGING TOWARD THE OPTIMUM LIST FOR STARTING READING AT THE MEANING-EXTRACTION STAGE

The second example of engineering will attempt to show how to design a reading program that starts at the top with the overall concept of reading and has children extracting meaning from the very beginning. The argument is that most reading programs have a high failure rate because they impose a memory burden that far exceeds the young child's attention span and memory capacity. They require the child to learn as many as 100–500 words before he begins to read stories that approximate his own semantic and syntactic patterns. They have extremely low incentive value because they start at the bottom and teach the child a progression of what is to him meaningless subskills such as the definition of letters and words, top-to-bottom progression, left-to-right progression (which in turn requires teaching him the difference between his left and right hand), and on and on.

There may be fundamental biological reasons for starting at the top, for having the child extract meaning from the very beginning. The human brain is built to extract meaning from language and there must be a considerable overlap between the neural circuits that process printed language and those that process spoken language. Perhaps the solution is to develop a technology that makes better use of the habits, concepts, and strategies that children use to teach themselves spoken language.

A. The Optimum List: An Unattainable Ideal

To start with the meaning-extraction stage and a high reward-to-effort ratio, we want to start the program with easily learned words that generate short, idiomatic, easily read sentences. There is a near infinite number of possible lists of words we could start with. It is intuitively obvious that some lists of words can be learned more easily and enable the student to read more sentences than other lists of the same size. The problem is to select—not the best; that is an impossible dream—but one of the several thousand or several million better lists.

To reduce the number of possible lists somewhat, let us assume a very young reader with a speaking vocabulary of only 2500 words. The 2500 most frequently used words are very familiar, the least frequent of them being words such as *dumb, castle,* and *Indian.* To further reduce the number of lists, this article will concentrate on a rather short list—the first 20 words that will be taught. Straightforward extensions of the techniques can select longer lists. The significance of the question in even this reduced form becomes apparent when one considers that these 2500 extremely familiar words will generate approximately 3,464,040,-997,412,500,000,000,000,000,000,000,000,000,000,000,000 ordered sets each of which has 20 different words. Clearly, some of these sets are better than others in that the child could (1) read more sentences with the words, or (2) that he could learn the 20 words more easily, or (3) that he would induce more phonic rules from them, or (4) that he would find the sentences of more interest, and so on. Some lists will be superior according to some of the above characteristics and some lists will be superior according to others.

To reexpress the problem in an easily visualized format, imagine that through some omniscient process each of the 3.46×10^{49} lists is calibrated according to an effectiveness index that considers all the above characteristics in its "proper" weight, and that the lists are then laid out from most to least effective, with the least effective ones lying quite a few light years beyond Alpha Centuri.

Let's see how much room for improvement we have. Even typed in a column and using small print, each list will require about 1 in. of paper or about 63,360 lists per mile of paper. Note that the number of possible ordered lists has 30 or 40 zeros. To type the 10 billion or so better lists that get out to the first 11 zeros requires a piece of paper over one light second long. By 16 zeros, the lists are ones that lie a light day from the optimum, and the lists at 18 zeros are about a light year away.

After that, the distance of a list from the theoretical ideal **really** starts increasing. The next zero, the nineteenth, gets us to lists that lie 10 light years away, the twentieth gets us 100 light years away, and the twenty-fourth gets us 1,000,000 light years away. And we still have quite a few zeros left. In other words, there are a lot of lists for authors to happen upon, and so there is a lot of room for improvement by eliminating the poorer choices that have been made. It would be unfair to single out a specific publisher, but I assure you that if challenged, I can point to several preprimers, whose authors, communing with their intuitions, happened upon a list that lies somewhere out past Alpha Centuri.

Using halfway engineering based on the crude calibrations that currently exist, we can hardly expect to eliminate all the 3.46×10^{49} poorer lists and get to the theoretical ideal. But perhaps we can eliminate the ones that are so inefficient that they lie outside the solar system—or at least the ones that lie out beyond Alpha Centuri.

The 3.46×10^{49} lists should probably be arranged in slightly different orders for different categories of readers (e.g., suburban Whites, Black ghetto students, and Puerto Ricans will differ somewhat in the words each finds easiest to learn and in the sentences each prefers). At some future time, it may become possible to approximate the appropriate ordering for different groups, converging ultimately toward different orderings for each individual. The "optimum list" that lies at the base of any of these hypothetical orderings is an ideal that will never be attained, of course. We will be fortunate indeed if we ever get within the better 1,000,000. Nevertheless, the concept of a rank-ordering of possible choices that progressively increases in effectiveness and that has a single optimum list at its base is an insightful goal to strive toward. Even the exploratory techniques outlined in this section may get us within the better billion lists or so; at least they appear to yield a list somewhat more effective than any in current use.

The rank-ordering according to effectiveness would vary not only according to individual differences of students but according to those of program designers as well; some designers would weight certain characteristics more heavily than others. A heavy weighting on sentence meaning and matters that concern Goodman (1968) and Lefevre (1964) would yield a rank-ordering (i.e., one like that of Section VIII) that would differ from a heavy weighting on Venezky's (1967) spelling-to-sound correspondences (which might yield an ordering more like the one suggested in Section IX). The techniques that will be outlined in Section VIII may appear to place an extreme emphasis on sentence meaning, but simple qualifications could give heavier weightings to the more molecular characteristics. The unbalanced emphasis in Section VIII is dictated by limitations of space; considerations of learning the individual words have been dealt with previously, and considerations of phonics and phonic blending will be dealt with in more detail in Section IX (see Section VIII,C for an illustration of how the tables enable an emphasis on phonics to be meshed into an emphasis on meaning).

B. Selection Formulas

In brief, this section will summarize an article (Coleman, 1975) that used some simple rank-order mathematics to converge toward an optimum 20-word list that is able to skip the beginner ahead into the meaning-extracting stage of true reading. In selecting lists that get progressively closer to the hypothetical optimum, I focused on selecting a set that produced a maximum number of sentences that are simultaneously useful and easily learned. The first step, therefore, was to measure each English word's potential for generating short, familiar sentences. This in turn required a frequency count on such sentences.

The closest count available at that time were two that had been made on an insufficient number of 4-year-old children, one by Chitwood (1973) who attached a wireless microphone to 43 children and recorded their total production for a day, and one by Newman (1973) who asked 39 young children to give several sentences each containing one of the 160 most frequently used words in English. Since resources were not available for making a more appropriate count on larger numbers, the best I could do was average these counts and refine them with subjective ratings by adults. Using such jury-rig procedures, I developed four rank-ordered tables—rank-orderings of the most frequently used one-, two-, three-, and four-word sentences in English. The ones for one- and two-word sentences will serve to illustrate the technique. From the ordering of 397 two-word sentences, I drew their most frequently used words: *what, can, I, we, will, did, mother, it, do, mine, that, this, he, have, get, had. . . .* For one-word sentences, the rank-ordering was: *No. Yes. Look. Stop. Run. See?. . . .*

Such rank-orderings of words were then used to devise a selection formula that would generate a large number of easily understood sentences. It is necessary to consult the original article (Coleman, 1975) to get the full flavor of the techniques; the basic notion, however, is that I started with a very simple selection formula, one that used only two selection criteria. Specifically, Formula 1, which might be coded as 1222, 1222, 1222 . . . , drew from the top of its lists the word that occurred in the largest number of one-word sentences (*No*), then the three words that occurred most frequently in two-word sentences (*what, can, I*). And so on, mixing the top words from the two rank-orderings in a ratio of 1 to 3: *No what can I. Yes we will did. Look mother it do. . . .*

The resulting set of 20 words was then used to generate a large sample of its possible sentences. The sentences were analyzed and additional selection criteria were tested for their potential in selecting 20-word sets that could generate larger numbers of sentences. Such test-refine iterations quickly showed which selection criteria resulted in sentences that could be further combined into longer sentences. Then a second formula adding the better criteria was tried, refined into a third formula, and so on. Here is Selection Formula 4:

1 2-S 2-M 2-VC 2-Ob 2-VP

where 1 means to select the word used most frequently as a **one**-word sentence and 2 means to select the word with the highest potential for generating **two**-word sentences, except that:

S means that it must be one that can be used as the subject of a sentence (*I, we, Mother . . .*)
M means that it must be a modal auxiliary (*can, will*)
VC means that it must be a content verb (*get, go*)
Ob means that it must be a direct object (*her, this*)
VP means that it must be able to serve as a verb particle (the *in* of *come in*, the *up* of *get up*)

1	2-S	2-M	2-VC	2-Ob	2-VP
No	*what*	*can*	*get*	*it*	*on*
Yes	*I*	*will*	*come*	*mine*	*in*
Look	*we*	*did*	*see*	*that*	*down*
Stop	*mother*				

The 20 words of Selection Formula 4 can generate a huge number of idiomatic sentences: *See? Stop! No. Yes. See that? What did? That did. I can. I will. Get on. Get in. Get down. Stop it. Stop that. Come in. Come on. Get it down. Get what down? Get that down. Come on down,* and on and on and on ad infinitum. Each of the 20 words can be combined with many of the others to generate short idiomatic sentences. Furthermore, the sentences themselves can be combined into many times as many additional sentences: *I can get down. Make Mother get it down. What can stop it? Mother can stop it. See what Mother can get. Come see what I did,* etc., etc., etc. As a second furthermore, many of the sentences can be transformed into questions: *Will (Can, Did) Mother get it down?* As a third and fourth furthermore, most of the sentences are idiomatic in most American dialects and they can be used in many different situations.

Although List 4 generates quite a few easily read sentences, it is still far from the optimum list. We could almost surely select a 20-word list that lay nearer the optimum by adding considerations of learnability. We might get one that lay still closer by using a different formula for choosing word classes. As additional tables become available, one could add other considerations and gradually choose lists that approach closer and closer to the optimum. Usually the added considerations will not provide a mathematically definite choice, only several equally plausible ones. The next step, therefore, is to conduct an experiment that chooses among them.

If a person is familiar with sentences such as *See Jane! See!* that predominate in beginning texts, he might be surprised that selection formulas as simple as the above would go a long way toward solving the problem of stilted sentence structure. The technique of calibrating complete sentences, however, has never been reduced to practice in designing reading programs. There is an infinite number of sets of words the designer could happen upon for initiating instruction, and lacking even crude measures of sentence productivity, there is little probability that he would approximate the set from which the student can most efficiently induce the concept of extracting meaning from print.

The techniques of this article have been described as "mathematical," but picking words from the top of a list may appear singularly **un**mathematical to some readers. The judgment is somewhat unfair; the mathematical essence of the method lies in the tables themselves and the fact that they are actually scales which rank-order their units according to a measure.

At any rate, during the early development of the strategy, concern with punctilious mathematics should not divert attention from the fact that the weightings in the selection formulas must be decided experimentally, not mathematically. The weight given to each index will vary with the goals of the reading program. The optimum lists for different populations may differ in their emphasis on phonics, spelling, printing, reading for meaning, etc.

To recapitulate, some simple rank-order mathematics have been illustrated that solve one problem in starting reading instruction at the meaning-extraction stage, namely, selecting a small set of words which generates a large number of easily read, idiomatic sentences. But perhaps some readers are not convinced that the techniques will continue to work when selecting longer sets. For their benefit, let's apply the techniques to the substantially larger vocabulary of an existing phonics program.

C. Combining an Emphasis on Phonics with an Emphasis on Meaning

Instead of miring the reader down in the details of selection formulas, this section will rest its case on his global value judgment. Specifically, it will provide an example of the use of the calibrations.

Most people are aware that the language of preprimers, especially phonics preprimers, could hardly be described as idiomatic. In fact, most of this language is so awkward that the beginning reader has considerable difficulty in using his knowledge of semantics and syntax to guess unfamiliar words. To make the point of this section (that the above computational techniques can fit colloquial language to existing plots even

when restricted to a phonics vocabulary), I selected the most nonidio-
matic phonics reader I could find and tried to see if my jury-rig calibrations could improve it. Figure 5 gives the story in the original.

In fairness to the program, it should be noted that it is a phonics
program and, in my opinion, one of the best. The following improvement
of the syntax, therefore, illustrates how experiment-station tables would

Fig. 5. This booklet contains the most deviant sentences I could find in current use.
Compare them to those of the booklet in the next figure, one which uses the same plot
told with exactly the same set of words.

Fig. 6. I think this book is quite an improvement on the preceding, but I am willing to let the final judgment rest with others.

enable a program engineer to mesh a bottom-up optimum list with a top-down list.

Using the same general techniques described for the selection formulas, I generated a large sample of the sentences that can be formed from the vocabulary of the story. Then I calibrated each sentence for idiomaticity using the Chitwood rank-orderings (1973) and my modifications of them (Coleman, 1975) as standards. Figure 6 gives the same story told in a refitted dialogue based on these crude calibrations. Leaning over as far

Fig. 6 (continued).

backward as I can without falling down, I still think my version has more idiomatic language and a sharper plot. I also suspect that it would teach a kindergartener a little more about plants and planting. The final judgment, however, I leave to the reader.

Summary. A major refrain of this article has been that educational experiment stations could duplicate the gains of agricultural experiment stations. I am not talking about small gains of say 50 or 150%; I am talking about **big** gains. To appreciate their magnitude, consider the history of corn.

Fig. 6 (continued).

Corn appears to have been first domesticated in Mexico. The earliest wild corn found in the Valley of Tehuacan had cobs no longer than a man's thumbnail. These miniature varieties were dated by radiocarbon at about 5000 B.C. Corn had been domesticated at Tehuacan by 3500 B.C., and by 2300 B.C. the Indians had developed it into a major food crop capable of sustaining the civilization that measured the seasons and computed the length of the year more accurately than the European civilizations of the same time. Despite this long history, in the early 1940s, the average yield per acre in Mexico was about eight bushels.

Fig. 6 (continued).

Compare that to the 200 bushels an acre yielded by hybrids developed by straightforward, almost mechanical, plant breeding strategies at agricultural experiment stations.

In my opinion at least, contemporary reading programs are at about the same level, and have the same potential for improvement, as corn farming in Mexico in 1940. Or, to paraphrase an earlier summary, calibrations on the sentences to be assembled into an enrichment program can lead to substantial improvements in instructional efficiency. It does not seem unduly extravagant to hope that the base concept of reading— extracting meaning from print—could be presented in a handful of animated cartoon lessons. Given sufficient distribution, the next generation might go into the first grade never remembering a time when they were not masters of the meaning-extraction stage of reading. As before, a more speculative hope is that because the concept was learned so young, it would be stored in a larger number of synaptic interconnections than is the case with ourselves. It would not be a problem these children had to think **about**; it would be a tool they thought **with**.

IX. A THIRD EXAMPLE OF ENGINEERING: OPTIMUM LEARNING HIERARCHIES? OR OPTIMUM FEEDBACK LOOPS?

Calibrations are useful not only for designing more efficient sequences of materials; they are equally useful for designing feedback loops, which, as often as not, will be more efficient than fixed, unresponsive sequences.

Actually, the third example will be more like a set of questions than an example of successful engineering. But a good indication that a discipline has advanced to the engineering stage is its potential for putting questions in precise enough form that they automatically suggest useful experiments to the researcher unendowed with the intuitions of genius.

A. Rank-Ordering of Phonic Blends

Recall the 24 types of blends that were calibrated in one of the blending experiments and the 24 concept-induction curves that resulted. These 24 types can be considered to be 24 concepts or blending skills that we need to teach the child. Clearly, these concepts are not separate and distinct, but overlapping; that is, some instructional programmers might group them into a smaller number of concepts, and some into a larger number.

The exact number has no great effect on designing the optimum learning hierarchy. The important point is that the 24 concepts can be ordered from easy to difficult. Moreover, by using the more fine-grained rank-ordering of consonant and consonant clusters given by other arrangements of the data, it would be possible to rank-order 20–100 exemplars under each blending concept. Thus, using the current calibrations on blends, it is possible to get a finely detailed rank-ordering of the 1000–5000 blends one intends to teach the child, for example:

tele.vision, tele.phone, um.brella, el.bow, alli.gator . . .
presiden.t, importan.t . . . spen.t, plan.t . . . ben.t . . . an.t
rabbi.t . . . spi.t . . . i.t

.

.

.

t.elevision . . . t.able . . . t.oot, t.ooth . . . t.oo

B. An Optimum Learning Hierarchy?

This rank-ordering would be considerably more finely detailed and considerably better documented than any learning hierarchy I have ever heard of, but would it be an optimum learning hierarchy? Probably not. Probably no such thing exists.

Most discussions of learning hierarchies appear to assume that the learner should master a lower order concept before advancing to the next higher order one. But an equally plausible assumption is that it would be more efficient for the learner to advance to the higher order concept a little **before** he completely masters the lower order one. Then, he starts killing two or three birds with a single stone; as he partially masters the higher order concept, he simultaneously completes his mastery of all those of lower order.

Choosing between the two assumptions need not be decided on the debating platform; it would be easy to compare the two by using the rank-ordering of phonic blends.

C. Or an Optimum Feedback Loop?

As a matter of fact, once a journeyman researcher has the rank-ordering before him, a large set of more sophisticated experimental questions automatically occurs to him. He would send experimental groups through the rank-ordering and start testing such independent variables as the following:

a. Level of mastery. Different groups would be skipped ahead when they attain levels of say 20, 40, 60, or 80%. Or perhaps when they attained 2, 4, . . . n successive correct blends.

b. Amount of skipping ahead. After attaining different levels of mastery, different groups would be skipped ahead by 1, 2, . . . n blends. Or to use bigger steps, by 1, 2, . . . n blending concepts.

c. Direction of skipping. One group skipped ahead only vs a group which is also skipped back when mistakes are made.

d. Error rate, and so on. More generally, once he has a finely detailed rank-ordering of blends, any reasonably ingenious researcher should be able to plot the functions that would enable him to describe a resonably efficient feedback loop for teaching phonic blending. It would, no doubt, entail skipping the child forward according to his correct blends and backward according to his mistakes. Moreover, a little experience with the loop would probably suggest how to make it respond quickly to an individual child's proclivity for guessing, tolerance for making mistakes, attention span, and the like.

D. A Complete Phonics Program

A major refrain of this article has been that there are massive differences in the learnability and productivity of the language units that are assembled into reading programs. Since the differences are not less than those between insecticides or fertilizers or seed varieties, it does not seem extrvagant to suggest that they could lead to a progressive increase in intellectual productivity similar to the increase in agricultural productivity that has been occurring throughout the past century and a half. It does not seem excessively optimistic to assume that much of the difficulty a child encounters with current instruction might be eliminated by a better budgeting of his effort, namely, by not starting him on units that are beyond his competence and by not wasting his effort with undue attention to skills that have slight value or that will fade into insignificance as soon as he gains an overall view of reading.

To be specific, a detailed analysis of the blending calibrations shows that although most words in English are difficult for 6-year-olds to blend (*t.oo, b.ee*), there are 20 or 30 that are within the competence of 2-year-olds (*tele.vision, um.brella, el.bow*). This surely reflects a difference in difficulty of something like 10 to 50 magnitudes. It may seem strange that differences of such magnitude are not reflected in any contemporary program for teaching blending, but the notion of calibrating language units has never been reduced to practice.

As a second example, out of all possible two-sound words, there are 14 that are roughly five times as easy to learn to sound-out as any other (*u.p*). And out of these 14, there is a smaller set that is several times as productive as the others (*a.t, i.t*); they combine with other sounds to generate larger numbers of three and four sound words. Without systematic tables, there is little probability that an instructional designer would chance to start his program with this small set of words.

But **with** the tables, even the halfway engineering that I used to get us a little closer to the optimum list of words can also get us a little closer to a list of phonic skills rank-ordered according to ease of learning. Given the rank-ordering, more elaborate versions of the preceding experiments might describe a feedback loop for working children through it.

E. How Can We Get the Skills into the Minds of 2-Year-Olds?

Perhaps with singing commercials. Institutional advertising. Public service spots.

A healthy percentage of the total annul budget for television goes for 10-, 20-, 30-, and 60-second commercials. In production polish, at least, the better ones are several times as sophisticated as the regular programming. Why not put them to a little better use? Like raising the intelligence of coming generations.

Consider teaching the 200 some odd words that would enable a young child to read the largest number of useful sentences. It requires no great ingenuity to arrange them into 50 or 60 combinations that could serve as names of products. For example, *the big brown cow* (obviously chocolate milk), *I can candy*, and so on.

Or consider teaching the sounds of the letters. Using pairs of image hierarchies such as Fig. 3, it is not overly difficult to devise products that teach the shape and sound of a letter and to fit them into a little drama of overlapping images like Fig. 4. Off the top of my head, mmmary mmmilkshake is a two-humped camel (candy or cookie or breakfast food shaped like an *m*) who loves good things to eat and is always saying, "mmm, mmm, good!" Or Calvin Cookie, the coughing crow (a cookie shaped like a *C*) who choked and is always coughing (or cawing), "c-c-c-." Or a gadget shaped like a *P* for puffing soap bubbles (when soap bubbles pop, they say p', don't they?). And so on.

Finally, here is a storyboard for a short commercial that advertises the soap bubbles and the instuctional toy, the bubble puffer (Fig. 7). The commercial not only teaches the shape and sound of *p*, but one of the easier blends as well. As I type this, it occurs to me: Why not name the product *get up soap bubbles*? Then we could work in two of the most useful words and one of the most useful sentences in English.

Summary. To continue paraphrasing a refrain that echos through this article, it does not seem unduly extravagant to hope that if our children had grown up exposed to hundreds of such spots, they would never remember a time when they were not complete masters of the phonic concept. Or to hope that this knowledge would be stored in so many synaptic interconnections that the phonic skills of printed language would

Fig. 7. Excerpts from a storyboard for a 30-second television spot that advertises a commercial product, *get up soap bubbles*. Note that the commercial (and the product itself) teaches the shape and sound of *P*, a useful sentence (*get up*), and one of the easier blends.

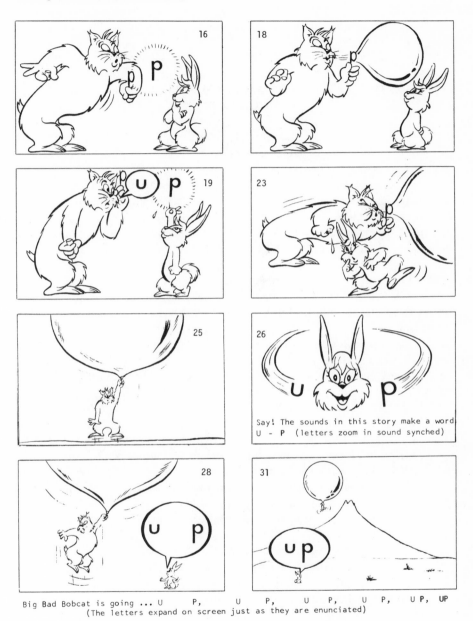

Fig. 7 (continued).

be almost as automatic and unconscious as the phonetic skills of spoken language.

X. THE MATHEMATICAL ARGUMENT FOR EXPERIMENT STATION RESEARCH

Contemporary basic research fails to provide the knowledge required for an applied science because it is based on a completely inadequate statistical model.

The necessity for experiment-station type research can be stated with mathematical precision in terms of nonrepresentative, fixed-effect restrictions. If basic findings in the psychology of learning were not hemmed in by large numbers of fixed effects, massive improvements in teaching efficiency might be possible. Consider the basic research on imagery. Experimental psychologists are reporting differences of up to 600% in favor of imagery presentations over nonimagery presentations (Bower & Clark, 1969). When an applied psychologist learns of a variable that exerts such a massive influence on learning, his work is cut out for him; how can he apply it? Unfortunately, most studies of imagery have used experimental designs that are so hemmed in by fixed-effect restrictions that the findings may not be generalizable to the learning of useful skills (see Clark, 1973 for an exhaustive review of the language-as-fixed-effect fallacy, one variety of statistical shortcoming that flaws a considerable percentage of experiments in basic research).

Or consider a different variety of the language-as-fixed-effect restriction. Most studies of imagery have drawn their language sample from a population of 925 nouns rated for imagery by Paivio, Yuille, and Madigan (1968). The demands of counterbalancing have further reduced this population to some 100–200 words and this has led to a multiexperiment variety of language-as-fixed-effect fallacy that Clark (1973) did not consider, namely, many imagery experiments had to be based on pretty much the same language sample. It is not possible to estimate how small this restricted sample actually is since the language sample is seldom published, but if one peruses the few that have been, the same words keep turning up. To the extent that the experiment must generalize to the language population, the practice is little different than if—after say a penitentiary psychologist uses a particular 100 inmates to show that an extra Y-chromosome affects criminality—many subsequent experimenters use samples that contain many of the same 100 men.

The point I am trying to bludgeon home is that there are fundamental mathematical reasons why applied psychologists must calibrate by direct experimentation the pertinent units they will use in their educational programs; the very nature of the contemporary experiment and its statistical model almost guarantee that the findings will not be generalizable beyond the fixed-effect restrictions of artificial laboratory paradigms.

A. Generalizing to a Single Population of Subjects

As a specific example of why the generalizability of the contemporary experiment is so severely limited, consider a series of experiments on imagery carried out by Postman and his colleagues (e.g., Postman, 1978; Postman & Burns, 1973). Although imagery exerts massive effects on learning, this series showed a reversed effect on memory; the low-imagery paired associates were actually better retained. Consider a simplified replication of their basic experiment (Coleman, in press): Subjects were taught high-imagery paired associates (*village–cigar*) and low-imagery pairs (*joviality–heaven*). A week later, more of the low-imagery pairs were remembered (5.25 lows vs 3.92 highs, which was essentially the same magnitude of difference obtained by Postman and his colleagues).

The contemporary conceptualization of such a Treatments-by-Subject Experiment can be represented by the expected mean squares of its F ratio (letting T stand for Treatments and S stand for Subjects):

$$F = \frac{\sigma_{TS}^2 + \sigma_T^2}{\sigma_{TS}^2}$$

This F turned out to be 5.63. Since 5.63 is significantly larger than 1.00, according to the traditional view of an experiment, I am justified in assuming that the treatments caused a generalizable variance in memory—that low-imagery pairs are better retained—that σ_T^2 is not zero— that it added something upstairs.[3] If σ_T^2 were zero, it would not have added anything upstairs, and the ratio would have been approximately 1.00 because a number divided by itself ($\sigma_{TS}^2 / \sigma_{TS}^2$) is 1.00, isn't it?

More abstractly, the accepted view is that this experiment and its F tests the null hypothesis that $\sigma_T^2 = 0$. This is a gross oversimplification; the traditional F tests only an extremely limited null hypothesis. It tests the null if, and only if, sampling effects are due to one population only; it assumes that all other effects are "fixed." Quite simply, a "fixed

---

[3] At the risk of hiding the message beneath an excess of accuracy, it should be noted that the expected F (since it is not for a population, but for a sample) would not be precisely 1.00, but slightly larger. It would be $df_{error}/(df_{error} - 2)$.

effect'' cannot be considered to be a sample that one can generalize beyond; if the mathematics the experimenter uses considers an effect to be "fixed," then he is not justified in generalizing to any representatives of the effect that were not actually used in the experiment. He is only justified in generalizing beyond "generalization effects," beyond samples that are in the downstairs part of the ratio, beyond σ_{TS}^2 for the experiment under discussion.

Continuing to be painfully elementary, the σ_{TS}^2 in numerator and denominator of the ratio is the interaction of subjects with treatments. In the example under discussion, it appears that the particular subjects used by Postman and by me remembered the low-imagery pairs better. But in the great population of subjects we both claim to generalize to, there may be many subjects who remember high-imagery pairs better. The difference of 5.25 to 3.92 that I found in favor of low-imagery pairs would be of no importance if it were due to the fact that I chanced to have drawn a sample with an atypically large proportion of the first kind of subject. If another experimenter repeated the experiment and chanced to draw a sample containing more of the second kind of subject, he would reverse my finding and get a difference favoring the high-imagery pairs. The mathematics of the typical significance test estimates the probability that my difference favoring the low-imagery pairs was not caused by such an atypical sample of subjects.

The problem with the mathematics of the typical significance test— which has been used for almost every experiment in the literature—is that it considers no source of sampling variance other than subjects. If it is not intuitively obvious, it is easy to show that because the hypothesis that $\sigma_T^2 = 0$ is almost always tested within this mathematical model, it is highly improbable that findings can be applied to a practical use. This model of an experiment provides no evidence that the findings (e.g., better retention for low-imagery pairs) would be replicable if any one of a great number of fixed effects—no matter how theoretically irrelevant they might seem—were changed (for example, changing something as apparently irrelevant as the sample of paired associates or changing the sample of materials in a reading experiment).

B. Generalizing to Two Populations—Subjects Plus Language

The above truism has been spelled out in strongest language in what Clark calls the "language-as-fixed-effect fallacy" (1973). For more neutral language, see either the earliest or the most recent discussion of the problem (Coleman, 1964, 1979), where it is treated more as a restriction than as a **fallacy**. But Clark and I are in complete agreement that most experiments in verbal learning will be of trivial import unless they use a more complex model than the above ratio. To take an obvious example, the findings of the exemplar (or an experiment in reading) will almost always be trivial unless one can make the assumption that the findings will generalize if the language materials are changed. The gist of the Coleman–Clark argument is that because this assumption changes language into a generalization variable, it automatically materializes a σ_{TL}^2 into the upstairs part of the ratio:

$$F = \frac{\sigma_{TS}^2 + \sigma_{TL}^2 + \sigma_T^2}{\sigma_{TS}^2}$$

(letting L stand for Language and simplifying the ratio somewhat, in particular by omitting the triple interaction). That is, in the exemplar under discussion, my F of 5.63 could have been larger than 1.00 because σ_{TL}^2, not σ_T^2, was adding something upstairs.

Stripped of the mathematical esoterica, the σ_{TL}^2 is directly analogous to σ_{TS}^2. The σ_{TS}^2 signifies that some subjects may remember more lows and others may remember more highs; the σ_{TL}^2 signifies that there may be some low-imagery (or high-imagery) paired associates that most people remember easily and others that they remember poorly. As with the subject sample, my finding in favor of low-imagery pairs would be of trivial interest if it was caused by my happening to have drawn an atypically large proportion of easily remembered lows (e.g., *joviality–heaven = Jove–heaven*). If, in an attempt to replicate my finding, another experimenter is not restricted to the exact pairs used in my study, he may happen to draw an atypically large proportion of easily remembered highs, thereby completely reversing the finding.

There is good reason for being so tediously explicit: Almost every experiment in the literature (and its significance test) is based on the mathematics of the first ratio; the mathematics of the typical F, formidable and intricate through they may seem, do not even consider the possibility that the finding could have been caused, not by σ_T^2, but by a happenstance σ_{TL}^2. It is not difficult to think of findings that one suspects are more a product of σ_{TL}^2 than of σ_T^2: think of research using sentences or passages manufactured by the experimenter; think of findings based on a single passage; think of series of studies that use the same language sample for experiment after experiment. If no such findings occur to you, see Coleman (1979) or Miller and Coleman (1972) for examples and explicit mathematical treatment.

There are several ways to deal with that pesky σ_{TL}^2. The best by far is the experiment-station technique of removing it entirely by studying the entire population. The preceding ratios were greatly simplified by omitting the sampling coefficient for each of the σ^2s. For example, the σ_{TL}^2 is actually multiplied by the sampling coefficient $(1 - l/L)$ where l = the number of language units actually used and L = the number one generalizes to. If the experiment uses the entire population, all is well; $l = L$, $(1 - l/L) = 0$, and σ_{TL}^2 disappears. Even if the population is too large to be completely exhausted, the experiment-station strategy is to exhaust it as much as possible. Recall that in one of the blending experiments, I gave each of 10 children a different sample of 240 words. Even though my resulting l did not quite equal L, it came sufficiently close that it substantially reduced the risk of generalizing to the primary school vocabulary.

If it is not possible to exhaust the population completely, standard statistics texts give, under the heading of "Quasi F," approximation mathematics that deal with generalizing to language plus subjects simultaneously. Or see Coleman and Miller (1974) for a simpler way that can be extended to generalizing to any number of populations simultaneously.

In an extensive review of semantic memory, Clark (1973) analyzed the experimental designs and statistics of the great majority of studies in the field; he concluded that, hypothetically at least, almost every finding could have been due to a happenstance σ_{TL}^2, not to σ_T^2. The thing to worry about is that Clark's evaluation, as hypercritical as it may sound, only exposes the tip of the iceberg.

C. Generalizing to Three Populations

Clark's evaluation does not go far enough because it is possible to list many sources of upstairs interaction other than language that are not considered by the mathematics of the typical experiment. One obvious source is measures. Continuing to use the high- vs low-imagery exemplar: In Postman's Introduction and Discussion, his terminology shows clearly that he was talking about memory-in-general. Thus, his measure of memory, 7-day recall, was not a fixed effect; it was an incomplete sample of the population of measures we lump together in our overall concept of memory-in-general (mathematically, the sampling coefficient, $1 - m/M$, was not zero). Therefore, just as for the subject sample and the language sample, there materializes into the upstairs part of the ratio a σ_{TM}^2:

$$\frac{\sigma_T^2 + \sigma_{TS}^2 + \sigma_{TL}^2 + \sigma_{TM}^2}{\sigma_{TS}^2}$$

(letting M stand for Measure and continuing to simplify by omitting three higher order interactions). Since the σ_{TM}^2, like σ_{TL}^2 and σ_T^2, has no counterpart below, it too must be considered as a hypothetical explanation of the F larger than 1.00 favoring low imagery. Actually, it turned out (Coleman, in press) that this σ_{TM}^2 was more than hypothetical; a different measure, relearning, completely reversed Postman's findings. According to relearning, the high-imagery paired associates were better retained. Summing up, in addition to the σ_T^2 considered by the traditional mathematics, my F of 5.63 could have been larger than 1.00 because either σ_{TL}^2 or σ_{TM}^2 or both were adding something upstairs (parenthetically, it is important to note that contaminating interactions like σ_{TL}^2 and σ_{TM}^2 can subtract from, as well as add to, the treatment difference).

D. Generalizing to More Than Three Populations

And clearly, there are still other boundary conditions that might change the findings if they were changed to generalization variables by generalizing beyond the values actually used in the experiment. As a matter of fact, some of my replications of the high- vs low-imagery experiment (Coleman, in press, Exps. 1B and 1C) showed that the results could also be changed by altering the acquisition technique. Letting A stand for acquisition technique and X, Y, Z for any other conditions you think might alter the results, the ratio of expected mean squares for an experiment could easily become something like:

$$\frac{\sigma_T^2 + \sigma_{TS}^2 + \sigma_{TL}^2 + \sigma_{TM}^2 + \sigma_{TA}^2 + \sigma_{TX}^2 + \sigma_{TY}^2 + \sigma_{TZ}^2 \ldots}{\sigma_{TS}^2}$$

Even this ratio, complicated as it appears, is still grossly oversimplified. In order to keep from using a page over 5 feet wide, I omitted from the upstairs a hundred some odd third, fourth . . . eighth order interactions with treatments. Summing it all up, the instant one generalizes a finding beyond the fixed effects actually used in the experiment, sampling coefficients become greater than zero and automatically materialize as many as 1? 10? 100? 1000? alternate explanations other than σ_T^2.

For simplicity of exposition, let us eliminate shades of gray and contrast two ways to handle these contaminating interactions: (1) nonrepresentative or pure science and (2) representative or experiment-station science.

1. Nonrepresentative or Pure Science

If one is a basic scientist interested in using his findings to build theory, the last ratio is a nagging reminder that future experiments must deal with the more serious restrictions that hem in the finding. The most desirable way to deal with them is to conduct additional experiments that plot the exact nature of each individual interaction with treatments, at the very minimum determing whether it adds to, or subtracts from, the treatment effect.

2. Representative Science

The experiment-station strategy provides a way to put findings to practical use without waiting 5? 50? 500? years for perfect analysis and the myriad of exact plots. Even when it is impractical to exhaust the population (or almost exhaust it) and reduce the sampling coefficient to zero (or almost zero), the experiment-station strategy provides a shortcut for dealing with contaminating interactions. The applied scientist does not have to have a plot of the effect alone, purified of all contamination, nor an exact plot of the effect alone, purified of all contamination, nor an exact plot of each interaction. The applied scientist can live with any number of contaminating interactions—*so long as they are representative*. He can get by with an overall resultant—the resultant of the treatment effect intermixed with a *representative* set of interactions.

Because the applied scientist can get by with that overall resultant, he can focus his concern upon representativeness, and postpone analysis until tomorrow. To get an acceptable resultant, all he needs to do is make sure that the boundary conditions of the laboratory represent the conditions of the application. Operationally, he carries out his experiments on the particular subjects of interest responding to the particular stimuli of interest under the particular conditions of interest. He carries out experiment-station type research.

Either strategy is a legitimate approach to science. It would mean, however, that while some problems are likely to yield to the first strategy, others are not. Problems most likely to yield to the strategy of pure science and complete analysis are ones that have a small number of contaminating interactions. Most likely, they would concern a single subskill of reading and a single well-defined response (e.g., the perception of isolated letters, paired-associate memorization, and the like).

The last ratio, expanded to its hundred some odd higher order interactions, shows why the pure science strategy will be unproductive for many questions in reading research. I do not intend to alienate the majority of the profession by listing all such questions, but I will risk describing their general nature. Basically, they are research questions whose laboratory paradigms permit changes in boundary conditions that substantially alter the treatment effect. The pure-science strategy, unfettered by the requirement of representativeness, gives the experimenter almost unlimited freedom in choosing the language sample, measures, presentation, instruments, and other boundary conditions. Frequently, this means that two moderately ingenious and tenacious experimenters on opposite sides of the theoretical fence can happen upon combinations that flipflop an effect from one direction to its exact opposite. For such problems, it would seem to be much too early for analysis; perhaps it would be more productive to settle for representativeness.

Perhaps it would be more productive to start the attack on such problems with the psychological equivalent of the kind of research that was conducted at agricultural experiment stations back in the 1840s. Recognizing that the complexities of plant nutrition were beyond the analytic powers of the chemistry and biology of that time, the stations measured the effects of representative mixes of fertilizers on representative crops under representative conditions. The result was a systematic set of tables that was not only of instant use to practicing farmers, but that solved in a very few years many of the major questions of plant nutrition (e.g., nitrogen fixation by legumes). Perhaps some reading problems now conceptualized from the viewpoint of pure theoretical science are likewise beyond the analytic power of current techniques, but would yield in time to the experiment-station strategy of dealing with an overall resultant— the effect intermixed with a representative set of interactions.

XI. SUMMARY AND CONCLUSIONS

There are parallels between the current state of affairs in education and those of agriculture before the first experiment station was established in 1843. The basic knowledge of the behavioral sciences is usually hemmed in by many fixed-effect restrictions such as the use of albino rats, and for this reason there are no mathematical formulas for transforming it into tables useful to an educational technology. As a consequence, before reading or any other field of education can be raised to an applied science, the units pertinent to the field will have to be calibrated by direct experimentation much as agricultural experiment stations weigh and analyze the elements important to agriculture. Experiments over the past 10 years have calibrated certain of these units and have shown that the differences among them are at least equal to the differences that provide the basis for the progressive increase in the world's agricultural yields.

Even unrefined, cut-and-fit engineering based on these calibrations can improve teaching efficiency to the point that much younger children can teach themselves to read. The magnitude of this improvement is not unusual in the history of science. When a discipline advances from methods of craftsmanship to methods of engineering, there is usually a quantum improvement in effectiveness. Besides the magnitude of the differences cited above, there is a more basic reason for expecting an educational experiment station to spark such a quantum improvement. An elemental technique that separates an engineer from a craftsman is nothing more subtle than that the engineer manipulates numbers before he manipulates things. An engineer does not develop a plane, or even a model for a wind tunnel, by putting in and taking out and rearranging steel and plastic and aluminum until he gets something that flies. He does his preliminary putting in and taking out and rearranging with numbers that describe his materials. An Educational Experiment Station in Reading would provide the measures that would enable education engineers to manipulate numbers to predict how children would behave when analogous manipulations are performed in the classroom. Since the first manipulation is several hundred times as inexpensive as the second, it does not seem unreasonable to expect rapid, cumulative improvements to follow the collection and use of the measures.

It has been estimated that the United States realizes $100 for every dollar invested in agricultural research. The returns from an educational experiment station might be of similar magnitude.

To give one example, local school systems spend at least $1.00 to teach a child each of the approximately 300 words he learns to read in the first grade. This accounts for a total cost to the national educational effort of well over $1 billion a year. Even the exploratory engineering described in this article makes it possible to teach many of these words at considerable savings. Perhaps at no cost at all if industry could be persuaded to shift some of their advertising budget into the aforementioned public service spots. But even if not, the examples given earlier argue strongly that an experiment station in reading could save local school systems massive amounts with a trifling investment. Saving such amounts—though not to be despised—is not the most important return that may be realized from an Education Experiment Station in Reading.

Man learns to talk during the years that lay the foundations of intelligence, and perhaps one reason that spoken language becomes the basic tool of thought is that this early learning engrains it deep into the bedrock of the mind. It does not seem beyond the realm of possibility that polished versions of the tables and techniques described in this article might give coming generations a similar genius for printed language.

REFERENCES

Battig, W. F. Paired-associate learning. In T. R. Dixon & D. L. Horton (Eds.), *Verbal behavior and general behavior theory*. Englewood Cliffs, New Jersey: Prentice-Hall, 1968.

Bower, G. H., & Clark, M. C. Narrative stories as mediators for serial learning. *Psychonomic Science*, 1969, **14**, 181–182.

Bricker, W. A. Errors in the echoic behavior of preschool children. *Journal of Speech and Hearing Disorders*, 1967, **10**, 67–76.

Clark, H. H. The language-as-fixed-effect fallacy: A critique of language statistics in psychological research. *Journal of Verbal Learning and Verbal Behavior*, 1973, **12**, 335–359.

Chitwood, A. *Recording the spontaneous speech of preschool children*. Unpublished masters thesis, University of Texas at El Paso, 1973.

Coleman, E. B. Generalizing to a language population. *Psychological Reports*, 1964, **16**, 219–226.

Coleman, E. B. Collecting a data base for a reading technology. *Journal of Educational Psychology Monograph*, 1970, **61**, Whole Part No. 2, 1–23.

Coleman, E. B., The optimum list and reading for meaning. *Theory into Practice*, 1975, **14**, 195–201.

Coleman, E. B. Generalization effects vs. random effects: Is σ_{TL}^2 a source of Type 1 or Type 2 error? *Journal of Verbal Learning and Verbal Behavior*, 1970, **18**, 243–256.

Coleman, E. B. Generalization tests and degree of representativeness: Their effect upon theory. In press.

Coleman, E. B., & Miller, G. R. The simplest experimental design that permits multiple generalization. *Journal of Reading Behavior*, 1974, **6**, 31–40.

Coleman, E. B., & Morris, G. Generalization tests: A terminology that focuses attention on fixed-effect restrictions. *Journal of Reading Behavior*, 1979, **10**, 377–392.

Coleman, E. B., and Morton, C. E. A modest plan to raise the national intelligence. *Educational Technology*, 1976, 7–17.

Deutch, M. *Rhyme and song in teaching reading to trainable retardates*. Unpublished MA Thesis, Ohio State University, 1975.

Donaldson, H. H. Laura Bridgman. *American Journal of Psychology*, 1890, **3**, 292–342; **4**, 248–294.

Goodman, K. S. *The psycholinguistic nature of the reading process*. Detroit: Wayne State Univ. Press, 1968.

Greenough, W. T. Experimental modification of the developing brain. *American Scientist*, 1975, **63**, 37–46.

Hall, A. D. *The book of Rothamsted experiments*. London: John Murra, 1905.

Horn, M. *An investigation of the vocabulary of kindergarten children*. Unpublished master's thesis, State University of Iowa, 1927.

Himelstein, P. *Printability of constituent strokes of the alphabet*. Unpublished Master's thesis, University of Texas at El Paso, 1971.

Karagiaouris, L. *Rank-ordering of lower-case letters according to the ease of reproduction through recall*. Unpublished Master's thesis, University of Texas at El Paso, 1969.

Laumbach, J. D. *Rank-ordering two-sound words as to phonic blendability*. Unpublished Master's thesis, University of Texas at El Paso, 1968.

Lefevre, C. A. *Linguistics and the teaching of reading*. New York: McGraw-Hill, 1964.

Marsh, G., and Sherman, M. Kindergarten children's discrimination and production of phonemes in isolation and in words. *Southwest Regional Laboratory Technical Memorandum*, August 9, 1971, TM-2-71-07.

Miller, G. R., & Coleman, E. B. The measurement of reading speed and the obligation to generalize to a population of reading materials. *Journal of Reading Behavior*, 1972, **4**, 48–56.

Newman, M. A. Word associations from preschool children collected by the continued sentence associations method. *Journal of Reading Behavior*, 1974, **6**.

Paivio, A., Yuille, J. C., & Madigan, S. Concreteness, imagery, and meaningfulness values for 925 nouns. *Journal of Experimental Psychology*, 1968, **76**, Part 2.

Poole, I. *The genetic development of the articulation of consonant sounds.* Unpublished doctoral dissertation, University of Michigan, 1934.

Popp, H. Visual discrimination of alphabet letters. *The Reading Teacher*, 1964, **17**, 221–225.

Postman, L. Picture-word differences in the acquisition and retention of paired assocites. *Journal of Experimental Psychology: Human Learning and Memory*, 1978, **4**, 145–157.

Postman, L., & Burns, S. Experimental analysis of coding processes. *Memory and Cognition*, 1973, **1**, 503–507.

Ranson, J. *The recallability of English words.* Paper read at National Reading Conference, St. Petersburg, 1970.

Rentel, V. *Ease of learning print-to-sound associations.* Paper read at Convention of American Psychological Association, Washington, 1969.

Rinsland, H. D. *A basic vocabulary of elementary school children.* New York: Macmillan, 1945.

SWRL-Ginn. *The seed.* Booklet No. 39 of The Kindergarten Reading Program. Lexington, Massachusetts: Ginn, 1972.

Templin, M. C. *Certain language skills in children.* Minneapolis: Univ. of Minnesota Press, 1957.

Valverde, F. Rate and extent of recovery from dark rearing in the visual cortex of the mouse. *Brain Research*, 1971, **33**, 1–11.

Venezky, R. L. "English Orthography: Its Graphical Structure and Its Relation to Sound." *Reading Research Quarterly*, 1967, **2**, 75–105.

Wellman, B., Case, I., Mengert, I., & Bradbury, D. *Speech sounds of young children.* University of Iowa Studies of Child Welfare, 1931, **5**, 7–82.

Washington, G. *The diaries of George Washington.* J. C. Fitzpatrick (Ed.). Boston: Houghton, 1925.

INDEX